fourteen

Aegir

fourteen

A Daughter's Memoir of Adventure, Sailing, and Survival

Leslie Johansen Nack

SHE WRITES PRESS

Published 2015
Printed in the United States of America
ISBN: 978-1-63152-941-2
Library of Congress Control Number: 2015940965

Pictures by chapters are available at www.lesliejohansennack.com

For information, address:
She Writes Press
1563 Solano Ave #546
Berkeley, CA 94707

She Writes Press is a division of SparkPoint Studio, LLC.

To Poo and Taunty

Nav·i·ga·tion/ ˌnavəˈgāSH(ə)n/ *noun*

1. the process or activity of accurately ascertaining one's position and planning and following a route.

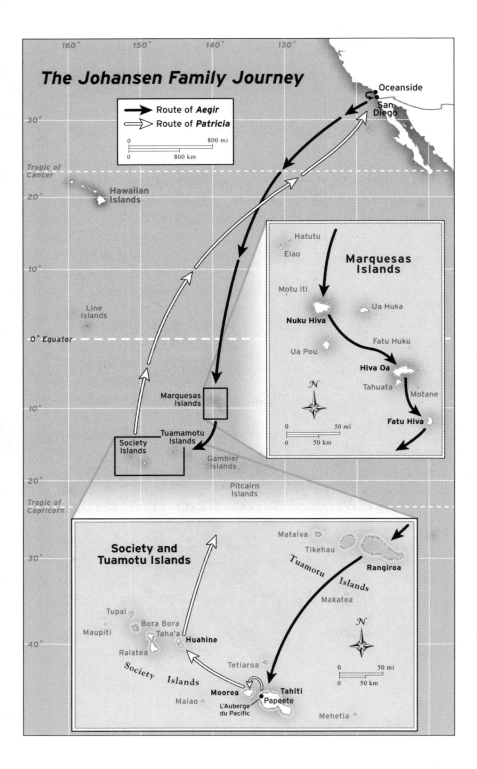

The Johansen Family Journey

→ Route of *Aegir*
⇒ Route of *Patricia*

0   800 mi
0   800 km

Oceanside
San Diego

160° 150° 140° 130°

30°

Tropic of Cancer

Hawaiian Islands

20°

10°

Line Islands

0° Equator

10°

Marquesas Islands

Society Islands

Tuamamotu Islands

Gambier Islands

20°

Tropic of Capricorn

Pitcairn Islands

30°

40°

Marquesas Islands

Hatutu
Eiao
Motu Iti
Nuku Hiva
Ua Huka
Fatu Huku
Ua Pou
Hiva Oa
Tahuata
Motane
Fatu Hiva

N

0   50 mi
0   50 km

Society and Tuamotu Islands

Mataiva
Tikehau
Rangiroa
Tuamotu
Makatea
Islands

N

Tupai
Bora Bora
Taha'a
Huahine
Maupiti
Raiatea
Tetiaroa
Society Islands
Maiao
Moorea
L'Auberge du Pacific
Tahiti
Papeete
Mehetia

0   50 mi
0   50 km

Part 1

Dad's Dream

One

In March of 1973, we picked up our new custom-built sailboat in Newport Beach and sailed south on our first-ever family voyage.

The forty-five-foot boat's name was *Serenity*, but Dad immediately renamed her, though he told us there were "old sea legends" of bad luck if a boat's name was changed. He added in a teasing and playful way, "I spit in the face of sailing folklore." The new name, *Aegir*, meant "lord of the stormy seas" in Norwegian.

Leaving Newport Beach harbor, we motored past the south jetty and headed into the open ocean. Toward shore, I saw surfers as black dots on their boards waiting for the next swell. Dad put up the main sail, hoisted the front sail up, and turned off the engine. The relative silence was beautiful with only the sound of water sloshing onto the sides of the boat. The salty ocean air carried the scent of fish and seaweed. The wind was light, the ocean flat and sparkling under the late morning sun.

It was chilly and I wore a pair of Levi's 501 Button Fly jeans, a T-shirt, and a blue windbreaker. Everybody but Dad was dressed in pants. He wore his favorite pair of cut-offs and a T-shirt.

"Leslie, grab that line there and pull it," Dad said from the captain's chair, pointing with his finger to a rope near him.

I jumped up from where I was sitting on the main cabin and pointed, "This rope?"

"On a boat, it's called a line not a rope, and when it's attached to a sail it's called a sheet."

"Well, that's confusing," I said.

"Just pull the sheet so the sail quits flapping."

3

I did and looked up at the sail.

"The forward sail is called the genoa," Dad said.

The genoa stopped flapping and filled with wind as soon as I tightened the sheet. "Good job!" he said. "See how that works?"

I nodded. The boat moved through the water, leaning over ever so slightly.

Mom sat next to Dad with a yellow scarf around her black hair and a puffy blue ski jacket on. She smiled when I looked at her. I hoped she was having a good time. My sisters, Monica and Karen, sat comfortably atop the main cabin. Monica first held onto the railing, and then laid down. Karen looked at ease and happy, her cute little smile showing crooked teeth, her shoulder-length brown hair blowing in the wind. She stared forward as I did, watching the boat cut her way to sea. The gentle forward motion felt natural to me. I liked the expanse of calm water in front of us. In a strange way it reminded me of the large view of the valley on our ranch: open and empty.

Dad, with a great big smile, yelled something in Norwegian to the sky or ocean. Then he added in English, "I'm home! We're sailing our very own boat. Our next big voyage will be to Tahiti, right?"

It was fun to see Dad so happy. He wore his floppy brown leather hat from the ranch to protect his bald head from getting sunburned, and the same blue wrap-around reflective sunglasses he wore on the ski slope. He looked comfortable at the helm. "Who's making sandwiches?" he asked.

Mom jumped up. "Who else is hungry?"

"I'll have a sandwich," I said, and Monica and Karen each asked for one, too. Mom went below deck but in a few minutes was back looking green and ready to heave. Her mouth curled as she said, "I'm going to throw up."

Dad yelled, "Not that side! Go to the low side."

Mom rushed to the low side, hanging on as she walked. She leaned over the side and threw up. I peeked around the edge of the cabin where I sat soaking up the sun.

"I don't feel well either," Monica said. She stood up and joined Mom on the low side of the boat to throw up. Dad shook his head slightly and smiled at me in an "I can't believe this" smile. I looked at Karen.

"How do you feel?" I asked.

"Fine," she said.

I went below and made sandwiches for Dad, Karen, and me while Mom and Monica endured the rest of the trip huddled together near the low side. We arrived in Oceanside five hours later and docked *Aegir* in her new home on T-dock, slip 14.

After that maiden voyage, our whole focus in life changed to learning about the cruising world. We had traded living on the ranch—a three-bedroom house on sixty-three acres—for life aboard a forty-five-foot boat, and I felt the reduction in space immediately. The boat's interior felt like the inside of the fifteen-foot trailer on the ranch.

Aegir had berths for eight, but nobody wanted to sleep in the main cabin where the galley, navigation station, and eating areas were. Mom and Dad settled into the aft cabin—the master bedroom—which had two individual bunks separated by a closet, a little bench to sit on, plus its own "head" (toilet) with a sink.

Monica, Karen, and I all shared the forward cabin which Dad liked to call by its official name just to trip us up. "You girls take the foc's'le. There should be plenty of room for the three of you."

The berth had a large trapezoid-shaped cushion, so we slept head to foot and sometimes got kicked in the face in the middle of the night. We knew better than to complain, so we made the best of it.

On the boat, there was nowhere to go for privacy. I missed my special place on the ranch where I went to get away from everybody, but found a new secret spot off of the boat at the end of the rock jetty on the nearby beach.

Dad enrolled me in sixth grade and Karen in fourth grade at San Rafael Elementary near the front gate of Camp Pendleton for the last few months of the school year. Monica had to go to seventh grade by herself at Jefferson Junior High. Working on the boat, finding a job, and getting us all settled living aboard the boat on T-dock occupied Dad's time and diverted his sometimes overbearing attention away from us.

Mom found work at Tri-City Hospital, but after several months she discovered that boating life, like pioneer living on the ranch, was not for her. Constantly sea sick, even on the dock, she couldn't stand the dampness, the smell of fish, the gusting wind at sunset, or the lack of privacy aboard the boat. Mom and Dad divorced when I was seven and had tried several times to reconcile. Their latest reconciliation wasn't going well—she and Dad fought constantly. Finally, Mom packed her bags and went back home to Canada. She said she was going to visit Grandma and would be back later. Although we exchanged letters and spoke on the phone occasionally, we didn't see her again for sixteen months.

After Mom left, the fighting stopped and peace prevailed on the boat. Dad laughed and made friends with other boaters in the harbor, meeting them for margaritas in the evening. Relieved, I began to relax into our new lifestyle.

Life on T-dock was unique. We had a special permit from the Harbor Master to live aboard *Aegir*, and during that first summer we explored the harbor, becoming affectionately known by the shop owners and other boaters as the "three harbor rats from T-dock." We played at the beach, learning to surf. We took turns cooking dinner at night because when Dad got home from working on other boats around the harbor he was hungry. Monica, Karen, and I worked on *Aegir*, sanding and oiling the teak railings, and learned to sail on an eight-foot sabot Dad purchased for us. Our homework was easy— Dad said: "Go sailing! Go two at a time. Sail around the harbor. Your job is learning to sail."

We took turns and sometimes all three squeezed into the sabot for fun. We rammed a few docks, flipped the sabot a couple times, and eventually learned to follow other sailors in the harbor and mimic their position and heading. The lessons we got from Dad, along with our hands-on training, had us entering the Yacht Club sabot races before the summer's end.

As the only live-aboards on T-dock, or anywhere close by, we had the dock to ourselves Monday through Friday during the school year. We each wore a key on a string around our necks, which opened the boat-owner's bathroom and laundry, and the T-dock gate. During the week we didn't have to share the laundry facilities or boat-owner's bathrooms with anybody else. On the weekends it was a different story. We had to wait in line to take a shower because there were so many people visiting their boats for the weekend.

Oceanside Harbor was U-shaped and T-dock was the closest dock to the beach, only a city block away. Between the beach and T-dock were the four-story Marina Del Mar condominiums, which cast a large shadow over us in the afternoon and evening. In my twelve-year-old mind, the harbor, with its hundreds of boats, was huge. But one day when we got supplies at San Diego Harbor, I understood why Dad had settled on small, quaint Oceanside. He could never keep track of us in such a huge place as San Diego Harbor with its thousands of boats.

Past the dive shop, near the lighthouse—a three-minute walk away—was a cluster of restaurants and shops. La Beaner's, the Mexican bar and restaurant, was a favorite of Dad's, along with the "greasy spoon" coffee shop The Dolphin Café. I loved The Candy Kitchen, where the manager, Forest, gave us free pieces of candy. We girls liked eating at Harbor Fish and Chips, watching the fishermen unload their catches from the commercial fishing boats docked right in front. There was a clothing store called Ye Olde Hawaiian Hut where we ogled formal dresses and puka shell necklaces.

Dad was happy the first six months, finding work on other boats in the harbor to earn money, and customizing our boat to go cruising around the world. He took classes at the Yacht Club on seamanship, navigation, and piloting, coming home at night and teaching us some of the lessons he'd learned. Dad's bald head became familiar and around the harbor they called us "Mr. Clean and the girls on T-dock."

By the fall of 1973, nearing my thirteenth birthday, I transformed from a little twelve-year-old girl into a five-foot-six-inch, curvy young woman. I was going to junior high with Monica now. I hated seventh grade, and dreamed about the day we'd take off sailing to exotic islands and could stop going to school altogether. Being only one year apart, Monica and I were in the throes of puberty together. Monica was tall—five-foot-eight inches—and skinny. Her breasts developed slowly and were A-cup sized. My breasts blossomed fast and soon were C-cups. Most people thought I was the oldest.

Monica and I rode the school bus every day to Jefferson Junior High with the military kids who lived on Camp Pendleton. The bus picked us up and dropped us off at the top of Harbor Drive, by the back entrance of the Base.

One day after we got off the school bus we walked lazily down the hill, stopping off at the Candy Kitchen to see if Forest, the manager, felt kind enough to give us a piece of chocolate that day. He did and as we walked toward home chewing our chocolate gift, I saw Dad talking to a man in the parking lot. "Hey, Leslie, come here a second," Dad yelled out.

Monica punched my arm lightly, smiled and said, "Bummer," and continued to the boat.

I walked toward Dad, watching his eyes travel up and down my body, as my sandals went flip, flip, flip. I looked down at my thongs, the most interesting thing in the world to me, trying to ignore him.

I waited by his side as he finished up his conversation. We were taught never to interrupt, never! Children were to be seen and not heard—that was the motto in the Johansen family.

"Why do you wear your bathing suit top to school?"

I had on my blue and white striped string bikini top under a white t-shirt. It was visible through the T-shirt and I thought it looked good—like I lived at the beach.

"I don't know. I like wearing it," I said.

"It looks like a bra to me," he said, "my girls don't wear bras. Only pregnant girls need bras."

I stared at the pavement. "All the other girls at school have bras."

"All the other girls aren't my daughters. We are European and European girls don't wear bras. Besides, you look beautiful without one—natural, like a young woman should look."

Across the parking lot, a surfer walked up from the beach, his wetsuit shining in the afternoon sun, carrying his board under his arm. I said nothing, knowing it was a losing battle.

"You're not shaving your legs or underarms, are you?" Before I could answer, he bent over and ran his hands up my shin, then lifted my arm to look underneath it. "Good girl. Don't be like all the other girls. Be a Johansen. Be proud to be European."

I spaced out, put up the invisible walls around me, the ones that had always protected me when he got too close into my space. My eyes looked ahead but everything around me was blurry, unfocused. I yearned for something I couldn't verbalize: the day my body was my own.

"You can go now. Get your homework done, then I have chores for you," he said.

He kept a close watch on me for the next few weeks, making sure I didn't wear my bathing suit top under my clothes. Monica didn't have to worry about any of this, she barely needed a bra and I was sure she didn't want the fight with Dad. She stayed quiet and never insisted on getting a bra. For me it became a game. I tried stuffing the tiny little string bikini top into my backpack but he found it. He never said anything to me, it just disappeared. I also tried stuffing it into the front pocket of my cut-offs, but he saw the bulge and just reached into my pocket on the dock before we left for school and pulled it out. He threw it in the dock box that held our ropes and extra sailing gear, daggers flying out his eyes at me. The silent war had begun.

I had no choice but to go to school feeling vulnerable and naked. The surfer boys sat on the wall by the cafeteria every day. Every girl wanted to go steady with a cute tanned surfer and I was no exception. One day as I walked out of the cafeteria, my breasts swaying with no bra, one of the guys on the wall yelled, "Hubba hubba. What's your name?" I could hear them laughing. Using the same strategy I used when Dad leered at me, I put up my invisible walls, blurred everything out and kept walking. I vowed never to walk across the blacktop after lunch again. The hoots and hollers faded to background noise as I focused on the library. *If I can just get into the library I'll be safe,* I thought, and then someone hooked an arm through mine and walked fast, shielding me from the boys on the wall. It was Raine Oliver, the girl who sat next to me in homeroom. If I was a C cup, then Raine was a D, or maybe a DD. She was only five-foot-two, with long brown hair, freckles all over her face, and big brown eyes. Her boobs were way out of proportion for her little body and as we walked arm-in-arm to the library another of the boys yelled out, "Hey look, Balloons has a friend—Baby Balloons."

Raine and I became instant friends. I told her the story of how we weren't allowed to wear bras because we were European.

"Let's go shopping tomorrow. I know where we can get you a bra for free," she said.

"Really? Where?"

"This store by my house has lots of them."

"I can't do that, even if it's free. If my Dad found me with a bra, he'd kill me."

"Hide it in your backpack. He'll never know."

"I tried that with my bikini top. He found it and took it out." I thought for a minute and said, "but maybe I have another idea."

The next day was Saturday so I met Raine at her house, telling Dad I was going to the beach. I left the boat wearing my bikini to keep my cover, but brought a shirt and shorts rolled up in my towel. I walked down the beach toward the pier and then climbed up to Pacific Street and found Raine's house one block back on Myers Street, about a mile from the harbor.

Her house was a small, white, old-style beach cottage that was totally far out—beads hanging everywhere separating the rooms, loud rock music, candles and incense burning. Raine's mother, Myrna Loy, had all kinds of older, foxy surfer guys at the house all the time.

In Myrna Loy's house, the front door was always open—

literally—and the guys called to people through the screen door as they walked passed. People came and went all day and night. There was always a potential party at Raine's house.

Myrna Loy wore beaded macramé headbands in her long blondish-red hair, string bikini tops and long gauze skirts. Whenever she saw me, she grabbed my arm with both hands and announced to everyone, "The sailor is here. Leslie's going to sail around the world with her family. Isn't that bitchin'?" The stoned surfers would raise their beer to me, and say, "Boss," or "Far out." It was so embarrassing.

The surfers at Raine's house smoked pot and drank the tomato wine Myra Loy made in the back room. I always felt on the edge of a cliff—in the most exciting way possible—when I was there. Raine didn't have the rules I had, and knew all about sex by the time she was thirteen. I loved her. She knew everything I needed to learn in life.

On the day we went to get a bra, we ran the entire way to the D.A.V., a second-hand store run by the Veterans on Coast Highway, about a mile-and-a-half from her house. When we entered the store I was hit with the musty smell of old clothing. Raine took me to the back of the store near the dressing rooms. To my surprise the bras were all in boxes on a shelf, and they were new. I took three different sized bras into the dressing room and tried them on. They were all white with a little pink flower in the middle front. They felt confining and tight, but at the same time safe and secure. When I tried on the 36-C it felt right. I jumped up and down in front of the mirror and my boobs hardly moved at all. I loved the bra and felt a surge of happiness inside as I thought about walking past those boys on the wall at school. I left the bra on under my shirt as Raine instructed, and skipped out with no problem.

When I got back to the harbor, I hid the bra on the ground behind the middle toilet rolled up in a ball in the boat-owner's bathroom because it seemed nobody used the middle toilet very often. It was the only private space Dad couldn't get to. It was my sanctuary—when I needed a moment to myself and couldn't get out to the end of the jetty, I went to the boat-owner's bathroom. I checked on the bra twice the next day to make sure it was still there.

On Monday morning I stopped in at the bathroom and put the

bra on. It felt tight and made my boobs smaller. I loved it. I swore Monica to silence, threatening her life. As we walked up the hill to get the school bus, she laughed a little and said, "I wonder when I'll be old enough to need a bra. I guess I'm built like Mom, small-chested."

I envied Monica. Life would be much simpler if I just had small breasts. No, life would be simpler if I was just born a boy. I hated my boobs. I hated my body. I hated my Dad.

I won the battle of the boobs and felt proud of the fact that Dad never found out. It was proof that I could take care of myself.

Early one Saturday morning a month or so later, I was asleep in the forward bunk with Monica. Karen was sleeping at her friend Shelly's, and it was nice having the extra room to spread out. I woke up with a headache clutching my stomach. I felt nauseated, with roaring cramps down low. The thin yellow morning light peeked through the porthole and I could tell it was barely light outside. Rolling over, I felt something wet. I pulled the covers back and found blood. I yelled, "Oh no!" which made Dad come running from the aft cabin, where he was just getting up.

I knew about starting my period. Monica and I had discussed it once or twice, and Raine and I talked about it a lot. I couldn't wait to be a woman and important. But finding the blood early that morning shocked me. I was sure there would be more warning when I started my period, not like I would receive a letter in the mail announcing its arrival on Saturday or anything, but something to indicate that my entire life was about to change.

Dad stood over our bunk, "Ah, Leslie, goddamn it," he said as he looked at the mess. I shrunk back.

"I guess I have to go the store and buy you some pads—just what I want to do at 6:00 a.m. on a Saturday morning."

"Sorry, Dad." I sank back into the cushions and pulled the covers over my head.

He turned and left the boat, "I'll be back with pads in twenty minutes!" he yelled.

The boat rocked as he stepped onto the dock and I waited a few minutes for Dad to walk down the dock. "I'm sorry Monica, I really am."

Monica jumped out of bed. "It's okay, Leslie. Don't worry about it. I'll help you clean it up."

I changed pajama bottoms, grabbed the sheet and sleeping bag, and took them down the dock to the boat-owner's bathroom. I wondered what Mom was doing at that very moment—why she couldn't be there to help me. She was never there for the important stuff.

It was bright out, one of those cold, clear, late fall mornings. The harbor was peaceful and still for a Saturday morning. I was grateful I didn't see anybody except the brown pelicans sitting on the end of the dock.

I got in the shower with the dirty linens, standing on the sleeping bag to keep my feet off the cold tile, and turned on the hot water. A lump grew in my throat as I stood in the steamy shower. Maybe it was the hormones, or the embarrassment of Dad seeing the bloody bed, but it was suddenly all too much. I couldn't stop the tears. They came in a flood, unlocking all the other pains I'd stuffed away. The well was deep and it scared me because once I let some of it out, controlling it was impossible. The pain echoed off the cement walls, ricocheting around the bathroom as I cried about Mom, Dad's weirdness with me, the bra, and now this. I cried so hard I struggled to catch my breath, hiccupping between outbursts.

I couldn't tell anybody what had happened that morning or how humiliated I was once again. Everybody thought we had such a great life. We lived on a boat—how fun! We were going to sail around the world—how lucky! But I wished I lived in a house like all the other girls I knew, wished I wasn't known and admired around the harbor, wished I didn't have to act happy about heading out into the open sea with Dad. I wished I wasn't the weirdo who lived on a boat with her father. I didn't want people to look at me and point. I wanted to blend in.

The bathroom door opened and then slammed shut. I stopped crying. Monica knocked on the shower door, "Leslie, I could hear you crying all the way down the sidewalk." I didn't say anything. "Take the belt and pads Dad got you."

"I don't want to wear that," I said.

"Why not?" Monica asked.

"Because I don't want to. I want to wear tampons."

"I don't think Dad would let you do that," she said.

Monica hadn't started her period yet, but I knew she was right. My pain hardened into anger. Anger at Mom for not being there, at Dad for yelling at me for starting my period, at everybody in the world who was so happy we were sailing around the world. Dad didn't scare me anymore. Letting those emotions out in the shower left room inside—room for some anger.

I reluctantly put on the stupid old-lady pad and shoved the sheet and sleeping bag in the washer. Filled with bravado, I stormed down the metal ramp, scaring the pelicans into flight. With each step I gained more courage. When I got to the boat I found Dad making coffee in the galley. Monica had followed me down the dock and stood behind me as I boarded *Aegir*.

"I don't want pads. I want tampons," I said.

"What are you talking about? Young girls don't wear those," he yelled.

"Yes, they do! How do you know, anyway?" I yelled back.

He stepped back against the gimbaled stove, looking a little surprised. Then he dug in, "Who wears them?"

"My friends. They all wear tampons."

"Raine? Raine wears tampons? I can tell she's that kind of girl."

"What kind of girl?" I asked with my hands on my hips.

"A girl that's easy."

"You don't know anything!" I screamed. "Raine's not easy! Stop talking about my best friend like that—I hate you!" I ran to the forward bunk and buried myself in Monica's sleeping bag.

Dad laughed, like he always laughed at me, "Ah, Leslie, misguided stupid little girl," he said. I peeked around the corner of the forward cabin just in time to see him leave. The boat rocked again as he stepped off and the sound of his flip-flops disappeared down the dock.

I buried my head in the pillow and screamed until my throat hurt.

Monica had been sitting quietly in the main salon. She came

forward and lay down on the bunk with me. "You really told him, Leslie," she said with a big grin.

I picked my head up from the pillow. "Yes, I did. And I'll tell him again and again if I have to. I feel like I could tell him off a hundred times right now."

"Did you see the look on his face when you said you wanted tampons? Oh my God, Leslie, he was stunned." Monica started to giggle, trying to keep it under her breath but it was contagious as I realized my victory. It felt good to stun him.

We laughed out loud, but only for a minute. The hatch above our heads was cracked open and we knew better than to be caught laughing after a confrontation.

Raine snuck me some tampons. I tried to put one in but passed out in the boat owner's bathroom, knocking my head so that I had a big bump on it. But I didn't give up. I kept trying and trying until I was successful. Monica stayed with me in the bathroom trying to talk me out of it the entire time.

Two

*W*e sailed *Aegir* every weekend, learning how to be crew members under our demanding father/captain. Dad invited old friends he owed favors and new friends we had just met to come sailing every Saturday and Sunday. It became like a show—the Bjorn Johansen show. Dad stood on the stern, floppy brown hat on, leaning back against the stainless steel railing, arms crossed across his chest with a preoccupied look on his face. Karen sat on the captain's chair, expertly steering us down the fairway toward the open ocean. Monica and I stood near the mast, waiting for the command.

Guests and crew looked toward the open ocean. "Raise the main," Dad would yell. Surprised to hear Dad bark orders, the guests turned to look at him. As soon as Monica and I began raising the main, they turned and watched us. When we were finished, he ordered us to raise the genoa. The guests watched in fascination as three young girls operated the boat. What they didn't know was Dad took Monica, Karen, and I out sailing during the week as dress rehearsal when everybody else was working. He made us practice our given jobs until we got it right.

Once the sails were filled with wind, he yelled, "Kill the engine," and Karen pushed the button, killing the diesel engine and the noise aboard. There was never a better sound than the wind in our ears and the water slapping against the hull.

All of Dad's guests would commend him and praise us girls on being such "good little sailors." For our reward, after sailing we'd tie up to the guest dock in front of the Jolly Roger where we ordered Hot Fudge Cake and the adults ordered wine and drinks, congratulating Dad on his fine crew.

One weekend in May, Dad let each of us bring a friend to see the circus in Long Beach. We sailed up on Friday after school, and then on Saturday afternoon saw the elephants and tigers perform at the Polack Brothers Circus. Sunday morning we headed back home to Oceanside. We left Long Beach Harbor at 7:00 a.m. The gorgeous morning was clear and bright with flat seas and calm winds.

After breakfast, all six of us sat in a row on the deck with our legs dangling over the side of the boat. Monica and her friend Kerima were closest to the bow with their long fourteen-year- old legs. Raine and I, now thirteen, came next. Sitting next to us was Karen, eleven and petite like her friend, Chris. They were closest to Dad, who sat at the helm. Excitement flew around the boat like electric shocks as we yelled indiscriminately at the ocean as it rose up to wet our feet. Dad played along, steering *Aegir* close to the wind, her rail in the water. What was he thinking when he agreed to a sailing weekend with six young girls?

The bright green sea rose up and the boat leaned into the wave as we screamed our excitement, stretching our legs to reach the water. Sitting hip-to-hip, swinging our feet and hanging onto the lifeline cable with both hands like we were riding a roller coaster, we didn't notice anything except our fun.

By 11:00 a.m. the seas had built to ten or twelve feet, the wind blowing a steady 25 knots. The puffy grey and black clouds gathered in the sky just ahead of the boat. An emerald wave rose up to the edge of the boat. We all reached for it, yelling in anticipation of the cold water on our legs, until the water rushed over the edge of the deck, soaking all of us in a flash. It was a rogue, a larger than normal wave. Our screams of delight turned to screams of fear. We hung on tight to the lifeline so we weren't washed overboard.

"Get over here, girls!" Dad yelled from the wheel, as he turned the boat up into the wind to bring the deck level. One by one, all six of us scooted over, got up on our knees, and inched our way to the main cabin hatch—Karen and Chris, Raine and me, and finally Monica and Kerima. Everybody was soaked, and quickly chilled by the building wind.

Everybody except Monica and me went below. The boat rode up

increasingly larger swells, plunging down into deepening troughs. Monica and I held onto the teak railings, feet wide apart on the deck to gain stability in the building seas. I imagined riding a bucking bronco. "Take the helm, Monica! Turn her into the wind!" Dad said. He looked at me and said, "Follow me."

We inched our way to the foredeck, holding on to the lifelines, so we could take down the genoa.

Monica yanked and pulled and tugged at the wheel but nothing happened. Dad yelled, "Start the engine to give you some power!" Monica reached down and turned the key. Normally we could tell when the engine was running, but I couldn't hear anything above the noise of the wind. Dad yelled again, "Turn the boat into the wind!"

Monica tried to turn the wheel but nothing happened. It stayed fixed. She looked desperate, with big eyes. "It won't turn!" she yelled as the wind carried her words away.

By now, the boat had turned parallel to the seas, and as each wave came up on us, we rocked back and forth more violently, and the railings on each side of the boat got closer and closer to the water.

Dad yelled, "Crawl back to the helm!"

I timed my crawling so that I was on the high side of the roll each time I moved. Dad followed me. Soaking wet, the wind blowing my hair around my head, I shivered from cold, but also from fear. Everything seemed to be going wrong at the same time—in just a short time, our day had gone from fun to frightening.

Dad grabbed the wheel from Monica, but couldn't turn it.

While we rocked violently in the trough of the next wave, I heard what sounded like a tree splitting down the middle. High above us, the top twelve feet of mast broke off, landing precariously on one of the yard arms—the vertical braces halfway down the mast. Holding on for dear life, I looked up and saw the broken portion swinging back and forth violently.

"Holy shit!" Dad yelled, "Look out!"

Before we could react, the boat rolled violently and the piece of mast broke free and came crashing down on deck, missing Monica by only a few feet. Monica raised her arms and covered her head. A look of panic flashed across Dad's face, and he grabbed her hard and bear-hugged her for a second. He gently pushed Monica back against the cabin for stability and looked over the side of the boat, only to see the mast slamming into the side of our fiberglass hull with every roll. The sail had covered the cabin, a section of it drooping into the water. The halyards, which normally held the mast in place, lay like spaghetti all over the deck and drooped in the water.

The main cabin hatch opened from underneath the sail. "What was that noise?" Karen said, as she pushed the sail away to see. Her hair was dry and she wore a dry sweatshirt. How calm it was below, compared to the chaos on deck.

"The mast came down!" Dad yelled. "Everything's fine. Now go below."

"Everybody's sea sick down here and everything's falling out of the cabinets!" Karen yelled back.

"I can't help you now. Go below and close the hatch," Dad insisted.

Looking scared, Karen disappeared below, pulling the hatch closed.

Dad faced me and shouted, "I need to go into the aft cabin and find out why the steering is jammed!"

Monica leaned over the edge of the boat and threw up. She looked pale and sick. "Go below and take care of yourself," he said sympathetically.

Monica's eyes were huge as she shook her head, "I can't go below. I'll be even sicker down there. I want to sit down."

Dad nodded his approval. Monica wedged herself on deck between the steering wheel and the pedestal that held the compass.

Dad dug out the drogue—a huge canvas bag—from the deck locker. He threw the drogue over the stern and tied it off to a cleat. The drogue immediately turned the boat perpendicular to the seas and we began riding up and down the waves again. The death roll stopped and we avoided "turning turtle." Then Dad went below into the aft cabin.

The wind whipped and the black sky began to spew rain. It felt like things would never get better. One section of the horizon was clear and blue in the distance, but the squall we were under took up three-quarters of the sky. I felt helpless standing on deck shivering so

I peeked down into the aft cabin. I watched as Dad discovered one of the boat's steering cables had popped out of the steering box.

"Come down here," Dad said. "See this cable here? It should be in there," he said pointing to a circular brass device. There was no way to move the cable back into position, the tension on it was too strong. Our bodies shook involuntarily from the cold, but Dad's eyes were focused and his voice was clear and steady. He smiled at me and brushed my cheek with the back of his fingers. "Get my tool box," he said kindly—we could finally hear each other without yelling—and his affection made me determined to persevere and assist him in any way I could. It was him and me against this storm. I retrieved his toolbox from around the corner in the engine room. "Check on the others," Dad said as his head descended into the cabinet where the steering components were.

I crawled through the engine area into the main cabin to find a silent, miserable group of girls. The floor of the boat was covered in magazines, books, discarded wet clothes, pillows, towels, and various items that had fallen out of cabinets during the violent rocking back and forth. The smell was a mixture of salt water and vomit.

"How are you?" I asked hesitantly.

Kerima groaned and laid her head back, closing her eyes. Raine said, "What happened? This must be a huge storm."

"Leslie!" Dad shouted from the aft cabin. "I think it's time for a May Day call."

I got on the radio and called the Newport Beach Coast Guard. They answered and said they could rescue the people but that we'd have to leave the boat. Dad shoved his way forward to the navigation station and grabbed the microphone, yelling profanities about not abandoning his ship *ever*, and turned off the radio. He looked at the wide-eyed girls and said calmly, "Everything will be fine," and stomped back to the aft cabin.

I followed Dad. As he looked into the steering box and compartment, he said, "I think I've figured out how to jury-rig the steering. I need to work on this some more." In his now-calm-and-collected voice, he said, "Can you check on Monica?"

I opened the aft cabin hatch and climbed out. Monica was wrapped in her bright yellow foul weather jacket, which Karen had handed up to her, protected from the wind and water as much as possible. Her hood was pulled so tight around her face I could barely see her eyes and nose.

"Monica! Are you okay?" I asked. She looked up at me in utter misery and then laid her head on her chest again.

It was so dark it looked like night. The horizon had disappeared completely. There was no more clear sky anywhere. The dark, water-laden clouds dumped their load on us relentlessly. The wind blew, occasionally gusting twice as hard and then returning to a steady blow again. Water crashed over the bow each time the boat climbed a wave and fell down into a trough. Glad I had put on my foul weather jacket, I stood on deck for a while, watching the storm ravage us—wondering if we would make it back.

I sat down next to Monica for a while, leaning against her, hoping my presence brought her some comfort. We locked arms, laid our heads on our chests, and tried to rest. There wasn't anything either of us could do until Dad fixed the steering.

About forty minutes later, Dad called me to the aft cabin. "I think I fixed the steering. I need you to stay down here moving this pipe back and forth as I call directions to you. Understand?" Dad had cut a hole in the top of the hanging closet and inserted a long pipe down through it to the steering component.

"Yes," I said.

"Good! We'll work together and get us to the harbor, okay, sweetie?" he said. I smiled and nodded at him.

Dad grabbed his foul weather jacket and went up on deck. He started the engine, filling the aft cabin with the smell of diesel. My mouth began to water, as my stomach flip-flopped. I thought about throwing up, but Dad kept the aft cabin hatch open which gave me some fresh air. He stood in front of the hatch on deck and yelled for me to turn to port. I pulled the pipe towards me and held it there. "Good! Keep it there until I tell you to straighten it out." The boat responded and we began motoring to shore. We no longer rode up and down the waves violently, instead the waves came from behind us and lifted the stern up slightly and we surfed them in to shore.

The rain had stopped and the wind had died down. The waves were not nearly as big as they were a few hours earlier. As the motion of the boat calmed down, Dad yelled down to the girls to come on deck if they wanted. They emerged tentatively, glad for the fresh air, I'm sure.

As we entered the calm interior waters of Newport Beach harbor, Dad said, "Would you look at this?"

I could see Dad's back as he faced forward on the deck, just outside the aft cabin doors. He stood with his feet spread apart for balance, arms crossed over his chest like the King of Siam.

"What?" I yelled from the aft cabin. "What is it?"

"I guess the weather is calm enough now because it's the Coast Guard on their way to rescue us."

I wasn't sure what that meant exactly—we were already coming into the harbor.

Dad yelled, "We don't need your help!" Then he held his middle finger high up in the air above his head.

Apparently the Coast Guard had been trying to raise us on the radio, which Dad had turned off in a fit of anger. They were obligated to investigate our whereabouts after the storm died down. Later Dad laughed about it, calling the Coast Guard "sissies."

We were able to tie up under on our own power at the visitor's dock at 4:00 p.m. I came up on deck to see the harbor, blue patches in the sky and beat-up ole' *Aegir* safely tied to a solid dock. The boat was a wreck, with the top portion of the mast tied down to the main cabin, halyards and shrouds bunched in a pile. With his chest out and his head held high Dad smiled at me as I took it all in, "We limped into the harbor, but we did it—you and me—and I'm proud of you," he said. I smiled back at him, glad it was over.

"Can we go ashore?" asked Raine.

"Yes, girls, go ashore," Dad said. He watched as we girls ran up the dock and onto the grass. We dropped to our knees, giving thanks to the heavens above. Raine hugged me sideways as her freckled face kissed my cheek in happiness. Without shame, but with lots of screaming and laughing, all six girls kissed the ground.

We moved *Aegir* to San Diego Harbor for repairs. The insurance company estimated the damage at $10,216. The report stated "the steering failed when the auto pilot jammed and held the rudder stationary." It further said the mast was glued together in diagonal sections, and that the top section broke off during the violent rocking back and forth when we were caught in the trough. The report also noted the winds gusted to sixty knots that day and some of the waves reached a height of eighteen feet.

This was the first storm we'd ever encountered. Over the past fourteen months of living on the boat, Dad had spent many hours teaching us how to sail, but now our training would take a new turn—preparing for storms and failed equipment. The biggest lesson Dad learned from the storm was that we all needed safety harnesses. The likelihood of falling overboard was high during a storm. "I can't imagine if I would have been washed overboard," he said one night at dinner. "What would you girls have done all alone in that storm with no mast and no steering?"

Monica's seasickness made her somebody we couldn't entirely rely upon. Karen only weighed ninety-five pounds, which made her more of a worry than a help on deck during a storm. I had to admit that Dad and I worked well together and that helping him made me feel capable, even powerful. I respected him as our captain and felt safe with him in charge. Dad respected me, too, which cemented my position as first mate on *Aegir*, although nothing was ever said out loud.

The repairs took close to six weeks so we moved into the Marina Del Mar Condominiums next to T-dock. We were still in our old neighborhood and could continue with school while Dad commuted to San Diego every day to work on the boat. The departure date for our around-the-world cruise was set for December 1, 1974, only six months away.

The apartment was a small, fully furnished two-bedroom. In one bedroom were two twin beds, in the other, a king-sized bed. Shirley and Bill Blake, a rich couple from Palos Verdes who owned the penthouse condo two stories above us, had learned of our upcoming voyage and helped Dad rent unit 206 from the owners at a reduced rate. Everybody seemed to want to help the Norwegian and his three daughters who were sailing around the world. Dad was very good at soliciting help in the name of a higher good: our education and world travels. Shirley and Bill took us under their wing, feeling sorry that Monica, Karen, and I didn't have a mother close by, and that Dad didn't have a wife.

Shortly after settling into the condo, a few weeks before summer break, Karen and I lay on our twin beds doing our homework like normal teenagers. Monica was visiting a friend who lived on a small ranch with horses, goats, and chickens. That was her love, not the boat and the harbor. She went there as often as Dad let her.

"I miss Mom so much," Karen said, "I can't wait to see her." At the end of summer Mom and Grandma were coming to visit and say good-bye before we left for Tahiti. It would be the first time we'd seen Mom in well over a year.

"Yeah, it'll be nice to see them, that's for sure," I said.

"How long are they staying?" Karen asked.

"A few weeks, I guess. Dad's keeping the apartment until she goes back to Canada."

"I wish we could stay in the apartment until the day we leave," Karen said.

"Yeah, that'd be nice."

I loved living in a condo, having real beds and real showers. We were silent for a moment, when the front door opened and slammed shut. Dad's words, spoken in rhythm with each step he took, got increasingly louder, "Why—are—those—jeans—still—hanging—on—the—balcony?"

Karen jumped up off the bed and ran toward the door as Dad rounded the corner into our bedroom. He grabbed Karen, picking her up by the waist, lifting her shoulder high. She screamed and grabbed the doorjamb near the ceiling and tried to hold on. Her miniature size was really pronounced when she was in the air—she looked like a doll. I watched her fingers slide across the doorjamb as she tried to hold on as Dad pulled on her as he walked toward the living room. She couldn't hold on any longer and her fingers disappeared.

I followed carefully.

"How many times do I have to tell you to get your clothing off the railing?"

Dad had told us not to hang our clothes on the railing since the wind had taken some of our clothes down to the rocks and into the water below. T-dock, the dock we usually lived on was right outside our balcony.

"You stupid, stupid girl, you never listen." He held Karen over the edge of the balcony by her waist. "Don't squirm or I'll drop you on the rocks."

Karen stopped moving. Her pale face and saucer-sized eyes stared right at me. I held my breath, didn't dare say anything. He held her out over the balcony edge for a minute while he yelled, "Maybe next time you'll listen when I tell you to take your clothing off the balcony."

Liquid trickled down as Karen peed her pants. Dad shook her a little and said, "You're peeing on me? You are actually peeing on me?"

He turned around and came inside, still holding her high. I lowered my gaze and stepped aside as he walked to the hallway and threw her into the bathroom, "Clean yourself up and get those goddamn jeans off the balcony before I get back."

Karen landed against the wall at the far side of the bathroom, between the toilet and the shower, letting out a yell as she hit, and then slid to the ground. She burst out crying.

The front door slammed shut as he left. The walls shook.

I ran into the bathroom to find Karen huddled in a ball on the floor. "I think he broke my shoulder," she cried. "God, I hate him."

"I know. I'm so sorry, Karen. What can I do?" I closed the bathroom door and locked it.

"I thought I was going to die. I was over the rocks, Leslie—I thought he was going to let go."

"He would never let go, Karen." Dad was all about the dramatic when it came to punishment, but I knew he would never drop her.

He said all the time that we were "brain dead" because we couldn't remember anything. He was always looking for ways to get our attention and impress upon us the lesson at hand.

I rubbed her shoulder softly, remembering Monica's punch in the stomach a few years earlier.

We sat on the bathroom floor together, "When's Mom coming?" Karen asked.

"Dad said August or September." The linoleum floor was cold so I stood up.

"I wrote to Mom and told her all about the storm and being dismasted."

"Really? You probably scared her to death," I said, brushing my frizzy hair into a ponytail.

"I can tell you're not excited about Mom coming. Why?"

"I don't know...she's never here when I need her." I told Karen how hard it was that Dad wouldn't let me wear a bra.

"Yeah. He gets weird about things."

A small laugh escaped me. "Yeah, he gets weird about jeans hanging on the balcony."

"Oh, God, I better get those right now." She got up gingerly and I felt her shoulder. It wasn't broken, just bruised.

Three

I was six the first time I realized there was something wrong with Mom. I pushed open the apartment door after school one day and saw the tipped over chair, the blanket strewn across the bedroom floor, and a pile of pillows in the corner. Dad sat on the green plaid chesterfield. He wore a red and blue Norwegian sweater over an old pair of blue jeans. The light from the hanging pendant lamp bounced off his bald shiny head. If he'd had hair it would have been disheveled. His blue eyes found Monica and me and then stared intently at the floor again.

"What happened, Daddy? Where's Mommy?" I asked.

He closed his eyes, took a drink from his highball, and said, "Your mother fell off the bed."

The white walls were bare except for a rustic wooden bookshelf that hung from the ceiling by two thick chains. The splintery planks held books about home construction, gardening, and sailing, along with stacks of *Sunset* and *National Geographic* magazines. One shelf held Mom's books: Rod McKuen poems, classics like *Gone with the Wind* and *The Grapes of Wrath*.

Mom dressed Monica and me as if we were twins. We had long blonde hair that Mom curled into ringlets and put in pigtails each morning with ribbons. We had matching dresses, matching shoes and socks, and matching pea coats, mine red, hers blue. We stood together at the front door of our apartment.

"Why, Daddy? Where is she?" Monica cried out as she ran and buried her face in Dad's chest. I stood motionless.

"She's tired girls, and needs a rest." Dad hugged Monica. My eyes followed Dad's as he looked toward the bedroom.

"Where's Karen?" I asked, pronouncing it the Norwegian way Dad insisted, *Car-in*. Not that she herself pronounced it correctly, at five years old she couldn't say her R's so she said "Cahwin."

He nodded his head slightly toward the bedroom and I walked through the partially open French doors. I saw the ugly bare mattress, sheets dripping to the floor, and Karen hiding under the vanity. She wore a pink dress with mismatched bobby socks—one white and one blue—but no shoes. Her arms were wrapped around her knees, drawn up to her chest. Her hair hung lifeless around her face. She looked at me with wide brown eyes, as if astonished to see me, and whispered, "Mommy's gone."

That first time Mom left rocked me deeply. I'd lay awake at night, scared to ask Daddy again where she'd gone for fear of a spanking; scared to think of the black hole she'd seemed to disappear into. I cried into my pillow, not knowing if she was alright.

Living without the screaming, fighting, and crying was easier, but not having a mom to help with dinner, baths, or laundry was harder. Monica, Karen, and I learned to be independent fast. Dad didn't allow any crying or feeling sorry for ourselves.

It was only years later that we learned that "falling off the bed" was code for her illness. She was battling mental illness, alcoholism, and prescription pill addiction. She would disappear many more times over the years, always in the middle of the night, it seemed—she was there and then she wasn't. Dad did a good job hiding the reasons from us, but he couldn't hide the fact she was gone. As I grew I began to patch together the reasons for Mom's disappearances. Dad said stuff like, "she's weak and needs help," or "mental illness runs in her family." I also heard words like manic depression, paranoid schizophrenia, and electric shock during discussions of treatments and diagnoses Mom received over the years.

Leslie, Karen and Monica

When I was seven, Dad and Mom got divorced. As we drove toward San Francisco one day without Mom, Dad made the announcement.

"Girls," he said as he laid his arm across the entire length of the front bench seat of the car and turning his head slightly backwards, "I have some important news. Your mother and I are divorcing."

He liked to talk to us like we were adults.

None of us had to ask why. It was obvious they weren't happy. Dad turned the radio off and continued, "You girls are old enough to pick who you want to live with, but you must stay together. Do you understand?"

I stared out the window as the car sped down the freeway. The full moon hung low over King's Mountain. It was big, and I could see the dark spots on it. I studied the moon silently, wishing we could stay with Dad always and marveling at how the full moon followed us all the way down the freeway, wondering if we Johansen's were somehow special. Silence thickened in the car. I looked over Karen's head to Monica and mouthed, "What do you want to do?"

Before Monica spoke, Karen said, "I want to live with Mommy."

Monica chimed in, "I want to go with Mommy, too."

I said quickly, "I want to stay with Daddy."

I thought my Dad was a god and was convinced, without needing him to explain a thing, that the divorce was Mom's fault. I felt important and proud to be his daughter.

We moved back to Canada with Mom, leaving Dad alone. He quit his job as an instrument technician at United Airlines, moved out of the Norwegian community we'd all lived in on King's Mountain and got a job selling life insurance on Market Street in San Francisco.

Mom, Monica, Karen, and I moved into an old fourplex apartment on St. Luke Road in a poverty-stricken part of Windsor. It wasn't far from our grandmother, aunt, uncle, and cousins, but it was very different from our nice neighborhood in Henrik Ibsen Park. The apartment and city of Windsor felt wrong, like we didn't belong there. I didn't hide the fact that I wished Dad would take us back to California. Mom yelled and cried and drank and threw things.

We lived very close to the Hiram Walker Whiskey Distillery, which filled our noses with barley until we almost barfed. Our neighbors were different than the Norwegian families we knew, and even at seven years old I could tell we had lost everything important. We used to be special, and now we weren't.

As if to confirm her fall in stature from married woman to single mom, Mom stopped coiffing her hair, cut it in a bob, and began working the night shift as a Licensed Vocational Nurse (LVN) at Lakeside Hospital, across the river in downtown Detroit.

I settled into second grade. We missed our dad, and survived on Sunday evening phones calls when he would call to tell us how much he missed and loved us.

Dad seemed to have forgotten about us for almost two years, until the second Christmas Eve when I heard a rap at the door. When I opened it, a huge Christmas tree stood in my way and then Dad leaned the tree to the side. He had a huge smile on his clean-shaven face. His small blue eyes and great big smile never looked so good. I screamed at the top of my lungs and leapt into his arms. Dad brought us presents and hugs and took us to the Bahamas for Christmas. He told us stories of a ranch he'd bought in California where he said we were all moving so we could be a family again.

I couldn't have been happier.

We drove to California with our belongings piled high atop our brown 1964 Buick Skylark, through Michigan and Montana and west from Yellowstone through the rolling green hills and raging rivers of Idaho, right into Nevada's dead and barren desert lands. Sand knolls covered in cactus spread for miles in every direction. We drove straight over the Sierra Nevada Mountain Range, through thickly wooded mountain roads, until we arrived in the plains and valleys of Butte County near Paradise, California—and not a moment too soon. I was sick of being in the car after ten days so when Dad turned onto a dirt and gravel road, I jumped up on my knees and said, "Are we there yet? Is this Paradise? Are we there yet?"

"Yes, we are. Welcome to Midgaard," Dad said as he got out of the car, adjusting his cut-offs and opening the big swinging metal gate, "The name is from Norse mythology meaning 'enclosed yard!'" he yelled as he walked back to the car.

We headed slowly through the gate and drove onto the property. Swaying golden grass covered the earth as far as I could see. Old oaks grew together in groups across the landscape, along with red Manzanitas, small shrubs, and an occasional tall green pine. The gravel road crunched under our wheels and led us down through a wooded section into a larger open area that looked south over a large valley.

I was amazed to see buildings on our ranch already. There was a brand new barn, a matching outhouse, and a big slab of concrete where Dad was building our house. We'd all expected land in the middle of nowhere—just like Dad described to us—but he hadn't said anything about the work he'd done. He kept turning to check our faces to see our surprise, obviously proud of himself. Best of all, the barn had two horses in it.

We settled in during the summer of 1970, when I was nine, sleeping in a fifteen-foot travel trailer that looked big enough for Barbie and Ken, but not a family of five.

Mom holed up inside the trailer and didn't come out for weeks, sleeping days and nights away. She wasn't keen on hiking, riding horses, climbing rocks, or pounding nails. Her escapes were reading and sleep. She wasn't drinking yet, as I remember, but she kept a bottle of pills near her bedside. She'd come out of the trailer with messy hair, squinting at the bright day, and sit at the little picnic table where we ate all our meals, head in her hands, smoking a cigarette.

"What's wrong with Mom?" I asked one day while helping Dad pound nails in the two-by-fours.

"She doesn't like pioneer living. She keeps asking if we can move to town," he said. "Do you want to move to town, Leslie?"

"No way, Dad, I want to be here with you building the house, and playing with the horses," I said.

My heart was secretly divided. There were days when I would have loved to take a real shower, and curl up to watch *Wild Wild West* in soft clean pajamas like all the other kids in the world who had flushing toilets. But I kept up the brave front. The bond between Dad and me grew stronger every day. Monica and Karen watched him pick me for tasks, glad to be excluded because Dad was volatile and demanding. He looked to me to help him and I never wanted to let him down. He pushed me outside my comfort zone and each time I succeeded, whether it was riding Duke, our ornery Quarter Horse, or going with him to the lumber store for supplies, it set me apart from my sisters and mother. He chose me as his companion and I couldn't have been happier. It was exciting walking near the edge of the volcano, never knowing when or if it would explode. When it did explode, it usually didn't explode on me. It exploded on Monica and Karen and Mom, who were not participating in whatever Dad and I were doing.

We found a family of four kittens one night and rescued them. I picked the orange one for myself and named it Margo after Dad's favorite movie star, Ann Margaret, who came from Sweden like his mother. Monica named the two blue/grey ones Dusty and Stormy. Karen picked the black one and named it Sambo since Dad liked Sammy Davis, Jr.

The next day I tried to show my kitten to Mom. I entered the dark trailer midday and whispered loudly, "Wake up, Mom."

Curled up under the sleeping bag, she moaned and stretched at the sound of my voice.

"Look! We found kittens. Isn't this one cute?" I held Margo by the belly, stretching my arm toward Mom.

Mom rolled over, eyes cloudy, smacking her mouth softly—trying to find moisture—and pointed with her long, skinny finger, "Hand me the water glass. I'm dying of thirst."

She leaned on one elbow, her black hair sticking up and a thin pink sleeveless nightgown hugging her thin body. She took a careful drink, trying to focus on me, then reached for the prescription bottle on the shelf, opening it and downing two little white pills. Margo's tiny mews filled the trailer, which smelled musty and thick.

"What did you say, honey?"

"I have an orange kitty and we named her Margo. Isn't she cute?"

"That's nice, Leslie, but don't put that dirty cat on my bed. Take it outside and I'll see it later, okay, sweetie?" She collapsed onto her back.

"When Mom? When will you get up?"

"Soon. Now go outside and leave me alone. I have a headache."

I left the trailer and found Monica and Karen with their kitties on the picnic table outside the trailer.

"What did she say?" asked Monica.

"Nothing. She's tired and has a headache," I said, hurt she cared more about her pills than me and my new kitten.

Dad came up to the trailer, tool belt still wrapped around his waist, sawdust on his shirt. He went inside and boomed, "Get up, Paula, we need to talk." We all looked at the screened trailer door, surprised at his harsh voice. Dad came back outside carrying bread, peanut butter, and jam.

"Girls, make me a sandwich. I'll be right back," and he went to the barn.

"I want to do it," said Karen, "I get to make Daddy a sandwich."

We put our kittens back in the box. A few minutes later, Mom came to the door of the trailer, barely covered in her thin pink nighty, blinking, scanning the area. The cool morning breeze had disappeared with the dew on the ground and the heat had already built to a smoldering hot temperature.

"Where's your father, girls?"

"He went to the barn," Monica said.

"I'm making him a sandwich for lunch," announced Karen proudly.

Mom looked at Karen trying to smear peanut butter on top of the jelly, "Leslie, help your sister," she said, and disappeared back inside the trailer.

When Dad returned, Mom emerged from the trailer, coffee in hand. She wore shorts and a tank top, and fluffy pink slippers on her feet. She brushed away the leaves from the picnic bench with her fingertips, her rear end high in the air in a dainty feminine way, and sat down. She took a sip from her coffee, surveying the rest of us.

"Enough Valium, drinking, and sleeping to avoid everything, Paula, you need to get a job in town at the hospital," Dad said.

She held her coffee cup with two fingers through the loop and her pinky finger up. The cup shook just a little, "How dare you talk to me like that in front of the girls. You go get a job, Bjorn, and support this family." She loved to use his name whenever she could, it rolled off her tongue with such authority. He told everyone it was pronounced like "urine" with a "b"—"Burine," which always made people squirm but Dad loved it.

She slammed her cup down on the table, the coffee sloshed out, as she added, "I can't believe I moved here from Windsor to live in squalor."

He stood there like the King of Siam—Dad's favorite movie was the *King and I*—his hands on his hips, shiny bald head held high, gaze cast downward on his subjects. "This isn't squalor," he proclaimed. "The trailer is our home for now. And don't talk to me about getting a job. I made all the money to buy this property and the materials to build the house. The girls are happy being outside all day." He winked at me.

I looked down at the dirt, not wanting to watch her scream, not wanting to watch Dad yell at her, just wanting everybody to go away.

"You need to get a job so we have money for food while I finish building our house," he said. With that, he walked away.

Mom stood up from the picnic table and yelled after him, "You didn't earn the money to buy this property by working. You won the money gambling in Vegas. So don't say you earned it through a job."

After their argument, for many evenings in a row, Mom took the only good car we owned—a sky blue 1968 Impala—into town. She returned drunk and brazen, sure she could take him on and fight him better with the liquid courage. They had some horrific battles. But when she was sober, she cowered. The more she backed away the more he moved into her space like the King advanced in power by clapping his hands and demanding silence. But in the movie, Deborah Kerr never cowered from Yul Brynner.

Anytime Monica, Karen, or I complained about how hard we had it, Dad called us "sissies" or "softies." He compared us to Mom when we whined about not having any milk for cereal, or a flushing toilet, or heat when it was cold, or medicine for painful mosquito bites, or being scared of walking to the outhouse at night, or having ticks in our hair, or biking ten miles into town to bring back Kentucky Fried Chicken for dinner. He grew up in Norway where he had barely anything, skiing miles to school each day, living a tough life. He made fun of Mom's prissy need for things like hot showers, clean clothes, and fancy dinners. He used her as an example of how not to be, so I mostly kept my mouth shut about any grievances I had.

"Men don't like prissy girls, so don't be prissy," he'd warn us during our nightly dinner of bologna sandwiches or granola. "Be the kind of girl that helps out and isn't afraid of getting dirty." He expected us to dig in and work as hard as we could for our age. No quitters were allowed. Whining was not an option.

I hated that he lumped me in with Mom. I didn't want to be anything like Mom, sleeping all day and crying about things. I tried very hard to make him proud, following him around while he built the house, handing him nails, bringing him sandwiches and cold water. It strengthened the bond between us, but created a rift between my mother and me.

I found my secret place by accident one day when I followed the horses up to the edge of the property. At the farthest point from the house on the edge of the canyon, I found two giant boulders under a family of oaks. The trees gave plenty of shade and during the hot summer months the rocks were cool, comforting, and protective. I took a towel from the trailer and sat between the two boulders, leaning back against the rocks with my bare back, absorbing the coolness. Atop the smallest bolder, the silence broken only by the hawks that circled over the canyon, I hung on an oak tree branch admiring the view. In front of me were miles of valley, dry ranch land, and oak and red manzanita trees. I could see our "bath tub" spring at the very edge of the meadow.

It became my special place and I didn't tell anybody else about it. I went to the boulders to get away from the fighting, and wrote in a notebook I took from the trailer. I wrote about riding the horses, or hiking to the bottom of the canyon and swimming in the river. I never wrote about the sadness and hurt of our family.

I alternated between feeling sorry for Mom and being mad at her for causing so much trouble. I wanted to comfort Mom but she was enemy territory. If Dad saw me cuddling with her he would give me the silent treatment for a few days, avoid eye contact, make me feel unwanted. He stopped winking at me, and brushing my cheek with the back of his fingers, which nearly made my heart burst out of my chest with pride. When he stopped doing that, I was crushed.

Karen, being the youngest, would often curl up in Mom's lap after a bad fight, rocking back and forth, trying to comfort her, "Mommy, I love you. Please don't be sad."

Monica took her grief inward, often crying into her pillow. Dad worked us against Mom, talking about her drinking and pill taking. "You girls better never drink and take pills like your mother. She's weak and soft."

Not only did Monica look like Mom—tall, thin, and lanky—she acted like her, too—ditzy and not very clued in on her surroundings. Dad's questions frequently called her back from space or wherever she went daydreaming.

I looked like Dad with my round pudgy face, two dimples, and big smile. Though we were almost the same height, Monica had bird legs and I had thicker, muscled legs. Dad called me "healthy looking," which I was sure was code for fat.

Karen was petite and thin. She looked to be a mix between Mom and Dad with her freckled nose.

Leslie, Bestefar, Monica, Karen and Mom

Mom moved to town as the rest of us settled in on Midgaard, in the three-bedroom house Dad had finished. Water was scarce, and except for the natural spring on the meadow above the house we had to haul all our water in bottles from town.

Dad solved our water problem by purchasing a huge metal tank, which he put on the ridge above the house. He paid a guy from town to come fill it with water monthly. After Dad hooked the tank up to the house, we could take short showers (timed by him), do dishes in the kitchen sink, and flush the toilets—but only at night, using the outhouse was still mandatory during the day.

Not long after we had "running" water, Monica and I decided to combine our three-minute allotment of shower time into a six-minute shower by taking one together. We plugged the tub so we stood shin-deep in warm water. After we washed our hair, I said, "Give me the soap," but Monica held the soap over her head with a teasing smile. She turned around and began soaping herself up. I reached around her, "Give it to me!" I said, and grabbed it. Monica turned and shoved me against the wall, grabbing the soap back. I thudded against the wall and my legs slipped out from underneath me. I landed with a slosh, screaming, "Monica! Stop it!"

Dad burst into the bathroom. Monica stood over me as I sat in the water.

"What happened?" His eyes were wild and menacing.

"She shoved me," I said.

Without another word, Dad grabbed Monica's skinny wet arm and punched her in the stomach. She landed face down in the tub on top of me. He grabbed her by the waist and hauled her folded, naked body down the hall, setting her down by the wood burning stove in the living room. She screamed and cried, "No! Put me down."

"Stop wasting water and don't ever push Leslie again!" he yelled.

I peeked around the corner from the bathroom and saw Monica naked against the wall, dripping wet, covering her face with her arms, ready for the next blow. Dad stood looking at her naked body for a moment and then turned and left through the sliding glass door. Monica fell to her knees, grasping her stomach, crying in a huddled lump. I took a towel and draped it over her back.

"I'm sorry, Monica," I whispered.

Monica hobbled into the bedroom and I followed. There was a big red circle below her rib cage where Dad had punched her. Water dripped from her long hair. Her big brown eyes were filled with tears, her long black eyelashes clumped together.

"I guess we know for sure who the favorite is now," she said.

"I'm sorry, Monica. I really am."

"Dad loves you the best," she said.

Dad told us we might never have electricity because PG&E didn't have lines anywhere close to our property. The only way to have lights after dark was to hand-crank the generator Dad had bought. We all learned the routine and took turns cranking it at night like we took turns building a fire in the Franklin stove. Once in a while, we were allowed to watch Dad's favorite TV show, *The Sonny and Cher Show*. The TV was in Dad's room so we'd all pile onto the bed in our nightgowns and slippers.

One winter night I remember Dad laughing at all the jokes and lusting after Cher in her skimpy outfits. "Isn't she beautiful, girls? So exotic."

Cher held Chastity, their cute baby girl, and was making some joke about Sonny when the generator sputtered to a stop and we were swallowed by darkness. Nobody moved. I could almost hear everyone thinking, *Who's going to put fuel in the generator and crank it on again?*

"Monica," Dad said, "go put some gasoline in the tank and crank the generator back on."

I knew Monica was scared, so it didn't surprise me when she said, "Leslie, can you help—?"

"No!" Dad didn't even wait for her to finish. "Karen, go with Monica and hold the flashlight so she can fill up the tank. You two work together."

I couldn't believe Dad didn't pick me—he always picked me to do everything—but I knew better than to say anything because he'd change his mind and make me go outside. I lay very still waiting for the lights to come back on, with only silence and darkness surrounding me. It felt weird to have my eyes open and not see anything so I closed them.

"Leslie, where are you?" Dad's voice sounded silky and soft.

"Right here, where I was before."

"Come here and sit next to me."

"Why, are you scared, Dad?" I said, teasing.

"Get up here *now*." His voice was curt, strong, and abrupt.

My heart jolted at the change in his tone and I rolled over and sat up. But before I could move to the top of the bed, he grabbed me and hugged me, wrapping his big arms around me, pinning my arms against my body. His mouth came down on mine hard. His tongue pried my lips apart. I tried to get loose and close my mouth, but he was too strong. He held me tighter and moved his tongue around inside my mouth. I couldn't fight him so I went limp. My mind saw flashes of light as I waited for it to end. Then the kiss changed, softened, as I lay rigid in his arms. He released some tension from the hug at the same time. I stayed still.

When he was done kissing me, he laid me back down on the bed, cleared his throat, and shook the bed as he fixed the pillows behind him and straightened himself up.

I crawled back to my original position. Adrenaline pumped through my body. I wanted to run, but I stayed frozen in place like an animal whose life depends on stillness to avoid capture. The silence buzzed. The blood in my ears rushed. My eyes were wide open, though it was still pitch black. Then he spoke in a regular tone of voice, as if nothing had happened. "How long does it take to fill up the tank and crank that generator?"

I didn't respond. It had been about ten minutes since they left. I closed my eyes, knowing the lights would be coming on soon, and I buried my head in the blanket. *God, just let me act normal like nothing happened, let me act normal, act normal, normal, normal, normal.*

The familiar sound of the generator started up—putt, putt, putt—and the lights flickered on. The TV blasted Sonny and Cher, "*Babe, I got you babe/I got you, babe*," in perfect harmony.

I was looking intently at the TV without seeing it when Monica and Karen burst into the room, followed by a rush of cold air.

"We did it. We filled it up and started it right back up," Monica panted. They jumped on the bed, breathing hard, and found their spots.

"Okay, now be quiet. The show is on," he said.

Cher introduced The Jackson 5. My mind followed their singing and dancing routine, eventually becoming engrossed in the show. A commercial came on and I remembered the kiss as Raquel Welch sold Quasar TVs. I turned my head slightly to see him. He was leaning on some pillows, up on his elbow. When he saw I was looking at him, he leaned over farther, maybe to see my expression. The bed shook as he moved. He smiled at me and squeezed my foot. I turned my head back to stare at the TV, willing time to go faster so the show would end and I could leave this bed. I concentrated on Raquel Welch and the show came back on. Somehow, as if by magic, I forgot about my father. I forgot about everything. Nothing had happened. It was a nightmare and I made it up.

Often, after that, I caught Dad watching me intently. He studied me in a new way. He'd size me up from across the room—staring at me with a half-smile, half-smirk on his face. I didn't know if he wanted to kiss me again or spank me. I didn't know if I was a good girl anymore, or a bad girl. I didn't know if it was my fault or not. I became ultra-self-conscious about my body and my movements. My nose or my leg would itch, so I'd scratch while he watched in utter fascination. He seemed to relish my awkwardness, laughing quietly under his breath. I felt naked and exposed but tried to deny it, telling myself that everything was back to normal.

One rainy day during PE, the teacher said, "Today you must climb this rope to the ceiling." We stood in a line around the gym, shorts and T-shirts on, mumbling our discontent. The red gym shirt I wore felt funny over my chest, not flat like it did before. I was almost eleven years old, with tiny buds on my chest that made me self-conscious. A yellow tri-braided rope hung from the ceiling near the middle of the gym floor.

My best friend Patti and I stood near the end of the girls' line and watched as the first boy climbed the rope with ease, one hand over another, pulling himself expertly to the top. His legs didn't touch the rope but instead hung freely below him. A few girls tried and some of them got a few feet off the ground before they fell back down.

When it was my turn, I stepped forward and grabbed ahold of the rough rope with both hands. It was so thick that my hands just barely went around it. I pulled up hard, leaving my legs free and away from the rope just like the boys did. A zing inside went straight to my crotch and I fell to the ground on my knees, shocked by my body. I had never felt anything like that before and at first it startled me, and then it felt good down below. As I sat on my knees holding on to the rope, Patti leaned over and said, "Are you alright?" I nodded. The kids in the gym played basketball and ran around the outside of the court, yelling. Their voices echoed off the walls. The PE teacher yelled from the sidelines, "Try it again."

I saw that he was talking to me, so I stood up, grabbed high up on the rope again, and waited before pulling up. I didn't want to feel that warm soft glow start in my armpits, go through my breasts and down to my crotch. As I pulled up hard again on the rope, my knees and arms became instantly weak, my breath uneven. I fell to the ground again, landing on my knees, hitting the hardwood floor with a thud. I cried out. The feeling was so incredible, and unexpected and shocking to me—my scream was in pleasure, not pain. The noise in the gym covered my cry so nobody except Patti heard me. I tried to act hurt, grabbing my knees and bending over them. Patti helped me up and over to the bleachers where I sat for the rest of gym class.

I went home that day and couldn't wait to get up to my special spot by the boulders. The feeling in my crotch had stayed for the rest of the day as a warm, dull ache. I touched the little buds on my chest. They were so tender, I didn't remember them ever being that way before. As I leaned back against the granite rock, warm to my bare back, I touched myself softly and I felt the same zing in my crotch. I closed my eyes and did it a few more times. When I opened my eyes, Dad was right in front of me, watching me with a big grin. He towered over me, only a few feet away with his brown leather hat on, no shirt, and dirty cut-off jean shorts. "What are you doing, Leslie?"

"Nothing," I said. I lurched up and ran away from him.

"Well, don't play with yourself because your boobs will sag," he called after me, laughing.

When I came home that night for dinner he winked at me and smiled. My face turned beet red and I wished I were dead. In the following days, Dad continued to grin at me with that awful knowing look. That face—with those hawk eyes—is burned into my memory and even now I can conjure it in a second. He watched my every move, examining my walk. He stared, watching everything I did. I felt like a bug under a microscope. I wanted to die, to disappear and leave no trace that I'd ever been here.

After living in town alone for more than a year, Mom finally started coming around more consistently. She was happy that at least we had running water. Dad looked the other way when Mom used the bathroom during the day, just to keep the peace. She'd arrive after work to have dinner with us and watch us do our homework. One day she announced she would read us *Dove,* by Robin Lee Graham, the true story of a sixteen-year-old boy who sailed around the world alone. Each night after dinner, we sat on the porch overlooking the canyon, riveted as Mom read in her elegant and mesmerizing way, using different voices as she read different characters. Gripped by the adventure of this boy Robin sailing to exotic places, I couldn't wait to get home each day from school, racing through my chores and homework, eager to hear the next chapter.

The day she finished the book, we were gathered around the Franklin stove in the living room, curled up under blankets because the evenings had turned cold. Dad leaned on the couch staring off into space. Mom always said you could hear the wheels turning when Dad was cooking something up. "Why don't we sail around the world like Robin did?" Dad asked.

I didn't have to think twice about it. Sailing in the tropics was an extension of my favorite vacation ever—a trip to the Bahamas two years earlier.

"Yeah! Let's go," I said.

Mom hugged the book to her chest and said, "I'm ready."

"I don't want to leave the ranch and all our animals," said Monica hesitantly.

"Would we sail all the way around the world?" asked Karen.

"Yes. We could take five years to make the trip. You girls could do correspondence courses, and attend school in the countries we visit," Dad said. He was sitting up on the couch, watching us for a response. "I've thought about this for a long time now. My goal is to end up in France so that you girls attend high school for one year and become fluent."

I bounced up and down on my knees, "Yes, let's go. When can we leave?" We all knew he was serious. Oh, yes. Dad never talked about stuff unless he was serious.

Monica sat back against the wall and covered herself with the blanket, wearing a sad expression.

Dad said, "Think about it, Monica, maybe you'll change your mind."

Karen went and sat next to Dad on the couch. He put his arm around her. Karen said, "It sounds exciting, and I won't have to bike five miles to the bus stop anymore." Dad chuckled and kissed her cheek.

It was obvious Mom and Dad had already discussed the plan. They were going to reconcile again, though no formal announcement was made and all they seemed to do was fight.

Over the next six months, Dad talked about sailing and traveling every moment. He left to see boats in different harbors up and down the coast of California, Oregon, and Washington. He bought charts and maps and put them up on the walls of the house, marking out the route we would take on our around-the-world journey.

Then, in late 1972, Dad found a sailboat in Newport Beach he was excited about. "She's a custom-built sloop that's forty-five feet and could be the one to take us around the world," he said as we drove home from town one day. "I want you girls to come with me to Newport Beach to see her."

Four

*I*n Oceanside in the summer and fall of 1974, we sailed constantly, sometimes with a boatload of Dad's friends, mostly just the four of us so we could work on specific skills. During this time, Dad worked long hours to save money for our trip, but managed to pay close attention as boys began hanging around me. He scowled and peered at them, limiting my freedom by thinking up chores to keep me busy. His jealousy upped the ante between us.

He looked at me, studied me, with a smirk on his face. His smirk turned into laughter when I caught him studying me. The laughing disarmed me and made me self-conscious. *I'm not yours*, I thought. *I am not your girlfriend.* He ogled at me with his camera held up to his face so all I could see was one closed eye and his leering mouth.

He photographed me doing everything—the director filming his star. But I was a horrible actress, too self-conscious to be natural. His favorite stage for me was the boat. He took pictures of me sailing, doing all sorts of jobs on the boat. In one, I'd be holding the sail line in my hand, feet spread apart in a balancing stance, staring at the top of the sail to see if the sail was luffing. He taught me that pose and loved to photograph me in it. "Good, hold that pose for a minute," he'd say. He also photographed me sanding the teak railings, or washing down the boat with fresh water after a sail. He'd say, "Can you turn a little more this way so I can get the sun on your face?" He took pictures of Monica and Karen, too, but he *hovered* near me.

When I was younger, maybe six years old, he took his camera out at Half Moon Bay beach. "Take off your clothes, girls, and stand in the water," he said. It was cold and overcast, the wind blowing hard.

"No, Daddy, I'm too cold." I said, "I don't want to take my clothes off." But he made us get naked and stand in the ankle-deep water holding hands by height: Monica, then me, then Karen. He took shots of us, with our long blonde curly hair blowing toward the sea, the waves breaking behind us and getting us all wet. Karen, only four years old, began to cry. "Stop crying right now, Karen, or I'll spank you!" he yelled. But she could not stop—she shivered and cried, lips turning blue. I began crying too, and then Monica. He continued to take pictures as we sniveled and screamed. People stared as they walked past. I couldn't make my teeth stop chattering.

I was scared of Dad after that and didn't trust him as much. I didn't want to climb up in his lap, or let him tickle me before bed.

As I got older and caught him staring at me, I'd sometimes smile a little and then look away. He photographed me relentlessly on the ranch, doing chores, riding the horses. I also posed for him under the hot lights in the mock photography studio he set up in the extra bedroom. Afraid of making him mad, I shoved down my fear and acted like nothing was wrong. I'd sit quietly, smiling outwardly but cringing inwardly. After a while, I realized it was best not to make eye contact with him, but to look into the lens of the camera where I could see my own reflection and pretend I was alone, or go somewhere else with my mind. I got good at hiding my feelings, stuffing them down deep, never to see the light of day. He'd stare and I'd act like it didn't matter.

When we moved into the condo after losing the mast in the storm, Dad decided that because we only had two bedrooms we had to take turns sleeping with him in his king-sized bed. We all protested.

"We don't need to do that. All three of us can fit in two beds," Monica said.

"Yeah, we can put both beds together, or push one twin bed against the wall and two of us can sleep in it," I said.

"Yeah, Dad, we're used to sleeping in small spaces on the boat," Karen said.

"That's ridiculous. You'll each take a turn sleeping with your ole dad," he said, trying to make it sound fun or something.

Dad not only slept naked but walked around the condo naked before bed, or after his shower to get a bowl of ice cream from the freezer. His nakedness made me extremely uncomfortable. I avoided looking at him, but sometimes he just appeared around the corner and stood right in front of me. *Gross.* My eyes couldn't move away fast enough. I tried not to shudder, because he only would have laughed, I was sure.

One of the first nights we spent in the condo, while we watched Dad's new favorite show, *Kojak,* he casually said, "You girls need to embrace being European, so there's no reason you, too, shouldn't sleep naked."

I didn't miss a beat and quickly answered, "I'm American—not European at all. I don't want to sleep naked." I was the only American in my family, having been born in St. Paul when Mom and Dad first moved to the United States from Windsor, Ontario. Monica buried her face in a pillow. Karen stayed quiet. They weren't Europeans, either, they were both Canadian, but they stayed quiet, letting me fight the battle with Dad again.

With a stern look, he said, "Well, I didn't ask you. I told you. You are European because I say you are. You will sleep naked from now on. There's no reason to be ashamed of our bodies."

There was no discussion, and no way to get out of the new rule of sleeping naked. I dreaded, even feared, my nights with Dad. My sisters and I begged each other to switch when our night was up, but nobody ever switched. When I slept in the twin bed, I always felt bad for whoever had to sleep with Dad, but never bad enough to trade. Silence was a key strategy for me at least. I wasn't going to tell anybody why I was afraid of sleeping with him. I buried my fear inside, never talked to anybody about it. Monica reminded him of Mom, so she got the brunt of Dad's anger, while I got the seduction and yearning. Karen was young, only eleven, petite and still looked like a little girl. He loved her, I'm sure, but didn't see her as an object of affection, like he saw me. In both my sisters' eyes, this attention made me his favorite. He invaded my space, stalking me, nearly suffocating me.

I imagined solid steel armor around myself, turning the invisible energy field I'd created as a little girl into something more solid. Every third night when I was in bed with him, I envisioned myself wrapped in a hard steel case. I convinced myself it was real and it gave me courage. Impending doom hung over me as I held my breath and waited for him to make his move. The bed was in the middle of the room, with the headboard against the wall. Dad's side of the bed was closest to the door, which meant ours was on the other side—by the window and nightstand. When he was out drinking for the evening, the process of getting into bed wasn't any big deal. I took my shower and went to bed and tried to sleep.

But on the odd nights when he was home for the evening the fear was choking. He would sit in bed with his *Cruising World* magazine, watching me. After finishing in the bathroom, I would wrap my naked self in a towel until I got to my side of the bed, then drop the towel quickly and jump under the covers. He would smile. As soon as I got into bed, I turned off the lamp on the nightstand, positioned my pillow like a barrier between the two of us, faced him with my eyes closed, and tried to fall asleep. I had to face him so that if I heard any movement I could open my eyes. I wanted to see him coming, so I could scream.

On nights when I had my period, I slept in my underwear and was prepared to defend that right, turning my fear into rage toward him. As time went on I got better at converting fear into anger quickly—if I attempted to wear my underwear two weeks in a row, he'd question me.

The summer of 1974 went by and we all took our turns sleeping in Dad's bed. Even after the boat was repaired and returned, Dad said we could stay in the condo until after Mom's visit in August. In the evenings, he usually went out to dinner or drinks with Shirley and Bill at La Beaner's, the Mexican restaurant in the harbor. La Beaner's was our second home—we ate dinner there at least three times a week. Dad and Bill had some business thing going. They were great friends, always planning and scheming. Bill had to go back to Palos

Verdes during the week to work, leaving Shirley at the penthouse all alone. Shirley looked like Ann-Margaret, Dad's favorite actress, and they were sloppy hiding their affections while Bill was gone. It wasn't unusual to catch Dad pinching Shirley's butt, or see them walking down the corridor of the condo complex arm-in-arm. Dad and Shirley were hot and heavy. Bill was blinded by his admiration for Dad and Dad's dream of sailing around the world. It was a perfect situation for Dad, and for me, because when he was happy, my life was good.

As the summer progressed, Shirley and Dad became closer—she even defended Dad's bad behavior in our presence. After Dad held Karen over the rocks and threw her into the bathroom wall, Shirley came down from the penthouse, where Dad had gone to confess his sins, and tried to explain the pressure Dad was under. Although I hated her for making excuses for his bad behavior, it kept the focus off me.

Dad's preoccupation with Shirley didn't take away my worries of sleeping naked with him, though, because I knew when he drank—which was often—anything could happen. It was like somebody holding an open hand in front of your face, threatening to slap but never doing it. The anticipation was unbearable.

Monica, Karen, and I never discussed sleeping in Dad's bed because there was nothing we could do about it. We gained nothing by whining about it to each other. It was just a fact in our lives, another thing we accepted and learned to deal with.

Every third night I'd prepare myself, "put on" my armor and then nothing would happen, until I finally began to relax a little.

One night in August, a couple of weeks before Mom came to visit, it was my turn to sleep with Dad. Nobody would trade so I prepared for bed. Dad was out with Shirley that night, thank God! I showered and walked to bed in my towel, sliding under the covers, making sure the towel was within reach on the floor. As usual, I laid on the very edge of the huge king-size bed, facing his direction with my pillow in front of me. I fell asleep quickly, at the edge of the mattress.

I didn't hear him crawl into bed and only woke when I felt his hand on my breast. My pillow—the one I used as a barrier—was gone. He slurred something about Bill being mad at him and Shirley slapping him. His hands covered my body, rubbing up and down all over. Kissing my neck, he started to shift himself to get on top of me. My reflexes took over and I screamed, "Dad!" and shoved him back.

I jumped out of bed, ran to the bathroom and locked the door. I grabbed a towel and wrapped myself in it. I stared at my face in the mirror, hyperventilating. My eyes were wild, large, and fully awake, and I could still feel his hands on my skin.

My breath finally slowed. I sat on the edge of the bathtub staring at the locked door. Maybe he'd fallen asleep. God, he stunk. Maybe he was too drunk to get up. Maybe he didn't even remember what he had just done. I stared at the space between the bottom of the door and the linoleum floor for a long time, waiting for a shadow or a sound.

The condo was silent.

I needed clothes. I needed to get to the other bedroom and get dressed. If he was there when I opened the door I would scream and wake up Monica and Karen.

The door creaked when I opened it. I waited. No sound. I ran by his bedroom holding my breath. Once I got into the bedroom with Monica and Karen, I let out my breath. I got dressed quietly, facing the door, waiting for him to round the corner. I tiptoed into the living room and sat down on the couch.

The clock said 3:37 a.m.

Looking out, I saw the lights on the other side of the harbor where the fishing boats were getting ready for their day. The lights felt welcoming. I belonged out there in the friendly world, not in here.

My thoughts started looping: *I have to leave this house. I can't go sailing around the world with him.* Like a tire stuck in a rut, my mind spun the same thoughts over and over again: *I have to go away. I have to move out. I'm old enough to take care of myself. Yes, I could do it. I could move to Mexico and live on the beach in a tent with the surfers. Maybe I could live with Raine. Maybe I could move to Windsor with Mom and Grandma.*

When I closed my eyes and thought of living with Mom, I saw myself at age nine, living in a rundown fourplex, seeing her drunk every night from the bottle under the kitchen sink, sleeping all day long, working at the hospital, but mostly gone. She looked so pretty on the outside—hair like Jackie O, smile like Mary Tyler Moore—but that's not who she was. What I felt so often as a child came back to me: *She's empty inside and has nothing for me. She despises me, her middle daughter who her husband adores. No, Mom's been gone more than she's been here. Her looks are deceiving. I don't want to live with Mom. I'd rather live on the streets of Hollywood and become an actress. I can act. I am getting better at it every day living in this family.*

As the sun began to light the sky ever so slightly, I relaxed a little and leaned back on the couch and let my mind wander. Dad came into the kitchen. I saw his bare butt walk past me.

"What are you doing out here?" he asked, as if he didn't know, as if he didn't remember.

"I can't stay here. I have to go somewhere else," I stared out the sliding-glass door at the now empty fishing docks.

He stopped filling his glass with tap water and turned around. The counter blocked everything below his waist, thank God. I sat on the edge of the couch, ready for battle.

"Where would you go?" He sneered. "Who would take you in?"

I sat up straighter. "Lots of people. Raine would take me in," I said.

"You can't live with her. She isn't your family. You're coming to Tahiti, young lady, and there'll be no more discussion about it."

"I can't live with you. I can't go on the boat."

He belly-laughed, throwing his head back like the amused but irritated King of Siam. "You try, Leslie. You try to go somewhere. I will find you. I will drag you back here."

I didn't say anything more. I knew he was right. He stood in the kitchen for a minute staring at me as I looked out the window, and then he went back to bed.

I lay down on the couch and covered myself with a blanket as I stared out the window until sleep came. Monica woke me an hour later, wanting to know why I was sleeping on the couch.

"Because Dad's too weird. I won't sleep in there anymore."

With her brows together she said, "What happened?"

"I don't want to talk about it, but I can't stay here. I'm leaving today."

"What do you mean, you're leaving?"

"I can't live here with him anymore. I don't want to be part of this family."

Karen came in and began making herself a bowl of cereal.

Nothing more was said.

A few minutes later Dad got up and continued to act like nothing happened, talking to Monica and Karen about sailing with a bunch of people. He ignored me. After coffee he left, saying he was going to work on the boat.

I had breakfast and packed two peanut butter and jelly sandwiches into a backpack with clothes and ten dollars from my jewelry box, and left.

"See ya," I said to Monica and Karen as they stared at the cartoons on TV. I tried not to make too big of a deal out of it. I didn't want Karen to shout over the balcony to Dad that I had left. I walked right past T-dock and didn't even look. I walked with vengeance and purpose.

The day was clear and bright blue, a day for surfing and hanging at the beach with Raine. But that wasn't my plan. I walked past the restaurants and shops, past the Dolphin Café and the empty fishing boat docks. Where to go perplexed me. I wanted a place I'd never been before so he couldn't find me, but if I'd never been there before, how would I know where it was?

I followed Harbor Drive two miles, past the Jolly Roger to the ritzy condos at the dead end, the Marina Suites. The two-story complex had a pool and overlooked the entrance to the harbor. We often saw this place from the boat, but I had never actually been there before. It felt close but unfamiliar. The buildings were surrounded by large boulders, making a sort of barrier of rocks around the complex, protecting it from crashing waves or storm surges. I sat on a boulder, down by the water looking back at T-dock and our condo complex across the bay.

I watched a hawk carry a mouse in his talons right across the water, fighting with each flap of his wings to get higher and higher. A seagull chased the hawk, diving and squawking around it, trying to grab the mouse. The mouse squirmed and wiggled.

It hurt to admit there was nobody I could turn to. I called Raine but she wasn't home. It was better not to involve her anyhow. Dad would go there first. It infuriated me to admit Dad had accurately predicted my lack of options.

I spent the day blending in with guests around the pool, wandering around the condos, the boat docks, and the jetty until dark. I felt alone in the world, and stuck. Afraid to go to sea with my Dad on our boat, I felt cornered without any choices. I needed to find a safe place to live. I could be a cashier at an ice cream store like Forest, collect my check and live quietly without bothering anybody. In desperation I thought about asking Shirley and Bill's foxy sixteen-year-old son Scott to drive me down to Tijuana in his fancy car so I could disappear, but got scared at the thought of living alone in Mexico.

I wandered between the Marina Suites and the Yacht Club all day. I used the key around my neck and went into the other boat-owner's bathroom—larger than ours with three showers instead of two. I felt safe and stayed in the bathroom for a few hours, sitting in a shower stall by myself, eating my sandwich. I walked back to the condo area, and sat on the boulders again, until it was dark and little crabs started crawling out of every crevice. I couldn't relax. I went back to the bathroom and fell asleep in the shower stall using my backpack as a pillow. A few women came and went from the bathroom, opening the big thick steel door and letting it slam. My night was restless and sleepless.

I startled awake as the door slammed and a woman turned on the water in the other shower stall and began to hum "California Dreamin.'" I sat up, feeling low and desperate and achy from having slept on the cold tile all night.

I left the bathroom and sat on the park bench at the top of H-dock, hungry and cold. I couldn't live in the boat-owner's bathroom forever. Just peeking over the hills, the sun's weak rays didn't warm me. I rubbed my arms for some friction, hugging the backpack that sat in my lap. The day promised to be another great beach day—sunny, clear, and warm. A line of pelicans flew low on the water in a straight line, headed for their favorite tree by the Jolly Roger. The seagulls cawed in the distance. Down the sidewalk, two raccoons climbed out of the trashcan, stared at me, and then ran toward the hills of Camp Pendleton. The world was waking up.

As I sat on the bench, trying to make a plan, a car door slammed behind me and I turned to see Dad standing next to our red Opel Kadett. He wore a white pullover Mexican-style shirt with jeans and flip-flops.

In a nicer tone than I expected, he said, "Where have you been, young lady?" He walked toward me.

My heart raced at seeing him, sure he would beat me senseless. I stood up, clutching my backpack to my stomach. "Here," I said.

"Get in the car. We're going home." He reached for my backpack but I clutched it harder. He turned around and walked to the car. I followed him.

We didn't speak during the five-minute drive to the other side of the harbor. I stared forward, he stared forward. We entered the condo to find Monica and Karen watching *Rocky and Bullwinkle* and eating Cocoa Puffs. They turned around and smiled at me.

"Hey, Leslie, where have you been?" Monica said.

"Shhh," Dad said. "Leave Leslie alone. She's home. That's the most important thing."

I poured a bowl of cereal and joined them in front of the TV until Dad went down to the boat to work. Monica and Karen never asked about what prompted my night away. Later they told me Dad forbid them to ask any questions about it, and I never offered any information. It was one more secret between Dad and me.

I never took my turn in Dad's bed again after that, and he never bugged me about it. It felt good to have stood up for myself. In my mind, I'd won. He stopped watching me so closely, and I didn't feel so threatened. I always knew I could go back to the boat-owner's bathroom on the other side of the harbor and lock myself in. When it was supposed to be my night to be in the king-sized bed, I slept on the couch instead. Monica and Karen wanted to sleep on the couch, too, but Dad refused to allow that, which created even more tension between my sisters and me, with raging accusations that I was Dad's favorite and could do whatever I wanted.

I tried to formulate a more thought-out plan of escape. I had to hurry because our departure date loomed—only three months away. If I couldn't find a place to run to, I would need all the courage and stamina I could muster because that damn boat was only forty-five feet long, and unless I jumped overboard, there was no place to go.

Five

Dad didn't speak to me for weeks after I ran away, although he didn't act mad at me either. He avoided me and treated me as a non-entity, which was heavenly. I liked the space. He also stopped walking around the condo naked as often, and stopped watching me in that creepy way. He gradually started speaking to me, saying, "Pass the milk," in a nice tone of voice, or, "It looks like a good day for sailing," listing the people who were coming sailing that weekend. Even Monica and Karen picked up on his sweetness, staring at me with questioning looks. My one-word answers eventually turned into small sentences.

He was killing me with kindness, and it scared the crap out of me. I was completely off balance and suspicious, like—whack—out of left field might come the punch that would bring me to my knees and return our relationship to "normal."

During that summer of 1974 while Dad was occupied with Shirley, I started hanging out with Shirley and Bill's son, Scott. Sixteen and a stone-cold fox with long strawberry-blond hair past his shoulders and dark blue eyes, he drove a new red Datsun 260Z. He was two-and-a-half years older than me, exciting and mysterious, and I dreamed of driving away with him and never coming back. Scott had a thing for me too—sometimes. One weekend he'd be all over me, wanting to hang out at the beach, surf, sail, and make out after dark on Life Guard Tower #9. The next weekend he'd show up with a girl from Palos Verdes and ignore me altogether. My heart went up and down on his whim.

I tried to focus on boys at school. A cute boy named John De La Cruz liked me. John was shy and I liked him for that—he was the opposite of Scott. John sent me notes in class and sat next to me during lunch. He was soft-spoken, with deep, delicious dark eyes and long, gorgeous, straight black hair.

One day in early summer, tired of being yanked around by Scott, I ran into John at the Candy Kitchen. "Oh, hi," he said, his eyes darting around the store. I stammered out "Hi." John bought us ice cream cones and we sat outside and watched the seagulls duck and dive around the fishing boats. Nearly whispering, John said, "I come here a lot, hoping to run into you."

"Wow, really?" I said.

"Yeah—you're the prettiest girl at school by far," he said. My face turned red and I looked away. When we finished our cones, he breathed, "Let's go to the beach." He got up from the table, and I followed.

We walked past the Hawaiian Hut, past T-dock, where I was glad not to see Dad, out to the end of the south jetty, where we watched baby seals sun themselves and surfers ride waves. John didn't notice, but on our way across the sand to the jetty, we walked right past Scott making out with his cute girlfriend-for-the-weekend. Scott and I had been making out just a few days earlier in almost the exact same spot. I hid my hurt feelings by grabbing John's hand.

As John and I sat at the end of the jetty and talked, I kept an eye on Scott and the girl. Eventually they left, Scott looking back as they headed for the street. My heart sang because it showed that he really did care. *He looked back*!

John asked me to go steady with him that day, and I said yes. It felt good to commit to John—solid, honorable, and true. But my heart was torn. I was intrigued by Scott and his fast racecar, and his knowledge of what seemed like everything.

The following week, Scott didn't bring a girl down from Palos Verdes. When he asked me out, I knew I should say no. "I have a picnic and a surprise," he said, holding up a backpack. He looked so good in his blue-and-white board shorts, blue T-shirt, and leather flip-flops, I had to say yes. The air around him was thinner somehow—I had trouble breathing when he was near.

We walked to the north jetty, the barrier to the entrance of the harbor. At the end of the jetty, we watched the boats enter the harbor. We shared a tuna sandwich, some chips, and his surprise: two bottles of beer. We talked and laughed and it felt good to be with him again. I didn't mention seeing him on the beach the weekend before and he didn't mention John. We had a truce of sorts. We stayed out on the rocks until dusk. He held my hand, told me I was pretty, and that he wanted to go all the way with me.

The beer made me sleepy and happy. He led me to Life Guard Tower #9 and we climbed the stairs, sat and stared as the waves broke on shore. He held my hand and kissed me. A warm feeling down low slowly rose up inside, like I had melted brown sugar in my body. I loved how sure he was of himself. He put one hand on my breast and the other between my legs and we slid down until we were lying flat. The passionate kissing felt good, but brought a flash of panic. *Oh God, John.* I stopped Scott's wandering hands. "We're going too fast. Slow down." Perturbed, he sat up abruptly and pulled away. "Someday, Leslie, I will have you—before you leave on your trip." He climbed down from the tower and I hurried after him, feeling shunned and awful.

John came to the harbor off and on throughout the summer, and even though I still hung out with Scott, I always made time for him. John and I had only kissed. His kisses were tentative and light and I wanted more. John was shy and unsure of himself, and even though I liked that sometimes, I didn't like it when it came to sex. I was anxious to learn what the story was on sex, and would have preferred to find out with John.

I played a game with Scott, teasing and taunting him with John the same way he purposely showed up with his girlfriends. When I was with John, I looked for Scott on the beach, at the pool, or on the jetty just to snub him.

The week before Harbor Days, the annual party in August, I had a
cold. John had been away on vacation and I was missing him. The sky
looked blue and cloudless out the window from the bedroom where I
lay in bed, coughing. A light breeze blew in.

There was a knock at the front door. Dad opened it and I could
hear John's voice as Dad interrogated him. "Who are you?" Dad
boomed. "I'm John De La Cruz, Mr. Johansen. I just came to say hi to
Leslie." His voice was more confident than the small, whispery voice
he usually used when talking to me. A few moments later John stood
at the bedroom door with beautiful garden daisies in his hands. The
look on Dad's face as he stood behind John was one of almost-pride
as he pursed his lips in a smile and nodded his head in approval.

Without knowing it, John had accomplished several firsts. He was
the first boy to ever knock on our door and ask for me, the first boy
to get invited in, and the very first boy ever to bring me flowers. Dad
scared off all the boys around the harbor without ever having to say
a word. He studied them with a squinty-eyed, suspicious, chin-up
stare. He completed the scare tactic by taking off his hat to show his
Kojak-bald head. Most boys didn't stand a chance when Dad focused
his stay-away energy on them.

Shy, sweet John was different.

"So how sick are you?" he said as he stood in the doorway.

"I don't know. Those flowers are beautiful, though. Thank you."

The phone rang in the living room. Dad answered it as John put
the flowers down on the dresser. We listened to Dad talk to somebody
on the phone—somebody I knew was Shirley because of his tone. He
hung up and the front door slammed shut. He was gone.

John watched me from the end of the bed and I soon forgot about
my father. I knew I looked horrible and I felt even worse, but I didn't
want John to go. He searched for something on the radio, stopping
on the Beach Boy's "Surfing USA," which made happiness bloom
inside me like a daisy. John sat on the edge of my bed and we listened.

"Where have you been?" I said, for something to say.

"To a wedding, my uncle got married."

The song changed to one of my favorites, "Another Park, Another
Sunday," by The Doobie Brothers. I sang along very lightly but then

started to cough. John took my hand and kissed it. I closed my eyes in embarrassment and listened. John lay down on top of the covers next to me, and we played handsies, massaging and touching each other's hands. Seals and Croft's "Summer Breeze" came on and I felt better suddenly, hearing my favorite songs on the radio. I wanted to get up and slow dance with John, but I tapped my finger on his hand to the beat. Happy and content, I drifted into a light sleep. John must have drifted off, too, because we never heard the door.

"Leslie! What's going on here?" I opened my eyes and saw Dad in the doorway. His face was red and he was yelling. John jumped up and turned the radio down.

"Nothing!" I said. "We were just listening to the radio."

"I can see what you were doing. John, you can go."

"Dad, you're overreacting."

"Sir, nothing happened. I'm very sorry," John said.

"I'm not overreacting. He was in bed with you," he said. He looked directly at John and said, "You were in bed with her."

"Dad, he wasn't in the bed, he was on top of the covers. We were listening to music."

"Quiet, Leslie. Get out of here!" he boomed. As John made his way past, he continued, "That's how it starts. First they're on top of the covers, and then they're under the covers. I wasn't born yesterday, Leslie."

John left, and Dad yelled after him, "And don't ever come back!"

"Dad, come on!" I pleaded.

"Don't 'come on' me, little girl. I don't ever want to see him again."

I rolled over and faced the wall. John was too perfect and innocent to try anything. Dad left the room, pulling my bedroom door closed.

It was ironic because Dad should have been afraid of my spending time with Scott, who had both experience and serious designs on me. But Dad thought Scott was harmless because he was Shirley's son and Dad loved Shirley.

After a few minutes of silence, John reappeared and whispered through the open window, "I'll see you later, okay?" I got up and pushed the curtains aside. "Okay," I whispered back. Then he blew me a kiss and left.

I blew him a kiss back. I didn't see him for the last month of summer. He never came back to the condo, too scared to confront Dad again.

With the boat repairs finished, *Aegir* was returned to Oceanside and her home on T-dock. The story of the storm and losing our mast was now well known around the harbor and everyone came to see as the new aluminum mast was installed. Monica, Karen, and I got new long dresses from the Hawaiian Hut and posed for pictures, standing on the bow of the boat. Dad even wore a suit, standing behind us, with his reflective sunglasses on, smiling large. It became our Christmas card that year, and appeared in the local Oceanside harbor bulletin.

The next order of business was to outfit each of us in safety harnesses made of heavy-duty nylon straps to be worn around our torsos. A heavy line was attached to the safety cable on deck and the new rule was to wear them always when on deck.

Dad began a new course of training for us, too. The four of us continued to go sailing during the week after school when everybody else was working or busy. Man overboard drills were at the top of Dad's safety checklist. He explained each and every step of retrieving a person. The training took place while under sail, miles off the coast of Oceanside. A cushion tossed in to the ocean represented Dad in the maneuvers.

Each girl had a specific job during the man overboard drill. Karen was the lookout because she was the smallest. Monica was the helmsman because she was usually seasick but could still steer pretty well. I was the sail handler and deck worker. We learned to react quickly and work together without fighting, so Dad eventually refused to speak during the drills. He threw the cushion overboard and wouldn't say a word. It was up to us to be aware enough to notice that the cushion went overboard. The stopwatch was usually the hint we were beginning a man overboard drill. It took us twenty-five minutes to retrieve the cushion when we began. We got our time down to twelve minutes or so—still not fast enough. The goal was under ten minutes.

The number of people who wanted to sail with us before we left on our around-the-world journey increased exponentially with each passing week. Every weekend we took out boatloads of people, testing out the new aluminum mast and steering box. We ran more of a free charter business than anything else and Dad thrived on showing us off.

On one particular Saturday sail, the show featured me alone. It all started at dinner the night before when I asked Dad if I could have a new pair of shoes to go with my new Hawaiian dress for a school dance. We sat around the table eating barbecued mahi-mahi we'd caught.

"No, we don't have money for new shoes now. Everything I make is going to the boat."

"But, Dad, the only shoes I have are flip-flops."

He turned his head toward Karen and Monica and ignored me.

"We're taking out a load of people tomorrow, girls. We leave at 11:00 a.m."

"Oh," I complained. "I want to spend the day with Katie. She invited me to a family barbecue. It's her dad's birthday."

Katie Clarke was a new school friend. She traveled in an orbit Raine and I both dreamt of ascending to, but realistically never would. Even though I hung out with her, I never felt comfortable with her inner group. She was the most popular girl in our school. Her face, her clothes, and her long golden hair, were perfect. She did not shop at the D.A.V.

After math class one day, Katie invited me to have lunch with her in the cafeteria. Raine was green with envy. Katie could have actually dated those foxy surfers that everybody else drooled over, but she didn't which made the guys go even crazier for her.

"Well, you can't go with Katie tomorrow. The manager of Security Pacific Bank is coming with his family to go sailing. He's an important investor in J&J Marine. Howard and Diane are coming, and a few other people."

Howard Benedict was our dentist and owned the boat next to *Aegir* on T-dock. J&J Marine was the business Dad had started, working on other people's boats. I was seriously disappointed because being invited to Katie's house was an honor. I loved her family. Katie had what I dreamed of having: a normal mother and father who lived in a normal house.

Dad didn't understand and I didn't dare try to explain it to him. He continued, "We will be practicing the man overboard drill tomorrow. You girls need to get the time down a few minutes. You aren't nearly fast enough yet."

"Dad, really? We have to do the drill in front of all those people?" Monica whined.

"Yes. If you can do it with all those people watching, you can do it at sea when there's a real emergency," he said.

"Dad, I really want those shoes. Please?" I said.

"No. Now drop it. I don't want to talk about your prissy shoes anymore."

He looked at Monica and Karen. "Can't you just see Leslie on the foredeck in her high heels pulling down the genoa?" He put his wrists high in the air like some floozy, pinky fingers up, and whined, "Look at me in my high heels and long, painted red nails. I am a sailor, can't you tell?" He laughed, and my sisters laughed harder than I thought was necessary.

Monica was a tomboy and would never in a million years ask for fancy new shoes. Karen was too little to want high heels.

I didn't think it was funny at all. My face turned red and I grabbed my food and took it to the kitchen where I started washing the dishes, my back to them.

After a few more minutes of laughing at me, Dad yelled, "I'll tell you what, Leslie, if you can sail the boat all by yourself tomorrow from the dock to the half-mile buoy, you can have your precious new shoes," he said.

I pivoted around from the sink, and said in an abrupt, determined tone, "Fine. I can do that, no problem."

They all stopped laughing. Monica and Karen looked at me like I was crazy. Dad looked intrigued. None of us girls had sailed the boat alone before. As unacknowledged first mate aboard *Aegir*, it was a good idea for Dad to challenge me to sail *Aegir* alone. There might be a time in the South Pacific when I would need this skill.

As I fell asleep that night I ran through the tasks I would complete in the morning. I had to motor out the mouth of the harbor, put
the sails up, and set a course of 180 degrees before I could turn on
the autopilot. The longer I thought about sailing *Aegir* alone, with
all those people aboard watching every move I made, studying me
like Dad always did, the more determined I became not to show any
nerves.

I would show him. He wouldn't win tomorrow. I would.

Calm seas and 10-knot winds blew at 11:00 a.m. that Saturday—a
clear sunny day. Dad added to the bet during breakfast by telling
me that I had to prepare the boat for sailing that day, as well as sail
her alone, which meant I had a lot more work to do before the guests
arrived. I had to ready the sails, the lines, the life jackets, and the
food. In addition, I had to check the oil in the engine and warm it up.
I was also in charge of where everybody sat. Monica and Karen were
ecstatic that they didn't have to do anything until we were out to sea.
They sat on deck in their favorite spots and watched.

Raine arrived at the boat at 10:00 a.m. to see if I wanted to go to
the beach, but came sailing with us instead. By 11:30 a.m. our guests
had arrived. The manager of Security Pacific Bank Dave Kimball, his
wife Anita, and their three children, ages 12, 15, and 18, got settled
aboard. Howard and Diane arrived looking like they stepped out of
a tropical magazine advertising a beautiful and happy life. Karen's
school friend, Shelly, and her parents were aboard, along with
Monica's friend, Kerima, and her parents.

Shelly, Kerima, and Raine had been aboard the boat when we hit
the storm outside of Long Beach and lost our mast. Their parents
were eager to see what sailing aboard *Aegir* was like, having heard
the harrowing story from their daughters about our adventure at sea.

Our fourteen guests were made comfortable aboard *Aegir* as Dad
told everybody about our new mast. I stowed all of their things below
deck, and found a cushion for each of them to sit on. Raine sat by the
wheel watching my every move.

"I'm ready to pull out," I said to Dad.

"What should I do, Captain?" he said with a smile on his face.

People within earshot gave Dad a strange look when he called me captain. I tried to focus and not get flustered.

"Please untie the lines and push her out of the slip," I said.

I took the helm and motored her out the channel to sea. That was the easy part. Once we passed the north jetty and were in open seas, I began my work. I put the boat into the wind, put the engine in neutral, and scooted past all our guests to raise the main sail. When the sail was up and trimmed, I returned to the wheel.

"Why is she doing that all by herself?" Dave asked after the main sail was up.

"We have a bet going today. Leslie will get a pair of new shoes if she can sail *Aegir* all by herself," Dad answered.

Of course everyone who heard that got interested in what was going on. Raine looked at me with a huge smile. I turned red but smiled as Dave Kimball studied me quietly.

I made sure the boat was still into the wind and then headed to the foredeck to raise the genoa. I pulled the line until the sail was up and flapping in the wind, then ran back to mid-ship and pulled in the sheets.

Back at the wheel, I turned away from the wind and both sails filled with air. The boat began to sail. I shut the engine down. We approached the half-mile buoy and I set a course of 180 degrees. The wind was steady and we moved through the water nicely.

I sat down in the white, leather helmsman chair that was mounted on top of the aft cabin making it a position of height over everybody else. My favorite position to sit in while steering the boat was leaning back in the soft chair, steering with my feet.

"What kind of shoes are you getting?" asked Dave's wife, Anita.

"Red ones with heels."

Dad stood on the stern in his King of Siam position, legs spread apart for balance, arms folded across his bare chest, brown leather hat that protected his already-burnt bald head flapping in the wind. His sunglasses reflected back at me so I couldn't tell where he was looking.

The boat was moving at about six knots—a nice clip but not too fast. Monica was lying on her stomach on the cushions of the main cabin with Kerima. She had taken Dramamine and she and Kerima wore headphones and listened to 8-track tapes.

Karen and Shelly were on the bowsprit, watching for dolphins. Everybody else was scattered around the boat, mostly near the wheel within earshot of Dad. I did my last job—setting the autopilot so it would steer the course.

"Okay, Dad. She's sailing to sea. How'd I do?" I asked.

He lifted his glasses slightly so I could see his small blue eyes, and wore a proud grin. "You made some mistakes we'll discuss later. But you've got the shoes."

"Yeah!" I said looking at Raine and high-fiving her.

"We're not quite done yet," he added. "Let's keep working for now and then we'll relax."

"Oh no," I muttered when I heard a splash. I turned to see Dad's brown leather hat sitting atop the aft cabin. He'd jumped into the ocean with a flotation cushion—a real-life man overboard drill. God, he had a flair for the dramatic.

As the boat sailed away, he waved and smiled at me. *Oh my God,* I thought.

"Man overboard!" I yelled. Karen peeked around the genoa sail and I yelled again, "Man overboard!" She left the bowsprit, walking around the three Kimball kids lying on deck.

"Get Monica," I said. She tapped Monica, who looked up and took her earphones off.

"Man overboard, Monica," Karen said.

"Oh, no," she said and got up on her knees to look around.

"Come on, you guys, into action! Dad jumped into the water and I can barely see him anymore!" I yelled.

"He jumped into the water?" Monica said in astonishment as she came back to the wheel. Karen took her position on the stern, throwing another cushion overboard to mark the area, and tried to maintain visual contact with Dad's increasingly smaller blip on the horizon. Monica took over the helm, and started the engine, while I made my way to the foredeck to take down the sails I'd just raised.

"Ready?" Monica yelled. I gave her the thumbs up.

Monica turned the boat into the wind and the sails began to flap around. I hit the winch lock and the genoa dropped to the deck, covering Dave and Anita's three kids.

I stepped back to the winch that held the main sail and unlocked it. The sail tumbled down on deck. Shirley and Bill helped gather the sail and keep it from falling into the water. Monica turned the boat around, and headed back toward the yellow cushion we could still see.

"I can't see Dad anymore," Karen announced as she moved from the stern to the bow of the boat, eyes locked on the horizon and the yellow cushion. We reached the cushion and brought it aboard with a boat hook while Karen and I searched the sea for Dad. We continued to motor back in the direction we came from until we finally spotted him lying on his back, floating on the cushion. As we approached him, we turned the engine off and threw out the swim steps. He swam over to the boat and came aboard.

Everyone clapped, hooted, and hollered.

"Well, you didn't break any time records, but you did find me," Dad said, dripping wet on deck. "For that I am grateful," he said, and he kissed me on the cheek.

"The girls are amazing," said Howard. "I think you should make a movie. You'd make a million dollars. I just can't get over how well they handle this boat."

Monica and I flushed as we looked at each other. Karen hid her face in her towel.

"It was really remarkable, Bjorn," said Dave Kimball. "What you're doing is nothing short of marvelous. Training these girls to sail this ship—it's incredible."

Dave Kimball's kids gathered around. They were confused about what had happened, and had many questions. After Dad finished answering, we all took a swim in the ocean and played around, jumping and diving off the boom and the bowsprit. Our work for the day was done, and except for lunch, we were off duty. We played our usual game of diving underneath the boat. Raine had gotten good at this game too, along with Kerima and Shelly, but the Kimball kids didn't want any part of it. They stayed on deck, watching us splash and have fun. Our game was another source of astonishment for the people aboard who were uneasy about diving into the open ocean. After about half an hour, Dad called the fun over and we all came on board and dried off.

"It's time for lunch," he said. "Girls, get going."

As Monica took the helm, Dad raised the sails. Karen and I went below to make sandwiches for everybody. We put out a bowl of fruit salad and offered a bag of potato chips. If their amazement with the man overboard drill and the swimming wasn't enough, they went on and on about what a great lunch we fixed. Wine was served, with sodas and juice for the kids. We sailed for another couple of hours, until Dad said the show was over and we went back to the harbor.

Except for Dad actually jumping into the water for our man over-board drill, every weekend was pretty similar to this experience. We always had a boat full of people who were amazed and astonished at the Johansen girls and their bald Norwegian father. Dad loved the notoriety he was attaining in our area, training up his three blonde daughters to crew his sailboat. He loved to sit back and watch us work, too. It may have been his favorite thing to do.

Dad picked up on the idea for the movie and bought a 16-milli-meter camera and began filming the preparation of our journey. Not only was he taking still pictures of us, he began actually directing us in chores we did aboard the boat for this movie of his. It was horrible, but at the same time it was kind of exciting to think of being famous one day. He planned to fly back to the States once a year and show the film at yacht clubs for a fee, which would give us enough money to sail for another year.

Mom and Grandma

Six

After I proved to him I could single-hand *Aegir*, Dad began to ask my opinion on plans for our trip, like all of a sudden I was important again. "How many books do you think you girls will need?" He sat at the kitchen table jotting lists on a pad of paper. It was a Saturday morning on a rare day we didn't go sailing. Monica had just left to spend the day on the farm with Kerima, and Karen was still asleep. I was going to the beach with Raine and just wanted out of there.

Immediately regretting sitting across from him to eat, I took a big bite of cereal so I didn't have to answer right away. *How am I supposed to know how many books the three of us will read on an around-the-world journey, I've never done this before!*

I didn't want to speak to him—I hated him and was still trying to think of a better place to run away to so he couldn't find me this time. It threw me off balance when he was nice to me because I yearned for his approval and kindness all the time, but he only chose to give it to me when I was mad at him.

He and I were playing chess again and I had to be careful not to give up any good moves. It was a few days before Mom arrived and I knew he wanted us all to be a united, happy family when she got there—points in his favor if Mom saw us happy.

After making him wait an appropriate amount of chewing time, I finally answered. "I don't know. Will Monica even be able read since she gets so seasick?"

"Maybe not, but we can read aloud the books I have on the Marquesas and Tuamotu Islands while we're underway," he said. "I just need to know which fiction books you girls need."

"I don't know," I repeated.

"We could bring all the classics, like what they read in high school. Monica can get a list from school."

"Yeah, that sounds good," I said mindlessly, shoveling cereal into my mouth as fast as I could.

He never asked me how I was feeling. Instead he assumed everything was fine and that I'd somehow forgiven him. It was like Dad and I were planning this voyage together with our—*with our what? Kids? Oh my God.* Things were getting weird again, in a whole new way.

I told myself I'd answer his stupid questions but still try to find some place to run. Thank God Dad planned to sleep on the boat while Mom and Grandma visited, giving us all some much-needed privacy in the condo. *Maybe I should reconsider living with Mom*—I would talk to her, during her visit. If I could convince her to get an apartment in Oceanside, I could still be with my friends.

Mom and Grandma arrived at the condo the third Saturday of August in a flurry of suitcases and restrained affection. Dad held the door and the suitcases as Mom and Grandma rushed in to find Monica, Karen, and me watching *The Price Is Right*.

We all jumped up, excited to see them, but then we just stood there. It had been sixteen months since we'd seen Mom and longer since we'd seen our Grandma. I just watched Mom, unsure what to do. She looked so beautiful with her jet-black hair teased high and her lips painted fire engine red. She wore a bright yellow and white dress with high-heeled white sandals. She smelled like gardenias and looked gorgeous in her "California" outfit.

Dad set the suitcases down and watched the reunion.

Mom glided to Monica. I watched as she took the tips of Monica's hair in her hands, "You're getting so tall, and your hair is so long now . . . and blonde. You're the California surfer girl, aren't you?" she said as she brushed her cheek against Monica's. Monica caught my eye and squinted—she wasn't the California surfer girl. That role belonged to me, if Mom had cared to notice. Monica was a bookworm who hid under a blanket all day with a flashlight. Her hair was blonde, yes, but her skin was snowy.

Mom approached and I puckered up, arms outstretched. Mom brushed her cheek against mine like we were French or something, never really making contact. I only felt a swoosh of air. Her attempt at hugging me felt like a cloud brushing over me. I was puzzled by this greeting. Maybe she didn't want to rumple her new dress?

"Leslie, you look more like Bestemor every time I see you," she said and looked at Dad with a smile. Dad winked at me, grinning.

Bestemor, our Norwegian grandmother, had died of a massive heart attack when Dad was twenty, two years before he immigrated to Canada. I had seen pictures of her—full figured, round cheeks with dimples like mine, and overweight in a soft and warm grand-motherly way. I was surprised Mom didn't call me "healthy." This got our visit off to a great start.

Next she glided to Karen and spoke to her like a little girl, "And Karen, you're getting so big." She held Karen's arms and bent down and brushed her cheek. Karen rolled her eyes and laughed. She always forgave Mom for missing the mark by a mile. It was in her nature to forgive, and she missed Mom desperately. Karen wrapped her arms around Mom's waist, laid her head on her chest, closed her eyes, and hugged her tightly.

"Okay, okay, now don't mess up my dress," Mom said, her hug barely touching Karen's arms and shoulders.

I didn't remember her treating us all like we'd break last time I saw her. Or maybe it was her who was broken. I felt the absence of something that should have been there: protection, love, pride, caring.

Years later, I found out that when she'd first left us in Oceanside and gone to Windsor, she stayed in the mental hospital and had elec-tric shock treatments. I don't know if that made her more sensitive to touch, or if it was the strong medication she took to control the para-noid schizophrenia she was diagnosed with in the early 1970s, but when she visited us that time in Oceanside, she wasn't the same Mom who'd left us sixteen months earlier. Nobody offered explanations, at the time; I thought she was acting strange, and recoiled from her.

Grandma's silver-grey hair was short and curly. She didn't wear lipstick and kissed me right on the lips and bear-hugged me. I felt connected to Grandma. She was safe and solid in her "grandma clothes"—dark blue polyester stretch pants and oversized floral blouse—so opposite from Mom that I leaned into her for balance. With Grandma, I felt I could tell her anything and that she would believe and support me. She never judged me or made me feel bad about myself. I loved writing to my grandmother, telling her everything that happened in school with my teachers and classes. I even told her when I got bad grades and citizenship marks. But I never told her about what was happening with Dad. I couldn't tell anybody.

"I read all your letters, and I so love receiving them," Grandma said, her arms around me.

Mom whirled around. "Yes, if Grandma hadn't let me read her letters, I'd never know what was happening here with you girls."

"I write to you," I said.

"Not like you write to Grandma," Mom said.

I looked down with a red face.

Dad brought us back to reality, "Well, I'm going to the boat to work a few more hours. I'll be sleeping on the boat while you're here, Paula. You and Beatrice can have the twin beds. The girls will sleep in my bedroom."

Mom nodded her approval.

"You girls catch up. We'll have dinner at La Beaner's around six." And then he left. The mood between Dad and Mom was still cordial, but it was only the first day of a weeklong visit—we always prided ourselves at starting our visits civilly, anyway.

Grandma and Mom wanted to see the boat, but not leave the dock. Seeing Grandma on *Aegir* made me realize how old and unstable she had become. Instead of sailing, Grandma insisted we go to the "world famous San Diego Zoo," since her friends in Windsor wanted pictures of the animals. I thought it was strange to come to California and go home with pictures of animals from Africa, but Grandma insisted. She treated us to new bathing suits and shorts and even some eau-de-toilette since she said we weren't "big enough" for perfume yet.

On the third day of the visit, Monica took Grandma for a walk on the beach at sunset to show her the crabs that lived in the jetty. She especially loved the teeny, tiny little baby crabs. Monica was a friend to animals, big and small, and still missed the Ranch terribly. Karen and I watched cartoons while Mom rested.

"Karen, come here sweetie, I want to talk to you," Mom yelled from the bedroom.

Karen ran to the bedroom and was gone for about twenty minutes. She came back sniffling and wiping away tears. Before I could ask her anything, Mom yelled for me.

I got to the bedroom and found her sitting up in bed in a thin, sleeveless nightgown. I could see through the filmy fabric and immediately looked away. A drink sat on the nightstand on top of Dad's

Cruising World magazine. She held a *Sail* magazine on her lap. A smile slid across her face. "Lezlie, come and sit with me a minute. Tell me how you're doing." I hated it when she said my name with a "z" instead of a hard "s."

"What's wrong with Karen?" I said from the doorway.

"Oh, never mind dear, Karen will be fine," she said with that same forced smile. "Now tell me about yourself."

"I'm fine, Mom. Why is Karen crying?"

"Lezlie! Stop asking about Karen. She's fine," she said, louder. She looked toward the window and cleared her throat, then picked up *Sail* magazine and hugged it to her chest. After a few moments she said, "Tell me what's new with you. And come here and sit beside me." She patted the bed.

I tentatively sat down. She smelled like liquor. Her smile was big and looked funny somehow—forced and fake.

"Why do you have that look on your face?" she said. "What's wrong?"

"What look?" I asked, my mind going a thousand miles an hour trying to find something safe to talk about. "I'm starting eighth grade in a few weeks. I have a boyfriend named John De La Cruz. He's really nice." I stared out the window so I didn't have to see the smile sliding off her face and her see-through nighty. For a brief second I wondered why I had such big breasts. Hers were miniscule.

"What else? What else is happening?" she said, pushing me like I hadn't said what she wanted to hear yet.

I grasped for appropriate details, trying not to look too uncomfortable. It was important because if I couldn't keep up the smooth and innocent flow of "interesting" conversation, then she'd ask me what was wrong and I didn't know how to begin that answer. She scared me.

"Dad has us sailing all the time. We got a new mast. We're taking lots of people sailing every weekend. Did you know we're supposed to leave on the trip December first?"

"Yes, Karen said that," and then she paused. I looked around the room at her luggage on the floor, the pill bottles on the nightstand, her shoes flung against the wall. I looked toward the doorway, wanting to go back to the living room. She took my hands and said, "Lezlie, I need you to do something for me. Look at me. Can you at least look at me?"

I looked, focusing on her brown blood-shot eyes, trying not to see anything else.

"Can you do something for your mother?"

"I guess," I said. "What is it?"

"I need you to ask your father if I can come to Tahiti."

"I thought you hated the boat."

"I don't *hate* the boat, Lezlie Ann."

When she used my middle name, I knew she was upset.

"Does Dad know you want to come?"

"Yes, he knows. We've discussed it," she said.

"What did he say?"

She took a sip of her drink. "You do want me to come, don't you, Lezlie?"

"Yeah, sure, but I thought—you get seasick."

She narrowed her eyes. "I can't go back to Windsor, Lezlie. I want to go to Tahiti, but your father said no."

Conflict bounced around inside. Even though she was weird, she could maybe keep Dad happy at sea, if—and that was a big if—they didn't kill each other. Either way, the focus would be off me, and that sounded good. But the fighting could be horrible. It might be so awful I would want to jump overboard anyway.

I couldn't look in her eyes any longer. I had to back away. She was too close, the smell of liquor too strong. I stood up from the bed to catch my breath. She swung her legs off the bed and took a sip of her drink.

"Why are you backing away? Come here now." It was an order. She grabbed my arm and squeezed it tightly and pulled herself into a standing position. She brought her face close to mine and said in a hushed tone, "Karen says you're still the favorite and that Dad listens to you." She lost her balance and sat back down on the bed, pulling my arm down with her so I had to bend over. "You have to tell him you want me to come to Tahiti, Lezlie. You just have to!" After a pause, she added, "Can you do that for me?"

"You're hurting my arm. Please, stop," I said and twisted my arm loose.

"Listen, you've always been the favorite—right from birth, he preferred you to the rest of us, so you have to do this."

"Okay, I'll ask him, now let go of my arm."

She was suddenly soft as butter. She changed so fast I had whiplash. She rubbed her hand down my arm, her eyes widened again, and she took a sip from her drink. "I love you, Leslie, you know that right?"

"Yes, Mom, I know."

"Now, kiss me goodnight," she said.

I bent over and kissed her cheek lightly. I left the room and shook my whole body to get the weirdness off. I slid in next to Karen on the couch. "Mom's being weird," I said.

"Yeah, I know. She wants me to ask Dad to give her some money."

"She wants me to ask Dad if she can come to Tahiti."

"What are you girls whispering about?" Mom asked loudly as she walked into the kitchen.

"Nothing. We're not whispering about anything," I said.

"Bullshit. You were whispering and I know you were talking about me, so tell me, now."

"We were just talking about going to the beach tomorrow," Karen lied.

"Yeah, Mom. We weren't talking about you," I said.

Mom refreshed her drink, rolled her eyes, and headed back to the bedroom.

Three days before Grandma and Mom were set to leave, Monica, Karen, and I worked on the boat sanding and oiling the teak railings. The wind was still and the scorching sun beat down on us. Sweat rolled off my forehead as I moved my hand back and forth against the wood, making it smooth. I stopped to breathe.

"Karen, when are you asking Dad about the money?" I said.

"Wait, what?" Monica said. We explained everything to her. She was shocked and said, "Why didn't Mom ask me for something?"

"I don't know, but count yourself lucky. If you really want to, you can ask Dad if Mom can come to Tahiti with us."

"No, thank you. Never mind."

"I'm scared to ask him for money. Will you do it for me, Leslie?" Karen said.

"No way, Karen. I'm not doing everything." I took my sand paper and moved to another part of the deck to work.

"Man, she's sensitive," I heard Monica say.

A few hours later, Grandma yelled down to us from the condo balcony that it was time to get ready for dinner. Dad had just finished inspecting our work for the day and as usual he wasn't happy with the job, but he dismissed us when we promised to fix it the next day. We ran up to the condo and showered quickly. I was starving. I put on a yellow halter top with an exploding sun on it, and my white cords. We drove to Felipe's Pizza, by the pier on Mission Avenue, in a friend's car big enough to fit the six of us.

Felipe's was a small but very popular pizza place with only a few tables large enough for a party of six. It was packed and we got the last big table, in the middle of the restaurant. The restaurant was decorated in red-and white-checkered tablecloths with matching curtains on the windows. A candle in a red glass jar sat in the middle of the table with the Parmesan cheese and red pepper flakes.

Our pepperoni and sausage pizzas were almost gone when Shirley, Bill, and Scott came into the restaurant. It was the first time I'd seen them since Dad drunkenly blubbered about Shirley and Bill found out about the affair. They'd been gone for three weeks, but now they were back, seemingly ready to forgive Dad.

Bill approached our table and said a polite but stiff, "Hello." Plates and glasses clanked as the waitresses delivered pizza and pasta to tables. Shirley stood behind Bill peering at Dad silently. She looked beautiful in a flowered sundress, her strawberry-blonde hair up in a bun with wisps hanging around her face.

Dad introduced Mom as his ex-wife and Grandma as his ex-mother-in-law.

Scott's tank top showed his tanned muscles and he wore long red and white board shorts. He put his hand on my shoulder, which made my stomach flip over and sent the nerves in my body into overdrive. I was glad I'd worn my yellow halter top. I knew Scott liked that top.

The Blake's found a table across the restaurant. As Bill concentrated on his menu I saw Shirley staring at Dad over hers. I saw Dad wink at Shirley slyly when he thought nobody was watching. Shirley looked visibly relieved, exhaling so deeply it made me wonder if she'd been breathing earlier.

Mom caught the wink, too, and her gaze dropped to the floor.

From across the room, Scott smiled at me a few times. We had lots to talk about and I missed him. I could tell by the look in his attentive eyes that he missed me too. His smile promised heated moments. He wanted to have sex before we left for Tahiti. I wanted it too, but was scared in that anxious, hurry-up-slow-down kind of way.

We left the restaurant a few minutes later, waving good-bye to the Blake's from the doorway. Scott pointed to me with a smile and mouthed, "Later."

Nobody spoke on the drive home. I was lost in thought about Scott but felt the heavy silence. When we arrived at the condo, Mom made herself a scotch and water and Dad grabbed a beer. I caught Dad eyeing Mom. A storm was brewing.

"Why don't you girls go to the community room and play some pool for a while?" Dad said.

We readily agreed. A few minutes later Grandma climbed up the stairs to the game room, which looked out over the pool and was above the community barbecue and kitchen. "Your mother and father have some things to discuss so I thought I'd check on you girls," she said.

"Want to play the next game, Grandma?" I asked.

"No dear, I want to sit and watch you. Those stairs killed my knees."

Grandma read *Life* magazine on the couch while Monica read her book, curled up in an egg-shaped wicker chair that hung from the ceiling on a hook.

After the second game we decided to go to bed. We helped Grandma down the stairs slowly, one step at a time. Before we even reached the condo, we heard Mom yelling.

"Bjorn, I want to come. They're my daughters too and I want to come," she pleaded.

"Paula, no, you can't come and I'm done discussing this."

We entered the condo and they stopped talking. Mom's hair was messed up, not smooth and pretty. When she looked up I could see make-up smeared around her eyes. Dad, as usual, looked calm and collected in a chair at the kitchen table. He sat back in his power position with his fingers laced behind his head.

"I'm going to bed now," Dad said and left to go to the boat. He smiled at us as he walked out the doorway, winking at me.

Mom cemented us to Dad in a way nothing else in the world could. Her behavior, instead of bringing the family together, often resulted in aligning us with Dad. The tide moved us toward Dad this time. She sat at the kitchen table looking disheveled and red-faced.

Grandma said in a cheery voice, "Girls, why don't you brush your teeth and go to bed."

" . . . and then come and say good night to me," Mom added.

As we walked toward the bathroom, Mom caught my eye and waved me to the kitchen table. She whispered, "Why didn't you ask him?" Her breath smelled like booze and cigarettes.

"I don't know . . . I didn't have a chance."

"Well, now I'm stuck. He's making me go back to Windsor. Do you think you could ask him tomorrow? He might reconsider if you ask him."

"Okay, I'll ask him tomorrow," I said.

I didn't want her to come with us, but I didn't want to go without her either, and I knew I couldn't go back to Windsor with her. I was stuck, too.

Monica and Karen sat down at the table in their nightgowns. Grandma was on the couch trying to find the eleven o'clock news.

"Monica and Leslie, why don't you go to bed, I want to talk to Karen," Mom said.

"No, Mom, leave her alone," I said. "She can't ask Dad for money for you. Dad doesn't have any money."

"Oh, ho, ho, you don't know your father very well now, do you?" she said. "He has more money than you or I will ever know."

"I'll ask him tomorrow, Mom," Karen said.

"Why don't you want me to ask for anything?" said Monica.

The question hung in the air.

"Okay, here's a question for you, Monica," Mom said, after a moment. "Did you know your father was having an affair with Shirley?"

Monica's eyes got big, her mouth opened a little, and her face turned red. She sat straight up in her chair and said, "Yes, we all know he's having an affair with Shirley." She got up and stomped to the bedroom.

I was proud of Monica. Mom looked astonished.

"Paula, leave the girls alone," Grandma said. "Let them go to bed."

"Fine, nobody cares about me anyway. I'll just go back to Windsor and be unhappy."

"Don't be unhappy, Mommy," Karen said. "I'll come with you."

"Oh, sweetie, you love me, don't you? But you can't come to Windsor with me. Your father insists that all three of you go on this trip."

We rose from our chairs to go and she added, "But I haven't given him full custody of you girls yet, and it's my only bargaining tool."

"What does that mean?" I said.

"It means your father needs a signed piece of paper from me, and I don't intend on giving it to him without something in return."

"Paula, stop now," Grandma said. "Girls, off to bed."

We lay in the dark in the king-size bed in silence for several minutes. Karen finally said, "Mommy is sad she can't come with us."

"Mom's weird," I said.

"Yeah, I'm glad Mom isn't coming. She is weird," Monica said.

The next day I got up early and went down to the boat to find Dad. He sat at the navigation station, studying charts and writing in a notebook when I arrived.

"Mom wants to come to Tahiti," I said straight out.

"Yes, Leslie, I know. What do you think we fought about last night?"

"Well, she wanted me to ask you, and now I've asked you, so I can tell her I did."

"Oh, I see. You're merely doing your duty."

"Yes, and now it's done," I said. "She said something about custody papers last night. Is that true?"

"Yes, it's true. I need her signature to take you girls out of the country."

"How are you going to get that?"

"I don't know. I haven't figured it out yet, but I'm not giving her money, and she can't come sailing with us."

I found myself on unfamiliar ground. The divide between Dad and me had become smaller since Mom arrived. I had taken Dad's side more often than not in the last week. It was confusing. A week ago I wanted to get away from Dad. Now I wanted to get away from Mom.

Mom had a hangover and slept until noon. Grandma spent the day in the condo tending to Mom and knitting. Monica, Karen, and I lay around the condo watching TV and munching snacks until Dad insisted we go sailing with him. Dad hated it when we were "lazy butts."

We took *Aegir* out in the early afternoon and sailed for a few hours. The weather was beautiful, not a cloud in the sky, and the wind blew a perfect twelve knots. It was an uneventful afternoon, but by the time we returned, we were starving.

Grandma had cooked a pot roast dinner with all the favorites—mashed potatoes and gravy, peas and carrots, and sourdough bread. She found a tablecloth, and the vase had flowers in it. Mom said almost nothing during dinner except "pass the mashed potatoes," and "does anybody want more milk?"

Always a believer in looking good, she had on a crisply ironed blue dress, her hair was combed neatly and she wore red lipstick. The façade appeared thin as she tried to make it through the last supper with dignity. She was pale with dark circles under her eyes. Her hands shook as she lifted the food to her mouth in slow motion. She held it together, just barely.

It's the job of the child in a home with an alcoholic and mentally ill parent to act as normal as possible. It was also our job not to see how thin the veil was between civilized conversation and outright chaos. So Monica, Karen, and I talked about starting school, and moving out of the condo in the next few days—all as if nothing were wrong. In years past, we had gotten good at pretending, and even though we hadn't played this game in a long time, we all fell into our roles easily.

The next morning Dad took Mom and Grandma to the airport. Grandma cried when she left us and hugged us for a long time. Mom also cried, begging up until the last moment to stay and sail with us. Dad continued to refuse her, and Monica, Karen, and I stayed out of it.

It felt strange to see Mom so child-like with Dad, begging him like I did for shoes or ice cream. We were on the same level with Mom. That was a revelation. Dad had all the power. That was not a revelation. It was crystal clear to me that running away from Dad and the boat would never include running to my mother. I didn't want to live with her—not in Oceanside or in Windsor. My options were disappearing.

To whom it may concern,

I, M.C. Paula Johansen do hereby give permission for my children Monica age 14, Leslie age 13 and Karen age 11 to travel with their father Bjorn Erling Johansen, a Norwegian citizen and permanent resident in the U.S.A.

I also hereby declare that the childrens' father, Bjorn Erling Johansen has full custody of the children.

Dated at Windsor, Ontario this 27th day of September, 1974

M.C. Paula Johansen

I discovered years later that Dad did end up sending Mom money to help pay her rent and buy groceries; in return she sent this custody letter, fully notarized and dated September 27, 1974.

Seven

After Mom left, we moved back on the boat. It was time to get serious about planning and preparing for our trip. The condo was a lovely vacation, but now it was over. On board the boat Monica, Karen, and I crammed into the forward bunk again, trying not to kick each other as we slept in a space meant for two.

Dad's dream of sailing around the world always ended with Monica, Karen, and I attending high school in France. So a few weeks after Mom left, Dad put an ad in three papers: *The Los Angeles Times*, *The San Diego Union*, and the *San Diego Log*:

"WOMAN to teach French to girls 11, 13 and 14. One year cruise South Pacific. 45-foot sailboat. Resume to Box 2013, Oceanside."

Twenty-nine women replied. I was excited about the prospect of having another woman on the boat. I knew Dad would be happier with a companion aboard and I hoped the French tutor could do both jobs well—a tutor for us and adult company for Dad. He interviewed each one carefully over margaritas at La Beaner's. Only two made the final grade: Jane and Amy. They were both in their mid-twenties, but that's where the similarity stopped.

Jane, the hippie, had just returned from a year in France. She had long frizzy brown hair and wore a macramé belt with her bell bottom jeans and tie-dyed halter top. She didn't shave her legs or under her arms so I thought for sure Dad would pick her.

Monica, Karen, and I were in the main salon when Dad brought Jane aboard the boat. She came below and was visibly nervous. Dad tried to smooth things over by offering her a soda or juice. She refused, so Dad sat down and watched as Jane gave us a lesson.

She taught us how to say our names, explaining first in English and then speaking the words in French, *"Je m'appelle Leslie."* All eyes were on Jane. We paid close attention because we wanted Dad to see that we were trying—if he caught us being silly or not taking the lesson seriously, there'd be hell to pay later. But as we carefully watched her, she became more and more nervous, sweat rolling down her temples and armpits. She was melting in front of us. Her mouth was dry, her lips stuck to her teeth, and her voice cracked uncontrollably. After about twenty minutes, she asked to get some air, went above, and we never saw her again.

"How could she just give up like that? What a quitter," Dad said. We went up and searched the docks for her, thinking she went to the bathroom.

We walked down the dock. "She was scared," Karen said.

"Scared of what? She should have just continued the lesson," he said.

"Some people don't like to be stared at and studied," I said. I knew how she felt.

"Oh nonsense, if that's all it takes to ruffle her feathers then I'm glad she took off. She wasn't nearly strong enough."

The following Sunday morning, candidate number two showed up: Amy. She wore glasses, a sundress, and sandals. She had long black hair and a pretty smile. She wanted to be a teacher and spoke French fluently because her parents took her to live in France during her high school years. It was exactly what Dad was planning so Amy seemed the perfect fit.

Amy was sturdier and more composed than Jane. When she arrived, she spoke only in French, identified each piece of fruit hanging from the fruit hammock in the galley, and smiled constantly. She was warm and friendly, yet professional in her lesson. She looked at home on the boat and I liked her immensely. Dad watched as she worked with us and she didn't buckle under his microscopic eye. The only thing left to do was to take her sailing, which we did that day. She did great. She loved the boat, sailing, and it seemed she liked us girls, too.

Dad took Amy out for dinner after sailing to finalize the deal. We stayed on the boat eating canned soup for dinner. "Do you think Dad will offer her the job?" Monica asked, as she sipped her minestrone soup.

"I really hope so," I said feeling excited and hopeful at having Amy join our expedition. If she came aboard it meant Dad would be focusing on Amy and not me. I was sure of that.

Two days later, Amy showed up at the boat with a pie box in her hand, "Where's your dad?" she asked.

"He should be home soon. He's been in Newport Beach all day," I said. "Come sit with us while I make dinner."

She wasn't very friendly, and didn't ask how we were doing. She seemed focused and serious.

"What's in the box?" Karen asked.

"Apple pie, your dad said he loved apple pie," Amy said.

"Did you know our mom taught Dad how to speak English?" Monica said. "It's true. When Dad came here from Norway he didn't speak any English and all he could say was 'apple pie and coffee' when he went to the restaurant. He lived on apple pie and coffee for a long time until Mom taught him how to order something else," Monica said.

With wide eyes, Amy said, "Wow! I didn't know that."

"So we're going to celebrate tonight when Dad gets home?" I asked.

"Yes," she said.

About half an hour later, Dad came aboard looking tired. He was covered in sawdust and blue paint, but when he saw Amy he perked right up and smiled. He sat down across from Amy.

"It's nice to see you again," he said.

"Yes, I brought you an apple pie. I thought we'd celebrate tonight," she said. She opened the box, took the pie out, and held it up to Dad's face. Dad leaned in a little and began to smell the pie when Amy shoved the entire thing in his face, twisting the pie pan so she could get all the crust out of the bottom. "You're a pig," she said, and then she left the boat.

It was a flashbulb moment. Nobody moved. Monica, Karen, and I sat across from Dad with our mouths open. Dad wiped pie away from his eyes so he could see. Pieces of apple and crust slid off his face and onto his lap. He looked up the hatch and stood up like he was going after her. The pie pieces fell to the carpeted floor and he sat back down.

"Daddy, she threw the pie in your face!" Karen said.

I was afraid at any moment the volcano would explode. I took off, down the dock to find Amy, but she was gone—vanished into thin air. Karen came running after me, and then Monica. We stood in the parking lot above T-dock, baffled.

"Where'd Amy go so fast?" I said.

"I don't know, but she has guts," Monica said. "I wonder what Dad did to her."

"He made a move on her," I said matter-of-factly.

"Do you think he'd do that?" Monica said.

"Duh! Where have you been? He's been dating a married woman and he ogles me every chance he gets, and all my friends, too. Come on Monica, wake up." I knew I'd said it too harshly, but I couldn't help myself. Sometimes she was just so ditzy and acted like she didn't understand anything.

"Stop fighting, guys," Karen said.

I turned and went back to the boat. They followed me.

Dad had cleaned himself up. "Well, girls, I guess you won't have a French tutor on the trip."

None of us had the courage to ask why Amy had done what she'd done. I knew exactly how Amy felt but if I were her, I wouldn't have been so eloquent or kind in my refusal of his affections. I would have shoved that apple pie in his face twice as hard. The apple would have been up his nose and in his eyeballs, and then maybe I would have punched him in the belly while he was blinded by the pie. Oh yes! Or maybe I could have just asked him out to the dock for a private conversation and then kicked him in the balls and run, hoping he'd fall off the dock, hit his head, and drop into the water.

After the fiasco with Amy, our lives returned to the Johansen version of "Father Knows Best." After Labor Day, Monica, Karen, and I started school. We continued to sail with a full crowd of people every weekend with the reality of actually going to sea upon us. Our departure date was pushed back to January 5, 1975, so Dad could attend a court hearing in late December on a lawsuit he was involved with regarding the ranch. I didn't know any details about the lawsuit, but I wasn't upset about pushing back our departure date.

We had more freedom than we'd ever had with Dad going to Newport Beach every day. He made us promise to be good and stay close to the boat. I promised, of course, but couldn't have cared less. Mom's weirdness and Amy's refusal to come on the trip had left me feeling anxious. I didn't know what to do about the upcoming trip. I was ready for something crazy and irrational. I was ready for Black's Beach.

Black's Beach was a good surf spot, but was infamous as a nude beach. Scott invited me and I insisted we pick up Raine, partly as guide and partly as protector. Scott's hands wandered more aggressively every week and I felt pressure to give in and have sex with him.

The three of us crammed into Scott's red Datsun 260Z with all our beach gear and sped down Pacific Coast Highway. I felt reckless and excited—I would get naked on a public beach today. With the windows down, we screamed out the words to "One of These Nights" as our hair blew in the wind. I had never felt so good—so free—so ready for an adventure!

We arrived at Torrey Pines State Beach and parked on the dirt near some bushes, hiding the red car as much as we could from the highway. Signs warned of danger on the cliffs. The police tried to keep the public away from the cliffs because they were unstable and gave way all the time and people were stranded and hurt. If the police caught hikers, they gave tickets.

Raine led the way, and we carefully hiked down the crumbling sea cliffs, jumping down from boulders to sand and dirt shifting under our feet.

Excitement pulsed through my body—I wouldn't just be lying in the sun naked, but lying in the sun naked next to Scott. I was playing with fire and it felt good.

On the beach, we stood on the warm sand trying to catch our breath. Surfers littered the water like a collection of full-size *Playgirl* centerfolds, all lined up and ready for inspection, white butts in the air as they dove under waves. I giggled and pushed Raine a little.

"Rad," I whispered.

"Hey, you're not checking out those naked surfers, are you?" Scott said. He stood behind me, arms around my waist, resting his head on my shoulder so he could look where I looked.

"No way, José," I said, lying playfully.

The high school and college girls strewn up and down the sand had perfectly slim shapely bodies, some only topless, others fully naked. They lay with their brawny boyfriends, arms spread across each other's tanned bodies. My almost-fourteen-year-old body would never measure up to these women. Scott was sixteen, almost seventeen. He belonged with one of the girls on the beach, not with me. Intimidated, I felt like a little girl. Scott gawked at the girls, but tried to act like he wasn't staring by checking out the waves.

"Hey, you're not checking out those girls are you?" I said jokingly.

"Naaaaaah, I wouldn't do that," he said sarcastically.

We found a spot to sit on the outskirts of the nude bodies. Raine and I wore our bikinis. We had taken our T-shirts off on the hike down, now we took off our cut-offs. I felt self-conscious wearing a bathing suit, but I wasn't ready to take it off, either.

All my bravery—or was it bravado—quickly evaporated in the sun. I felt sick to my stomach. Under my breath I said to Raine, "I don't think I can do it."

"I know, everybody's just so damn perfect," Raine said. She had on a black halter bikini top that covered her unusually large breasts, which peeked out below, just a little. There was nobody on the beach that looked like Raine. I knew *Hustler* magazine girls had boobs that big—I'd seen my Dad's magazines hidden in a cabinet in the aft cabin.

"Oh, come on girls, I'll take off my trunks, and you two take off your bikini tops on the count of the three."

"I'm not ready," Raine said, scanning the beach and the surf.

Thank God for Raine. Again, I thought. I wasn't ready either. Scott looked at me and grinned a little, as if to apologize and said, "You girls look like all the other girls on this beach, so don't worry. You're both hot."

"I don't think so," Raine said under her breath. Suddenly the fantasy of lying naked next to Scott seemed far away.

"Let's get high and then maybe we'll have the guts to get naked," Raine said. She pulled out a joint and some matches from her backpack and lit up. I took a few hits off the joint. Instantly, my head felt thick and my vision slowed down in a cartoonish way. I looked from naked girl to naked girl on the beach and from naked surfer to naked surfer in the water and began to laugh. My own stomach looked deformed as I grabbed a handful of flesh and massaged it around.

"What are you laughing at?" Scott said.

I handed the joint to him and he took a long drag.

"Check out that girl over there. She's shaking the sand off her towel and making a show out of it," I said. Her long blonde hair blew gently in the wind. She flapped the towel a few times, lifting her arms a little too high to look normal. Her breasts were small and perky and her stomach flat and lean. I couldn't see any pubic hair from so far away. She was pretty and I tried not to gape at her. Several people were watching. She turned around and faced the cliffs and shook the towel a few more times so everybody could get a good look at her butt, which was perfect, of course. Finally, she sat down. Scott, Raine, and I looked away.

Scott began to laugh.

We tried not to make a spectacle of ourselves as we rolled around on our towels laughing loudly and commenting on various people along the beach.

"Shhhhh. Look at that dude walking into the water. Look how brown and cute his butt is," Raine said. "I'm going to talk to him." He held a long surfboard and had long blond hair half-way down his back. He looked a lot like the guys who hung out at Raine's house.

She walked toward the water in her black bikini. "No, Raine, come back," I giggled.

She spun around making a face like the Joker from Batman, flat and mouthy. She continued to the water.

Scott lay next to me, his body thin but scored with muscles. As if my thoughts called him, he rolled over on my towel, got right up to my ear, and whispered, "Let's go swimming."

He pulled me up to standing. I felt self-conscious in my yellow bikini. I looked at Scott and tried to force a smile onto my thousand-pound face. Everything felt so far away, yet the details were so close. Was I walking normally? I sure didn't feel normal. The ocean smelled salty, fishy with bubbles and seaweed. My arms and legs felt numb and heavy. We walked into the surf until I was waist deep and then dove under a wave, came up and exhaled.

"Ahhhh!" The water felt clean and refreshing like liquid silver spilling down over me.

"Want to body surf?" Scott stood beside me in his blue and yellow trunks. His hair was flattened back against his head, making his face appear bigger to me. I knew I was too high.

"No, I'm going to lie down," I said.

"Suit yourself."

I watched Scott from shore. He swam hard to catch a wave, put his arms to his side, lifted his head, and turned his body to steer down the wave. He was better at functioning high than I was. I felt warm and sugary inside as I remembered our kiss two days earlier. I felt the heat rise in me as I watched him become a dolphin.

Raine came back, looking pretty out of it. "Man, I'm so stoned, I have to sit down," she said. "That guy was really nice, but really straight. He might come over for a smoke later." Raine was good at talking to older guys. I admired her but wasn't sure I wanted to be like her.

"Why do you think Scott likes me?" I said.

"He wants to get you in bed. That's all guys want," Raine said.

"Yeah, but I think he really likes me too."

"Maybe he does. But he probably just wants to get you in bed."

We sat in silence for a while. I lay down on my back, closed my eyes.

"Do you think he likes you like John likes you?" Raine continued.

"Probably not, since he still brings girls down from Palos Verdes and ignores me." I said.

"Yep, he just wants sex."

"What's it like?"

"Sex?"

"Yeah, what's it like?"

"I hated it the first time, but now I kinda like it."

"How do you know what to do?"

"You don't. Just follow him. He knows what to do."

We stayed late into the afternoon, until we weren't high anymore. Scott and I made it back to the harbor just at sunset. I caught hell from Dad for coming home so late, but luckily he didn't ground me.

After dinner, Scott and I played pool in the community room. He was quieter than normal, as if the evening fog that had rolled in from the ocean had settled on him. We were alone and I felt brave now, like I could take off my clothes and not worry I wouldn't be enough. Maybe it was spending the day anticipating getting naked or coming down after being high. Halfway through the game, on my turn, Scott locked the community room door. His gaze was intense as he drew me in close. I appreciated how patient he had been all day at Black's Beach with Raine there. He slid my cut-offs down and backed me up to the pool table, clearing a space for me. I stared into his serious eyes. I let him lead the way and I followed, like Raine said. But something had changed in him since earlier in the day. There was no warmth, no tenderness, nothing at all from him. He was a robot. He didn't speak or say anything, and I didn't feel his usual passion for me.

He guided me to lie down on the soft green felt and then he climbed on top and entered me. I stared at the bumpy white ceiling and then at his face. He looked just past me, and I closed my eyes. It was too uncomfortable to look at him. He wasn't even in the room—he was someplace else. I flinched and scooted back from him. His eyes had an almost desperate look. He climbed on me again and forced himself inside of me. The pain diminished a little as he pumped three or four times and then it was over.

He rolled off me. We lay there in silence, staring at the ceiling.

"Go clean yourself up."

I got up slowly and went to the bathroom.

That was it? That was sex? I wiped myself off in the bathroom with a wet paper towel. I wasn't even aroused. I'd been more excited many times when we made out on the lifeguard tower. I wondered why he treated me so coldly. I had kept my eyes closed almost the entire time, and when I did peek, Scott was making a really strange face, straining—it looked like he was in pain too. I wondered what I did wrong. I wondered how many times he'd done it before. I wondered if I'd ever like it.

When I returned from the bathroom, Scott was staring out the window with his back to me, his hair still tucked into the collar of his t-shirt. He'd put his tennis shoes on. I sat down in the hanging wicker chair and swung a little, waiting for him to say something. The creak of the chair brought him back from distant places.

"Are you alright?" he said, without turning around.

"Yes." *No.*

"Are you hurt?"

"No." *Yes.*

"Let's go then. I have to get home."

My heart broke. *Did I do something wrong? Was he mad?*

He unlocked the door, opened it, and waited for me to join him. We parted ways at the bottom of the stairs without another word.

I walked to the boat. Tears filled my eyes as the cold night air rushed at my face. I'd given him what he wanted and he didn't even want to talk to me after it was over. Something was missing and it wasn't my virginity.

Eight

The next day after breakfast, I ran to find Scott, part of me not believing what had happened the night before, the other part of me wishing for a do-over. I found him on the beach with a mermaid, entangled in her long, thin arms and blonde hair. He didn't even notice me as I walked past.

Raine was right. All he wanted was sex. I was a fool, a misguided little girl. He must have gotten a good chuckle as he fell asleep. Maybe he'd tell all his friends he bagged another one, another easy mark conquered.

Scott disappeared from the docks and went back home to Palos Verdes without a word, and when he was in Oceanside he avoided me. In my mixed-up thinking about what would keep Dad away from me, I had promised myself and Scott we'd have sex. I was curious about sex and wanted to experience it before we left, but not like that. A small voice whispered that at least Scott had taken my virginity and not my father. If something was going to happen at sea with Dad, at least now I knew what "sex" meant. For that I was a tiny bit grateful. The experience of it cost me dearly, but maybe it would be worth it. In my thirteen-year-old mind I felt wise beyond my years.

My humiliation and embarrassment with Scott translated into anger at home on the boat. Karen, who was developing into a young lady, got the brunt of it. As we pulled out sail bags from the forward locker one sunny day, and unbagged them on the dock for Dad to inspect, I relentlessly teased her, "Look at those little nubs, aren't they cute?" She blushed and looked away as I bullied her. She buckled under the bantering, and as we pulled the sail end all the way down the dock together, stretching it out, away from anybody who could hear, I asked her if she would be wearing make-up and high heels soon since she was turning into a young woman. She blushed. We stood holding the end of the sail together as she begged me. "Leave me alone. Go away!"

Whenever Dad was away I teased and picked on Karen.

One night while making dinner I said, "My, it looks like it's getting cold in here. Karen, your little nubs are at attention." I laughed and poked Karen in the stomach. Monica took her side, "Stop it, Leslie. Leave her alone." Together they turned against me, begged and pleaded for me to stop. Without realizing it, I'd taken up position with Dad, on the side of hatred and vileness. I passed along to Karen the abuse I received from my dad, but at the time all I knew was that I wanted to lash out, and I didn't understand why.

We were two months away from our departure date. The reality of actually sailing away from the dock and leaving everything familiar for distant shores began to set in as a reality. One evening Dad had barbecued shark steaks and we were eating around the table in the main salon.

"How long will it take us to get to Tahiti?" Karen asked.

"We're not going straight to Tahiti. First we're going to Nuku Hiva," Dad said.

"How long will it take to get to Nuku Hiva?"

Dad smiled. "Twenty-five to thirty days."

All I could think was, *Great, twenty-five to thirty days of being the only one who could do anything on this sailboat.* My sisters weren't reliable. It would all fall to me—the only one Dad could count on. And the one fending off his hands and his looks. *Great!* I pushed my plate away.

With wide-eyes and genuine curiosity, Karen said, "So we'll be at sea for that many days without seeing anybody else?"

"Yes, dummy, what did you think when Dad said we'd be sailing around the world?" I said.

"Well, I didn't know," Karen said defensively.

Dad sneered at me but continued, "We'll probably see freighters and maybe an ocean liner if we watch the horizon carefully."

"What will we do all day?" Monica asked.

"You'll probably throw up every day and not do anything," I said.

"Shut up, Leslie. Gosh, you're so mean sometimes," Monica said.

"Gosh, you're such a dork sometimes," I fired back.

With squinted eyes and a stern face, Dad warned me. "Watch it."

But I didn't want to watch it. I wanted a confrontation. Dad continued to answer Monica's question. "I'll teach you navigation, we'll read about the islands. We all have to stand watch, and then there's laundry, cooking, cleaning, sanding the teak, and…"

Karen was clearing plates when she turned around with an exasperated look, "Okay, okay, stop." Dad had the ability to overwhelm all of us with too much information.

"The correspondence courses I wanted to buy for you girls turned out to be too expensive. So I will teach you myself," Dad said.

With those words, I got up and walked out onto the deck for some air. Dad would be there at every single turn of my life for thirty days in a row. There would be no escaping him.

I bent down into the main cabin hatchway and asked if I could go to Raine's house. Dad said yes and I took off running. It was unusual for him to say yes without asking me a hundred questions. I ran up the beach as fast as I could to the pier, feeling good but winded as I climbed the stairs. I called Raine from the pay phone on the pier and she walked down to join me. We got high together and sat on the cliffs overlooking the ocean in silence. The sun slipped into the ocean, first yellow, then orange, and then bright red. We stared at the horizon in a silent daze.

I felt trapped in my life. Going on this trip meant I'd have to keep my armor up the entire time. I laid my head on Raine's shoulder. She was my comfort and strength and understood me intimately. I loved Raine like a sister and felt so sad to leave her. We shivered and decided it was time to go home. I said good night and walked back to the boat, so high I forgot why I was angry in the first place.

The next morning was Sunday and we scoured the newspaper for sales on supplies for the trip— flour, dried eggs, dried milk, canned food, and all the soaps we'd need. We had to be careful of which soap brands we bought because they needed to lather in salt water, since all of our baths would be in the ocean. The boat had two hundred gallons of fresh water but it was only for drinking, cooking, and tooth brushing.

"Look! They have Suave shampoo on sale at Kmart," Karen said.

"What about the conditioner?" Monica asked. She had the longest, thickest hair of all of us and needed conditioner badly. Her hair was always a rat's nest.

"Yes, the conditioner's on sale too," Karen said.

Dad took a look at the paper, "Great! I'll go get some later today."

"Alpha Beta has corned beef hash on sale," Monica said. "I love corned beef hash," she said, licking her lips as she looked at the picture. Monica's carnivorous appetite was not obvious because she was as skinny as rope, but she was able to eat as much food as Dad, and her favorite meal was barbecued steak.

"Maybe a few cans," Dad said. "We'll be eating fish and seafood when we get to the islands, but I will get some for the ocean passage. Look for sales on rice and instant potatoes."

"What about Dinty Moore Beef Stew?" I asked. "It's on sale at Smart & Final."

Monica jumped right in. "Oh, please, Dad, I love Dinty Moore Beef Stew."

"Let me see the price. Canned meat is expensive," he said.

After looking at the ad, he agreed to buy a case, and Monica let out a squeal of delight.

I only had a couple of months of eighth grade left before we left on our trip so I focused on my friends and having fun. John and I were still a couple, even though he hadn't been down to the harbor since Dad threw him out of the condo in August.

One afternoon I was getting my books out of my locker for typing class when I was unexpectedly surrounded by three black girls. One of them shoved me face first into my locker. I bit my lower lip pretty hard and the other two girls laughed. They pinch-twisted my arms, yanked hard on my hair, and tripped me. They laughed at me on the ground and walked away.

They had picked me out of a sea of white girls for some unknown reason, and continued to harass me almost every day in the hallways and at my locker. They hated me and I didn't know why. I was alone the first few times it happened, but one day Raine was across the hallway when they shoved me hard. "Why are they picking on me?" I asked her when she picked up my scattered books and handed them to me.

"I don't know. Try to lay low."

"I'm not trying to stick out. I'm not prancing around saying, 'Hey! Look at me!'" I said.

"I know, but everybody knows who you are. You're the girl on the boat."

Beautiful and popular, Katie agreed to stick close to me during P.E. and after school. She told her Samoan friends to watch out for me. The Samoan girls and the black girls didn't get along very well. John helped, too, by having his friends watch out for me—the Filipino girls and black girls didn't get along any better than the Samoan or black girls. I took some comfort in everybody's help and hoped they'd be there when I needed them.

Never in my life had I noticed how different races treated each other. Dad had told us many times that the color of somebody's skin should never be a consideration. But here at Jefferson Jr. High it was a big factor in my day-to-day life.

The fear of being attacked kept me awake at night although I never told Dad. I knew he wouldn't intervene. He'd just lecture me about standing up for myself. Fear of their attacks woke me early in the mornings. As I dressed for school I wondered if today would be the day I got a real beating.

One day when Katie was out sick, while playing volleyball in P.E., I hit the ball across the net and it landed right on one of the black girl's faces. She was talking to somebody and not paying attention, so when the ball hit her face, she screamed out. I immediately apologized yelling, "Sorry," but I got the look of death from every other black girl on the court. The bell rang and I ran for the P.E. teacher knowing I was in trouble with the black girls, but she was locked in her office with the three Hispanic girls who had been caught smoking cigarettes. I waited by the P.E. teacher's window until she yelled at me through the glass, "Get moving, Leslie. Get changed."

The black girls were waiting for me. As I rounded the corner toward my locker, five or six of them surrounded me. "Why'd you hit Yolanda in the face?"

"I didn't mean it. It was an accident."

Two of the girls grabbed my T-shirt and pulled it so hard it ripped. They held me against the lockers while two other girls kicked and punched me, calling me "white bitch" and "honky." They pushed me down the row of lockers to the shower, shoved me down on the tiles, and Yolanda turned on the water and kicked me and then they all left. Nobody helped me. The locker room had cleared out. All the other white girls had left for class. When the second bell rang, the P.E. teacher found me still sniffling, lying on the tile floor in the showers soaking wet, but she never called Dad or did anything to the black girls.

I was bullied by those black girls until Dad checked us out of school on December 13. I couldn't wait to get out of Jefferson Jr. High. The following week I was featured on the front page of the school paper, *The Falconeer.* When I read the article, I was glad I didn't go to Jefferson Jr. High any longer. I could only imagine what the black girls would have cooked up for me after reading it. I had to laugh when I read what one student said she wanted for Christmas: "a bus ticket to Phoenix, Arizona." I would have joined her immediately, since in the back of my mind I was still looking for some place to run away to.

Falconeer

Vol. XX No. 12 Jefferson Junior High School Oceanside, California December 20, 1974

GIRL STUDENT LIVES ON BOAT

LEAVING FOR WORLD TRIP IN JANUARY

Not all people live in houses or apartments. Some actually live on boats. Take Leslie Johansen for example, she lives on a boat at the Oceanside Harbor.

Leslie lived on a ranch near San Francisco before, but her parents broke up. Her father bought a boat, and took the three daughters with him, including Leslie.

Leslie has lived on the boat for two years. Her family eats and sleeps there too. One of the disadvantages of livng on the boat is that sometimes when they have visitors it gets a little crowded. One of the advantages is that none of the girls have to mow the lawn.

Leslie has been on a lot of boat trips, and in a few storms like a gale. Leslie's next trip will be the biggest one of all. She will be going around the world over a period of five years.

Leslie likes living on her 45 foot boat better than living on the ranch with all the animals.

Her world trip is about begun. Leslie checked out last Friday to help prepare the boat as they are leaving on January 5.

by Nancy Pritchard

SANTA CLAUS STILL ALIVE FOR MOST

DO YOU BELIEVE IN SANTA CLAUS?

Louise Quigley: "I believe he did live, but he (Continued on Page 5)

THINGS FOR CHRISTMAS

WHAT DO YOU WANT FOR CHRISTMAS?

Anna Enriguez: "A bus ticket to Phonix Arizona"
Joe Magro: "An expensive Christmas Present"
(Continued on Page 5)

MEANING OF REAL CHRISTMAS

If someone asks you to tell them the true meaning of Christmas what would you say? Many people would not know what to answer. Some think it's waking up Christmas morning and seeing how many gifts you can get, others think it's just a quick vacation from school. But the real meaning has something to do with both of these. First

of all, the presents are just a way of saying "I Love You" or I'm thinking of you.

As for the vacation from school, it's a time for everyone to be with family and friends for the holidays. Also remember most important December 25, is the day we celebrate Jesus Christ's birthday. So remember when you wake up Christmas morning and see all those gifts under the tree, there's more to Christmas than meets the eye.

by Eddie Smith

Instead of getting a bus ticket to Phoenix, Dad surprised us all on Christmas Eve when he sat us down at the main cabin table and put a one hundred dollar bill on the table. We all eyed it. The last time we'd seen a one hundred dollar bill was exactly one year earlier.

We had always had regular Christmases like everybody else, with presents from Santa and from Mom and Dad, and a Christmas tree with tinsel that Mom and Dad fought over (Mom thought the tinsel needed to be placed on the tree one strand at a time, and Dad was more in favor of grabbing handfuls and just throwing it on). We always felt special because on Christmas Eve we got to open one present, in the Norwegian tradition. None of our friends got to do that. But now that we were teenagers, traditional Christmases stopped.

We sat at the table staring at the money. "The priests at the Mission San Luis Rey gave me the name of a family with three kids—two girls and a boy—who we will shop for," Dad said.

Last year, our first Christmas in Oceanside on the boat, we didn't have a tree or presents like all our friends at school. Dad told us then that the boat, and sailing around the world, would be our present. Instead he'd found a single mom with two kids and we used our Christmas money to buy her presents and food. This year would be the same.

I remembered the family's house, and how good it felt to deliver the gifts, so I wasn't too disappointed I wouldn't be getting any presents. Plus, I knew better than to expect anything from Dad, even at Christmastime. He felt we were very lucky and had to find ways to give back. To be honest, all I really wanted for Christmas was a train ticket out, but that would be impossible, so shopping for a needy family seemed like a good idea to me.

Dad managed to get an RV again this year from a friend so we could load up the presents and food and deliver them. Our car, a 1967 red Opel Kadett, was barely big enough for the four of us.

The best part of shopping for a needy family was riding in the cool RV. We got to sit at the table and play cards while Dad drove. As we drove to the toy store, Dad told us about the family. "The dad in our family lost his job six months ago and can't find work. The priests told me that the mom is in the hospital right now recovering from surgery. The family has no money and may have to leave their home and move in with relatives."

"How old are the kids?" Karen asked.

"The girls are eight and twelve. The boy is ten," and after a pause asked, "So, who's shopping for whom?"

"I'll take the twelve-year-old girl," I said. I figured that because I was only one year older I knew what the girl wanted. I would buy her girly things.

"I'll take the boy," Monica said, which was perfect since Monica loved to play all the boys' sports.

"Okay, then I'll take the eight-year-old girl," said Karen. "I bet she wants a new doll."

We each found two presents and loaded back in to the RV to wrap them. I found the girl curlers and a new purse. Monica got the boy a basketball and Monopoly. Karen found a doll that closed her eyes and peed her pants. We put ribbons and bows on the presents. Dad drove us to the grocery store where we bought all the food for Christmas dinner, including a pumpkin pie.

We arrived at a run-down adobe-style house by the Oceanside airport, and parked out front. Dad went to the front door, and we watched from the window of the RV as he spoke with the father. After several minutes, Dad waved to us, and we unloaded the presents and bags of food, putting it all down on the living room floor. As we came in the father said, "Thank you very much. We appreciate the kindness." He was dressed in an old dirty undershirt, dark pants, and work boots. The kids huddled together, peeking around the corner of the hallway. It seemed they were embarrassed we were bringing them food and presents. I tried not to look at them.

When we finished, Dad reached into his pocket and gave the man the one hundred dollar bill. "Let's get going girls, back into the RV."

"Thank you again, sir, you don't know how much I appreciate this," the father said.

We walked toward the RV, and as we climbed the stairs to go inside I turned around and saw the kids crowded around the open door watching us. The night was cool, but clear. The stars were out in abundance. And the moon was three-quarters full and hung over their house. Dad yelled, "Merry Christmas!"

I can't deny how good that felt. Those kids wore pajamas with holes in them, and the oldest girl wore a T-shirt so large it had to be her father's and ratty old sweatpants with bare feet. Their house was old and rundown. There was no car in the driveway. We drove back to the boat in silence. Even after what happened with Scott and my hurt over that, I felt lucky and blessed to have such a great life—one where we got to go to a far-off exotic land—while those kids didn't know where they'd be living next week.

I was conflicted with each turn of events about whether I wanted to go to Tahiti or not. I was glad I didn't have to be bullied anymore in school and I was grateful to have such a generous father. I still wasn't talking to Scott anymore, so it would be good to be away from him permanently. It would be hard to leave sweet John, but I felt undeserving of his innocent love. And Dad had been so kind lately. Maybe his wandering hands and eyes would stay where they belonged and nothing more would happen. Maybe I wouldn't feel angry and on edge all the time, waiting for him to make another move when I was least prepared. Maybe everything would go great and we would be a normal family now. Maybe Tahiti wouldn't be so bad.

Nine

The pressure of leaving for our trip had Dad preoccupied. The littlest thing set him off. We all walked carefully. We hid as much as we could, trying not to look like we were hiding. If he gave us a chore, we followed his orders to the letter, without a peep, attempting virtual silence at all other times. The day after Christmas, the three of us were in the forward cabin folding laundry when the shouting began.

"Monica, where did you put the charts I gave you the other day?"

"I don't know. I just set them down."

"Where?"

A long pause. "I don't know."

"Well, how in the hell are we supposed to sail to Nuku Hiva without them?!" Dad yelled. "Come out here so I can see you."

Monica cowered, pulling her shoulders forward and lowering her head to her chest.

"Monica!"

"I put them on the navigation station, I think." Monica walked into the main cabin.

Karen and I stopped folding the laundry and peeked into the main salon as Dad rifled through the documents on the navigation station.

"Well they aren't here now. Where could they have gone? Did they grow feet and walk away? Or did the little green man steal them?"

The little green man was my father's invention. Whenever something happened and nobody knew anything about it, Dad blamed it on the little green man. Eventually it became a family joke, and sometimes a tension reliever if we blamed something on the little green man and got away with it, which we sometimes did. He was always sneaking around the boat, responsible for all the ways in which we seemed to be letting Dad down. One time the little green man left the fire on under the coffee pot; another time he forgot to close the hatch before the rain started.

Dad walked toward the bow. "Leslie, Karen, have you seen the charts?"

"No," we answered in unison.

"Monica! This is serious! We need those charts!" Dad yelled.

The more he yelled, the larger Monica's eyes got and the smaller her body got. She folded herself into a small lump in the corner, her knees pulled up and her long blonde hair in front covering her body. He stomped back over to the navigation station, yelling so the whole dock could hear him as he swung his arms around the navigation station, "See! They aren't here."

Karen and I went into the main salon and sat next to Monica to watch the drama unfold. It was good to watch somebody else get chewed out, but I had to be careful not to show my enjoyment too much.

Dad's eyes searched the area up and down and then he bent down into the crawl space between the main cabin and the aft cabin and grabbed the roll of drawings wedged in between the floor and the engine. "Here they are!" he said, holding them in the air. They were splattered with drops of engine oil. He walked to Monica and swatted the top of her cowering head with the roll of paper. She lifted her buried head in astonishment, "I don't know how they got into the engine. I really don't."

The roll of drawings had probably rolled off the navigation station when one of us walked by too quickly and bumped them.

"You're just like your mother, Monica. You're ridiculous and I can never trust you with anything."

Our departure date, January 5, came and went without mention. We were getting to the point where none of us took Dad seriously anymore when he announced yet another new departure date. It felt like we would never leave for the South Pacific.

But on the morning of January 6, as I sat in the main salon eating my cereal, getting ready for a day of chores, Dad yelled, "Girls, come up on deck, I want to introduce you to someone."

Monica and Karen went on deck. I climbed out last and stood on the middle step of the entryway, poking my head just high enough out of the cabin to see a man standing on the dock. He was a surfer type, tall with blond hair. He held a notebook and a camera and waved, "Hello, I'm Steve Moore. I'm writing an article about your trip."

Mr. Moore interviewed Dad about our trip and we posed for a few pictures while handing supplies from the dock to the boat. Dad told Mr. Moore we were leaving on Sunday, January 19, which was news to Monica, Karen, and me. The article came out in *The Blade Tribune* the following Wednesday. It was almost like Dad needed the date to be printed in the newspaper so he'd abide by it.

Wednesday, January 15, 1975   The Blade-Tribune—1

Family Sailing Around The World

By STEVE MOORE
Staff Writer

OCEANSIDE — At 2 p.m. Sunday the 45-foot Aegir will sail out of Oceanside Harbor on a five-year, 50,000-mile trip around the world with a crew of four.

Bjørn Johansen and his three daughters — Monica, 15; Leslie, 14; and Karen, 12 — will begin their odyssey after four years' preparation.

Johansen, orginally from Norway, sold his ranch to raise the $55,000 for the boat and its equipment.

Their first stop, the Marquesas Islands, are 3,000 miles southwest of here in the South Pacific.

"That's the longest voyage a sailor can make without encountering land, but we expect good weather, so we aren't worried. The islands are the first stop on the way to Tahiti and are still part of the French colonial empire," Johansen said.

Although there is an auxiliary engine for emergencies, power for the family's voyage will be provided by the wind. The Johansen family will be aiming for the island of Nuku Hiva, a 14-mile-long stretch of land and one of about six islands they will visit in the south seas.

It will take them anywhere from 25 to 30 days to reach that destination, with the girls sharing watch duty, cooking chores and learning to navigate by the stars.

It will be an adventure in more ways than one for the family.

STOWING SUPPLIES aboard their sailboat for trip are Johansen and his daughters.

BJORN JOHANSEN plans circumnavigation.

"This is the longest voyage I've ever made, although I've wanted to go to sea since I was a kid. Before this, we've just sailed around the coast of California."

Johansen, 39, has lived in Oceanside for two years, doing custom work and technical installations on boats.

The trip represents a lifetime ambition for Johansen, but his real pleasure will come from seeing his daughters learn about the world first-hand and become bilingual.

After their stay in the Marquesas Island, the family will "drift" with no set itinerary until the fall. Then the Johansen's will land in France where the girls will live with a French family and attend school.

Johansen will sail to England where he will prepare the boat for its return trip.

During the voyage, Johansen will visit his native Norway where he used to be a deep sea diver.

During the first year, Johansen plans to shoot a 90-minute adventure film of his voyage which he hopes to show to harbor audiences from San Diego to Vancouver, Canada.

He will also write articles for "Pacific Skipper," a boating enthusiasts' magazine. The family will then leave their boat in Tahiti and fly back to Oceanside during the first year to promote the movie.

Each year there will be subsequent films which Johansen hopes will offset the $150 a month he has budgeted for the journey.

And now there are only the goodbyes to friends and relatives and some last minute packing. The girls' mother came down from Canada recently to wish the sailors well. And for the girls, 12-year-old Karen sums it up by saying, "It sure beats sitting in a classroom in Oceanside...we can't wait."

Two days before we left, Monica turned fifteen. Nobody mentioned her birthday to Dad. Karen and I snuck out and got her a cupcake and had a private celebration. Dad hardly even noticed us anymore. He rushed around all day collecting things, repairing things, and stowing things aboard the boat. In the evening he went to La Beaner's and came home after we'd gone to bed.

Finally, the morning of our departure arrived: Sunday, January 19, 1975. The weather was sunny, with blue skies and light wind. At noon we moved the boat to the visitor's dock by the Candy Kitchen and the large "Oceanside 95" fishing boat. Two television crews arrived and set up their cameras and lights on the dock. Steve Moore arrived with his notebook and a photographer. The fuss being made about our departure by the TV stations and the newspaper was fun and exhilarating. We were now truly "famous." I got wrapped up in the spectacle of it all. Maybe the kids from school would see me on TV.

Friends from around the harbor arrived and milled around the dock. Forest came down from the Candy Kitchen and handed each of us a bag of our favorite candy. Everybody watched the camera crews shooting us as we did fake chores, like coiling a rope, taking the sail covers off, and sitting in the captain's chair looking at the compass. Then they interviewed us on camera. Dad did most of the talking, but one reporter asked Karen how she felt about missing school, to which she replied, "Great!" with a big smile. The three of us agreed on that.

By one o'clock, fifty people had arrived, including John De La Cruz, who brought me a red rose. Raine brought me a puka shell necklace and made me promise to write, and Katie Clarke brought me a tie-dyed tank top and gave me a bear hug. Scott was there, but he only smiled at me wordlessly. I wanted to smile back but a huge hole in my stomach opened up so all I could do was look away. Shirley and Bill stood off to the side, watching the circus.

Monica's boyfriend, Bill Smith, came to say good-bye. I didn't even know Monica had a boyfriend! It was strange to see our resident bookworm teary-eyed over a boy. I had new respect.

Dad began a speech, puffing out his chest. I stood beside him, with Karen in front of him and Monica on the other side. He put his arm around me, resting his bicep on the side of my right breast, pushing it a little and flexing his muscle. I looked up at him with pleading eyes to stop. He ignored me. His fingers spread out wide around my hipbone. I wore a loose white blouse with red embroidery trimmings and white cord cut-offs. (After sneaking around with the one and only stolen bra I owned for more than a year, I had thrown it away just that morning in the trash can by the boat owner's bathroom. It wouldn't be possible to hide a bra from Dad aboard.)

My shirt crept up as he moved his arm and adjusted his hand around my hipbone, exposing my waist and stomach. I tried to squirm away and adjust my shirt but his grip tightened. He spoke loudly and people hushed when they heard his booming voice. "These are *my* girls," he said, as he looked deep into my eyes and held me still, then looked up at the audience. "They are accomplished sailors and I have the utmost confidence in them as deck hands and crew members. Thank you for coming to see us off today. We will be in touch with all of you. Please write to us in care of *Aegir* in Papeete, Tahiti."

Everybody clapped. The owner of La Beaner's stepped up, holding two carafes of margaritas. Dad let go of me, grazing my breast one more time. He grabbed the pitchers and I quickly adjusted my shirt. I was embarrassed and outraged. I searched the audience for someone who might have seen what had happened, but everybody was under his spell, not watching the sleight of hand happening right in front of their eyes.

I was his to do with as he wished. He had the upper hand—literally. I was powerless. Maybe I should have made a scene, cried and accused him publicly. But I was scared. I knew if I made a fuss, they would ask questions, and who could say if they'd believe me. More likely, they'd believe him. When the crowds and the TV cameras were gone and our trip was cancelled, I would end up with Dad. Alone. Just him and me. Then I would have reason to be afraid.

He was loved and admired by these people on the docks. This was his moment in the spotlight. We were his possessions and it was our job to make him proud. The image was all that mattered: the bald Norwegian sailor circumnavigating the world with his three young blonde daughters as crew.

My hands were tied behind my back with invisible thread that only he and I knew about. I silently vowed revenge.

Dad lifted the carafe high into the air and said, "Skol," and then drank from the decanter. The crowd burst into applause. He gave Karen, Monica, and me a long drink of the slushy lime liquid as everybody on the dock cheered.

It was time to go. Dad started the engine and shouted "Monica and Leslie, untie us and let's get going."

We performed our roles perfectly while the TV cameras recorded it all. We pushed *Aegir* out into the channel. I stood on the bow looking at all the people, but especially John. He was the sweetest, most thoughtful guy I had ever met. I silently vowed to remain loyal to him for the entire journey.

As we motored passed the gas and bait dock, boats followed us.

"Hey, Bjorn!" Shirley yelled. Dad waved and blew her a kiss right in front of Bill. Scott was next to her with a Cheshire cat smile behind black sunglasses. I looked away.

Fifteen or twenty boats followed us out the channel to the open ocean, including a Harbor Patrol escort. Monica and I raised the sails as we passed the half-mile buoy, though there was very little wind. The other sailboats did the same. There were a few powerboats which sped ahead of us, leading the way south. It got tiring waving to everybody over and over. All I wanted to do was go below deck and lay down on our bunk, but it felt wrong to avoid the happy people partying all around us. They watched us through binoculars. So Monica, Karen, and I sat on deck looking through our binoculars for a long time, waving occasionally. A quiet sadness settled on me.

As the sun dipped below the horizon, the boats fell off and turned back to the safety of the harbor. We smiled big, waved for the hundredth time, and shouted to the sky as loud as we could, "Good-bye." The wind had picked up but the seas stayed flat and still. Dad set the auto pilot so nobody had to steer and we motor-sailed south until we couldn't see any other boats.

This was it. We were on our way to the South Pacific. Hard to believe it was actually happening after two and a half years of preparation. The reality was here and yet it didn't feel real after so much hoopla and so many departure date changes. One door had closed, but the new door hadn't opened yet. I couldn't imagine our new world. Soon we would be in the Southern Hemisphere where it was summer in February, an odd thing to reconcile in my teenage brain.

Dad was below studying the charts. Monica sat cross-legged with the guitar and played James Taylor's "Fire and Rain" as I sang melody and she sang harmony. I was never good at harmonizing. That was Monica's gift.

We'd harmonized at every turn of our lives—driving across country when we moved from Windsor to Paradise, singing "She'll Be Coming 'Round the Mountain" when I was nine; on horseback together as we rode on the ranch singing "This Land is Your Land" when I was eleven; and now on our way to the South Pacific on our sailboat. Monica's eyes, dark brown with yellow flecks around the pupil, were a familiar place for me. We were different in many ways, but the same in so many more. We became one when we sang harmony.

"Let me play now," I begged her.

"What are you going to play?"

"'Mexico.'"

"You can't play that, we're going to Tahiti," she sang, strumming some made-up chordes on the guitar.

I grabbed the guitar, and played James Taylor's "Mexico." Monica harmonized expertly and we sounded good. Everything was right with the world.

Karen lay on a cushion, peeking out from a sleeping bag. At about six o'clock Dad came on deck and scanned the desolate horizon as we finished singing. It was completely dark.

"Okay, take it off autopilot, Leslie, and turn the boat to a heading of 165 degrees. We're going to San Diego. I have so many things to do before we can actually leave."

"Dad!" Monica yelled.

"Are you joking?" I asked.

Karen sat up, wrapped in her sleeping bag, her mouth hanging open.

"Nope, I'm not joking. And turn up the RMP to 2000 so we can make it by ten o'clock."

Part 2

The Reality

Ten

*W*e sat staring at Dad, astonished. He had to be kidding. Karen asked the question racing through my mind. "What if people find out that we didn't actually leave? Won't they be mad?"

"Nobody will know. We won't talk to anybody. I'm going to work as fast as I can and then we'll leave."

Monica and I sat on deck. I held the guitar. Our mouths hung open. "How long will we be in San Diego?" Karen asked.

"A week or two,"

"A week or two?" I repeated.

Dad looked at me with a sour face and continued in a stern voice. "You girls will sand and oil all the teak, do our laundry and clean the boat. That ought to keep you out of my way. And don't even think about sneaking off the boat to call your boyfriends. You will compromise everything if you do that." He stood staring at us, forcing us to be complicit in his lies.

I looked at Monica and then at Karen, truly flabbergasted. The past few weeks made more sense now. No wonder he'd been so angry. I wondered when he decided to fake everybody out – probably when the newspaper article came out announcing January 19 as our departure date.

After motor sailing the thirty-eight miles, we sneaked into San Diego harbor around eleven o'clock, tied up at the visitor's dock on Shelter Island, and went to bed.

The following two weeks were boring and frustrating. We worked on the teak railings, did the laundry twice, cleaned the boat topside and below, and dusted all the books on the bookshelves. I pulled down *Anne of Green Gables,* curled up, and read. I stayed out of Dad's way as much as possible. I hated him for tricking us, for pulling me away from John two weeks early, and for being such a bully. I felt like a hostage and we hadn't even gone to sea. As the time dripped by one day at a time, Monica, Karen, and I wondered aloud to each other whether or not we would actually leave for Tahiti, and what the reality of an ocean crossing would be like.

All I really wanted while we were in San Diego was to talk to John, and the more I couldn't have it, the more I wanted it. I began idealizing our relationship. I wanted to be innocent with him, instead of feeling tarnished and used by Scott, and thinking about what might happen in the next twenty-five days at sea with Dad. But I didn't betray Dad by calling John.

On January 22, three days after arriving in San Diego, I turned fourteen. The day went by uneventfully, thank God. Dad didn't notice the date and I was secretly happy. It was a relief to blend into the background and not be recognized. I couldn't stand him and didn't want his congratulations. Monica and Karen sang to me quietly in our bunk, playing "keep away" with my book, and tickled me until I screamed too loud and Dad yelled at us.

Dad made us take one last inventory of the food stores. He'd read in *Cruising* and *Sail* magazines that we needed items to trade with the native people in the South Pacific, so we bought bottles of perfumed lotion, eau de toilette, aftershave, cologne, and some inexpensive jewelry. We repacked everything so it was sea-worthy.

Finally, on Saturday, February 5, we left for Nuku Hiva. Without fanfare, we sailed away from the dock on the tail of one storm and just ahead of another. I sat on a sail bag on the foredeck when Dad came to photograph me. I had hardened inside in the two years we'd spent in Oceanside, and was able to ignore him by staring up at the sails while he took my picture. The winds were steady at ten knots under clear blue skies. We cleared Point Loma and headed out.

The waves quickly grew larger and the wind blew stronger. *Aegir* climbed each wave valiantly, fighting her way to sea while broken orange and red clouds filled the sky. The waves had white caps like they were topped with icing. Monica, Karen, and I sat on deck wrapped in jackets and blankets, watching California get smaller and smaller behind us. I wondered what the empty horizon in front of us held in store. Dad came up on deck with our dinner of bologna sandwiches and looked at the sky, "You girls know the saying, right?"

Monica didn't reply, her sour seasick look said it all. Karen and I remained silent as well. Nothing could squelch Dad's good spirits and so he recited the verse.

"Red skies in the morning, sailors take warning,

Red skies at night, sailor's delight."

I looked back at the brown lump of land as night fell on us, and said a quiet good-bye. After taking her Dramamine, Monica went to bed without eating.

Dad certainly was delighted—smiling and whistling as he adjusted the sails. He loved that we were headed into a storm, sailing close-hauled in twenty-knot winds, with the railing in the water. "*Aegir* is a fine boat. Look at the way she handles these seas," he said with a huge smile.

"Okay, Captain Bligh, I can see you're happy tonight," I said.

"Just think about it. Soon we'll be on the beach with beautiful natives in French Polynesia. If that doesn't make you happy, nothing will."

I rolled my eyes and looked away.

Our first night was rough. The winds howled and drove *Aegir* through the sea. In the forward bunk, all three of us felt queasy as the bow rose up on the swells, and then slid down the other side. In the endless up and down motion, my stomach was in the air while my body was already dropping down the next wave. I leaned against the netting, which held us in the bunk and kept us from falling on the floor. Watching Monica disappear into sleep to avoid feeling nauseous gave me compassion for her. I had only been seasick once before, when we lost our mast—I couldn't imagine feeling that way every day. But on this night I moaned and groaned and clutched my stomach, wishing I'd taken a Dramamine, trying to sleep. Dad took the overnight watch from midnight to 0500, the watch he would take during the entire trip.

Around 0200, Monica threw up all over the bed and then sat up and bumped her head, crying out loudly. I startled awake from my light sleep, queasy and just barely holding it down. Monica climbed over me and the netting, barely negotiating the three-step ladder to the floor. She bent over moaning, hardly able to stand. The smell was rancid as I climbed out of the bunk, slamming against the cabinets as the boat lurched forward. Karen followed me out of the bunk. For a brief time we all stood naked in the forward cabin searching for something to wear. Dad had insisted we continue to sleep naked "as European girls do," and although I resented him and his strange edicts, I complied without thinking. The cabin floor was littered with items falling from everywhere as the boat's angle became steeper and steeper—it was obvious we hadn't stowed things well enough and we would surely hear about it in the morning. Wrapped in a blanket, Monica threw up several more times in the head, the boat's toilet, which was only feet from our bunk. Karen and I grabbed T-shirts and covered ourselves up. We leaned back against the cabinets and watched Monica heave as the boat heeled over hard.

"Go on deck and get some air, after you flush that down, Monica," I said.

She nodded. Her face was pale, mouth hanging open, eyes drooping. She fought to get her pants and T-shirt on, grabbed a jacket and headed up on deck. The air was moist and thick with the smell of vomit.

Karen and I rolled the dirty sheets into a ball and stuffed them into a nook near the head to wash in the morning. While we put new pillowcases and sheets on the bed Dad poked his head through the hatch and yelled down from deck, "Leslie, take the bunk in the aft cabin! You girls are too big to share that forward bunk anymore."

Karen climbed into the freshly made forward bunk and said, "Lucky you. I have to sleep with Monica and you get your own bed."

At first I did feel lucky, but that passed as I realized what being separated from my sisters meant for me.

I climbed up the stairs and opened the hatch. The boat was heeled over sharply and I struggled to hold on. The moon, in its last quarter, barely peeked through the clouds. Dad and Monica sat on either side of the helmsman chair. The cold wind howled and they were bundled up in jackets and hats. Monica's drawstring hood was tied so tight only half of her eyes showed. She leaned against the helmsman chair, eyes closed, looking wretched.

"We made the bed up. I'll be fine sleeping in the forward berth with Monica and Karen."

"Leslie! What did I say? You sleep in the aft cabin from now on. End of discussion."

Monica never opened her eyes. I stood there for a moment staring at him. I descended into the main cabin and grabbed a sleeping bag and a pillow. "He's making me sleep in the aft cabin," I told Karen. She was already half-asleep and didn't respond. I stomped to the tunnel that separated the aft cabin from the main cabin and crawled back into the aft cabin to put my new bed together for the night.

The aft cabin was the master bedroom aboard the boat, with its own head and closet area. It was separated from the main cabin by a crawl space through the engine area. Each bunk ended in a cave-like nook, leaving only the top half of the bunk open. I considered sleeping with my head in the cave part, hoping it would make me feel safe and secure, but it wasn't big enough for my entire body. I dropped my T-shirt on the floor and crawled into bed, angry. The motion of the boat in the aft cabin was considerably less than the forward berth. I rolled back and forth a little, but it wasn't unpleasant at all. My grateful stomach began to settle once the constant pounding of the bow into the waves was gone.

The next morning I woke around 0800. The motion of the boat was softer, and we weren't heeled over so steeply. I peeked out the porthole to find blue skies and no white caps. I put on my T-shirt and crawled into the main cabin, relieved to find Dad sleeping on the double couch. I had fully expected him to take the other bunk in the aft cabin. I snuck into the bow and put on sweat pants and a jacket, with socks for my cold feet. Monica was asleep in the bow berth and the smell from the night before was still thick in the air.

I found Karen on deck doing her morning watch, bundled up like an Eskimo in a red ski jacket, ski gloves, and a wool hat, with thick socks on her feet. She sat with her knees pulled up to her chest near the helmsman chair.

Aegir was steered by an autopilot twenty-four hours a day, but one of us always had to be on watch, looking around for other boats, and filling in the log sheet every hour with heading, speed, and wind direction. Dad used this information in his navigation to determine our dead reckoning, or best guess position of where we were on the map. During rough weather we were allowed to stay below in the main cabin during our watch, but had to frequently poke our head into the clear bubble above the main cabin hatch to check the sails and look around.

The chilly north winds were steady, about twelve knots. The green ocean had turned a deep indigo blue—bluer than I'd ever seen. The sky was clear and the sun bright. The knot meter on deck showed we were moving at six knots. Karen held the hourly logbook to her chest.

"Crazy night, huh?" I sat down next to her.

"Yeah, I hope all our nights aren't that rough," she said.

"When did Dad wake you for your watch?"

"Around six."

"Have you seen anything?"

"Not a thing. We're alone."

I looked around. A horizon line surrounded us in every direction. *Wow! We were really at sea.* It was just the four of us on this forty-five-foot boat plowing toward infinity. I said a silent prayer that Dad would sleep in the main cabin every night until we reached Nuku Hiva.

Monica felt better in the calmer seas. When she came on deck a few hours later, she sat on the stern of the boat facing California with the transistor radio to her ear, listening to KFI out of Los Angeles, straining to hear the last words broadcast before we lost the signal.

On the third day at sea, I resigned myself to the aft cabin, moved my things, and made it my bedroom. The solitude and silence were heavenly while reading and writing, but fear that Dad would decide to sleep in the other bunk bubbled up like sour milk. I read *The Secret Garden*, where giant oak trees like the ones on the ranch protected the lush garden of pansies, sweet peas, and iris—a world so far away it was almost unbelievable. I looked up the flowers in the *Encyclopedia Britannica* Dad kept in the main cabin. As I read the book each day, my mind transported me thousands of miles away to a world very different than mine, but with a family also in the throes of conflict and secrets.

As we pushed through our fifth, sixth, and seventh days at sea, we felt winter upon us. It was cold and wet all the time with misty splashes from waves at unexpected moments. My face was cold and numb while on deck. I wore socks and tennis shoes at all times. When I licked my lips I tasted salt, and when I touched my face I could feel salt crystals.

Dad lit the fireplace in the main cabin to keep us warm at night, as the temperature dipped down into the forties. The head clogged twice within the first two weeks, which Dad blamed on us for using too much toilet paper. Monica, Karen, and I stuck together and denied it, blaming it on the little green man.

The watch schedule set by Dad had Karen taking the early-morning watch. I took the evening watches before and after dinner. Dad took 2400 (midnight) to 0600. And we all took the day watch because we generally hung out on deck. Monica's watch was the only variable. She was always on the verge of throwing up so Dad usually took Monica's late-evening shifts unless he was really tired, and then Karen and I took the watch for a few hours so Dad could sleep.

We saw pods of dolphins almost every day, and a few whales breached very near us. Flying fish landed on deck, flopping around until they landed back in the ocean. Occasionally one died on deck but that was rare. Two thick fishing lines with flashy feather lures tied at the end—one starboard and one port—trailed behind us as we trolled for fish. The fishing lines were attached to a long macramé string tied to a big copper navy bell hanging over the aft cabin. When a fish bit, the bell would ring.

Just after lunch on our seventh day at sea, the bell rang three times, then stopped, then rang continuously. Dad and I ran to the stern and pulled in a fifteen-pound Mahi-Mahi. I grabbed the net and scooped it out of the water. The fish glittered and sparkled in a rainbow of colors for a few minutes while it flopped on deck.

"Girls, fresh fish tonight for din-din," Dad said, as he bashed its head in with a broomstick. Blood flooded the deck. Monica arrived on the stern of the boat just in time to see all the gore. In a panic to get away, she turned the wrong way and threw up into the wind, causing vomit to come back in her face and all over her jacket.

"God, Monica, can you take that someplace else?" Dad yelled.

Dad had run out of sympathy for Monica's seasickness, like she could control it. I stood with blood and fish guts on one side, Monica's throw up on the other side, and almost heaved myself. Unaffected, Dad filleted the fish, cutting both sides off and throwing the remains into the ocean. I watched the carcass float away. Some lucky bird or dolphin would have a good meal.

"Can we have boiled fish and potatoes for din-din tonight, Leslie?" Dad asked with a huge smile on his face.

"Just like they make in Norway?" I said, knowing how much he loved boiled fish and feeling generous toward him for the moment.

"With lots of salt and butter," he added with a wink. Dad couldn't have been happier. It seemed he was in his element and completely at home.

I served the Mahi just as he liked it, with canned corn. The rest of the fish went into our small refrigerator, which held a few dozen eggs, two gallons of fresh milk, and mayonnaise. After a week at sea we had finished the store-bought bread, and any remaining fresh vegetables and fruit. Our menu from then on depended on my baking skills for bread, the ocean for fish, and the canned food we had aboard.

Monica was getting skinnier than ever, and I could tell she was famished as I cooked that evening. She ate a huge portion of fish and potatoes and corn with two glasses of milk. Dad warned her about overeating, but she didn't listen. Within ten minutes of finishing she quietly went to the stern and hung over the side. I watched her, wondering if she would make it without becoming seriously ill. We still had about twenty days to sail and although Dad had no compassion for her, Karen and I felt horrible. It was the same when we traveled in a car. Monica always threw up and was carsick. It had been a part of our lives forever but seeing her now in such a bad state, without any relief in sight, worried me.

That night on my watch there was no moon. As the boat plowed through the waves, a green phosphorescent glow surrounded the boat as if neon sparklers had been set off beneath us. The glow below and blackness all around were offset by the night sky. Speechless, I beheld the night sky in every direction, from horizon to horizon a hundred trillion million stars, some bright, others so far away I strained to see them. The sky hung so low I felt as if I could reach up and grab a handful of stars and scatter them to the wind.

Karen's voice woke me out of a dead sleep, "Leslie, Leslie, wake up."

I opened my eyes to darkness in the aft cabin. "What? What is it?"

"You were hanging off the side of the boat by your harness. Your feet were in the water and you were crying for us to come and get you. You were soaking wet and scared and you were pounding on the hull trying to get us to wake up." She took a short breath and continued, "You couldn't reach the bell because you weren't in the back of the boat. You were just hanging off the side. It was horrible, Leslie. You were half-dead."

I reached out for my little sister's hand, taking it in mine and holding on. I felt her trembling, but I could barely see her. "Here comes the light, watch your eyes," I said, flicking the light switch with my other hand. The sudden bright light was blinding. I closed my eyes but did not let go of her hand. Squinting through my eyelashes, I saw her pale face.

She frowned, whispering, "You hung there for hours and hours and none of us heard you. We were all sleeping. None of us heard you."

"Okay, okay, it was a dream, Karen. Calm down," I said.

I put my arm around her shoulders and she scooted up on my bunk. "It was your watch and a big wave took you overboard. You were hanging there and then a shark came and bit your leg off and you were hanging by your harness, half in the water and all these sharks were taking bites out of you."

"Karen, I'm here. I'm okay. Come here." I pulled the covers up and we both lay down on the bunk.

"Oh, Leslie, it was so awful. We couldn't hear your screams."

"I know, Karen. But I'm fine. It was just a nightmare, okay?"

Karen had read the book *Jaws* a few months earlier. I refused to read it after seeing so many of my friends scared to death of the ocean.

She still shook as she hung on to me. I was wide-awake. The visions she'd had were vivid and I could tell she was scared to death. I knew she needed comfort like a mother would give, but I, too, was scared of what lay ahead in our journey. I was glad to have somebody to hug that night. Karen had conjured this dream from her fears and I could completely understand how scared she was to lose me. After a few minutes of silence she stopped shaking and began to feel warm under the covers.

"Can I sleep with you?"

"Yes, of course," I said and scooted over to give her more room. I reached up and turned off the light. My eye caught Dad sitting in the crawl space between the cabins and the engine compartment. He was watching and listening. I turned back to Karen.

"Why didn't I blow the whistle on my harness?" I asked as we cuddled up.

"I don't know. Your whistle was gone. You didn't have a whistle."

"And that's how you know it's not real. I will always have my whistle attached to my harness, okay?"

"Okay."

And we slept.

Eleven

The weather was still cold, especially at night, even after sailing seven hundred miles southwest from California because we were still in the wintry Northern Hemisphere. We had sporadic warm days as we edged toward the Southern Hemisphere, but with the chilly wind we still wanted hot food for breakfast and dinner.

Cooking at sea was a challenge, like trying to tap your head and rub your belly at the same time. I could do it, but having so many things to keep track of pushed my coordination to its limits. It was a skill I figured out on my own through trial and error.

If the seas were flat, Monica ate. Otherwise she did not. When she was well, hunger descended on her as it does on the starving. She'd tear through the stores of food in the main cabin compartments grabbing cans of food saying, "No, not this. No, no that," tossing aside cans of peaches or soup. When she found the "right" can she'd yell, "Yes, this one, I want to eat this one" with such seriousness. We'd all laugh. She'd open the can, grab a fork, and start shoveling the food in cold, right out of the can. She craved protein and wanted anything with meat in it— she tore through cans of beef stew, chili, and beanie weenies. It wasn't pretty to watch, but my heart went out to her because I could feel how hungry she was, shaking and weak, wanting sustenance in her body as quickly as possible before the wind picked up and the swells starting rocking the boat again.

But the cooking part—which was often just the heating up of food—fell to me, not because I was such a good cook but by the process of elimination. Karen was too small and Monica too sick. All three of us had cooked while tied up at the dock. It wasn't any different than cooking in a house, except smaller. Monica loved to make Hamburger Helper or anything else with beef. In port, Karen used a step stool to reach the burners and dishes in the cabinets above the stove, but a step stool at sea didn't stay put and wasn't safe.

Cooking at sea required a completely different set of skills. We had a gimbaled stove, which swung with the motion of the boat. One morning we were heeled over pretty far when I tried to make a nice country breakfast for everybody. I mixed the Tang and put it in the refrigerator to get cold while I cooked. Then I reconstituted the freeze-dried hash browns in a bowl of water, which I carefully wedged into the sink with some dishes. I put dried egg mixture and water in a bowl and whipped up scrambled eggs. Everything went great during the preparation phase, but when I poured the hash browns into a big pan heating up on the stove, they slopped out everywhere because I'd forgotten to drain the excess water. The boat lurched forward, just at the wrong time, and I dumped the pan's entire contents over the galley floor. As I bent over to get the slushy hash browns off my bare feet, Dad came down the stairs from deck.

"What has happened here?" he said in an irritated tone.

Before I could answer, the boat lurched forward again and the bowl of eggs jumped out of the sink and landed right on Karen's head as she bent over trying to help me clean up.

"Hey!" she cried, looking up with yellow goop sliding down her hair and face.

It sounds like a Laurel and Hardy movie, and in any other family it could have been funny, but Dad was hungry and he looked stern and scary. I knew better than to laugh or make light of the mess. He wasn't in a playful mood. The happy Dad from the first few days of sailing had turned into a grumpy, impatient one.

"I'm hungry," he said, "When's breakfast?"

"In a few minutes," I said.

I dove down to the floor to help wipe off Karen's face and clean up. A huge mess covered the galley, with dripping egg and hash browns everywhere.

Dad sat across from the galley at the navigation station working while we cleaned up. Within fifteen minutes I served ham, bread, and butter to Dad with a large glass of cold Tang. He was happy, thank God! I breathed a sigh of relief at having avoided a yelling match.

Seeing the dolphins every single day never got boring or old. There were often twenty or thirty dolphins, maybe more because it was hard to count when they all came up at different times. I watched them from my favorite place on the boat, the bowsprit.. The thick metal bowsprit on *Aegir* extended about four feet. It was my hide-away and I'd curl up for naps at the bottom of the metal cage in a place just big enough for me to snuggle in, wedged between the chain and metal sides, only feet from the dolphins as they raced our boat. The dolphins looked up at me with one eye as they came out of the water and I talked to them, smiling and asking where they'd been. They made me feel calm and playful and I wished many times I was a dolphin so I could travel freely in the wide wonderful ocean.

I felt safer sleeping in the bowsprit during the day when the dolphins visited me than I did in the aft cabin at night. I had taken to pushing back as far as I could on my bunk so my back was against the hull. I wedged pillows and blankets in front of me creating a barrier, and burrowed in, hoping he wouldn't come.

After a week at sea, Monica, Karen, and I attempted not only a shower but hair washing. We had been scouting the cold days in preparation for our first shower and felt that even though the swells were still pretty big, around eight feet, the light wind was ideal and the sunny skies would warm up the deck by early afternoon to allow us to put our bikinis on. Right after I cleaned up the dishes from breakfast that day, I focused on nothing else but getting ready for my shower and trying to work out the logistics.

The actual shower part wouldn't be too difficult if we could manage to get some privacy on deck. But much to my disappointment, Dad seemed anxious to help in any way he could. We began first with figuring out about hair washing with Monica. She really wanted to untangle the massive knots that had taken over her whole head.

"Why don't you lay on deck with your head over the edge and we'll wash your hair that way?" Dad suggested. It was the same position as washing hair in the kitchen sink, face down. Dad scooped up a bucket of water from the ocean and poured it over Monica's head as she stared face first at the ocean. I kneeled down and lathered up her hair. Monica couldn't help because she had to hold on to the railing to make sure she didn't go over the side. She wore her safety harness over her bikini but still didn't want to let go of the railing.

"The soap's in my eyes," she said after a few seconds.

Dad scooped up a bucket of salt water and threw it on Monica's head and then quickly threw another bucket. Monica screamed for him to stop. As she lay on the deck, mostly blind from the salt and soap in her eyes, he affectionately swatted her butt and said, "This doesn't work. You must get on the foredeck and get your sisters to help. You girls can throw buckets of water over each other's heads."

"Not me. Not today. I'm done," Monica said. "I'm soaking wet now. I'm clean enough." She went below and we didn't see her again for some time.

Karen and I went to the forward deck and prepared to help each other bathe and wash our hair. Dad prepared his camera equipment back by the helm while we got ready on deck. "Take off your bathing suits because you may as well wash everything."

Karen and I stood together, facing away from Dad.

"Is he kidding?" I whispered.

"I don't think so. Does he ever kid?" Karen said.

"You go first," I said to Karen.

"No way, Leslie, you go first. You always cry about going second, so this time you can go first," she said smugly. It was true, I hated going second in everything after Monica and had objected since we were little girls.

Back by the captain's chair with his movie camera and still camera, Dad was ready to help us by taking pictures. "Girls, get going. We are losing light and sun here."

"I don't want to shower naked," I yelled back to him.

"Leslie! Stop being a baby. Get your shower over now!" he screamed.

I looked up and the clouds were streaming in, threatening to cover up the warm sun.

I quickly took my clothes off, facing forward on the boat so all he could see was my bare butt. I was so angry at Dad, but glad Karen was there to witness and assist me in hiding as much of myself as possible while he photographed us.

"We can hurry and get this done fast," Karen said.

I stood with my feet apart for balance, facing the bow so Dad couldn't photograph my entire naked body.

Click went the camera as he yelled directions. "Dump the bucket over your head and then soap up."

"I know how to shower, Dad. Leave me alone." I forced myself to say this in a jesting tone. I didn't want him coming up to the bow.

"Leslie, look back here."

I was fuming inside but laughed my nervous laugh. "No, Dad! Can you just go away?" I said as I turned only my head around.

Karen dipped the bucket in the water and scooped it up. I knelt down, facing forward, and she gently poured the water over my head. Then she squirted shampoo in my hand, and I lathered up my hair and my body all at once. The wind had picked up a bit so I began to shake with a chill. She scooped another bucket.

"Nice shot of your bum," he said. I could tell he was smiling and really enjoying himself by his singsong tone of voice.

I looked back again with another nervous smile, "Dad! Stop it!"

As Karen handed me a towel after the second bucket of water, she said, "I'll take my shower tomorrow, okay?"

"Good idea," I said. The weather had changed. As I dried myself off, I still felt soapy but didn't care. I was relieved the show was over, and ran to the aft cabin and got dressed.

That evening, when Monica and I sat on deck alone after dinner and Dad was below at the navigation station she quietly said, "Do you remember when Dad took our pictures naked standing in the surf when we were little?"

"Yes. I remember being so cold and crying."

"Yeah, me too. It's the same now, isn't it?"

"Yeah, except now we try to laugh and lighten the mood rather than cry."

Monica and Karen were eventually filmed naked while bathing on the foredeck as well. We never discussed it except to express our frustration to each other that Dad had his camera out again during showers. We all just endured it as best we could.

The terror existed just below the surface and if that surface was nicked and exposed to the air, the terror might leak out, and then who knows what would have happened. Time again to stuff it down and make the best of it—laughing and looking like it was fun.

The next morning as I woke up to Karen shaking my shoulder for my morning watch, these images were in my head: A light under the door. A shadow blocks the light. Warm hand rubbing. Kick off the covers. Hot. Eyes slowly close. Sleep. Rubbing. Rubbing my back. Nightgown is twisted up near my tummy. Long hair moved aside. Sleep and dreams. Lying on a blanket in a field of poppies. Warm sun. Rubbing. Caressing from my shoulders to my feet. Soft. Nightgown. Blackness. Nothing. Sleep.

I took longer than normal to come on deck. Karen yelled for me three times. I couldn't shake the eerie feeling, the body memory of something that happened a long time ago. *Was I a toddler? Was I five?*

Was it real? Did I make it up? When was he coming for me again? I stuffed the fear down into the black hole inside.

Dad had been threatening to teach us celestial navigation—how to plot our course on a map using a sextant—even before we left Oceanside. Being out in the middle of the big blue ocean meant we had no landmarks at all and didn't know where we were in relation to our island destination of Nuku Hiva. We were nine days at sea when he began his navigation instruction. Each day class began on deck at 10:30 a.m. and ended at 2:00 p.m., with a short break for lunch. Dad stood in front of us as we lined up on the deck like little students. It was awful.

We began with the basics. We learned how to find the meridian crossing, which is just a fancy way to say longitude. We also learned about lines of latitude, like the equator, the most famous latitude.

"In navigation, girls, you have to understand the difference between the two kinds of minutes."

"What? There are two kinds of minutes?" Karen said.

"Yes. Now listen to me. There are minutes on our watch, sixty minutes equals one hour. Right?"

"Yes." I said.

"In navigation, sixty minutes also equals one degree when we talk about longitude and latitude."

Nobody spoke. I stared at Dad. He stared back at us. He explained it again using different words but we were confused for days. We talked about it at every meal and during the day when we were all on deck. He explained it over and over and over and over again until the knowledge finally leaked in "our brain-damaged heads," as Dad put it.

"Now that you understand about the two kinds of minutes," he said, "I need to explain how to add, subtract, multiply, and divide by sixty instead of hundreds."

"Does that mean we can never go higher than sixty?" Monica said.

"Yes, exactly," Dad said. He was seriously impressed and happy we understood. But in fact only Monica understood.

The next day, encouraged by how "smart" we were, Dad got out the sextant and began our instruction. Our sextant was a black metal contraption about the size of Dad's open hand. It had mirrors and a viewfinder and required us to look through it with one eye, like a telescope.

A sextant "shot" of the sun was the only way to figure out how many miles we had sailed the previous day, and find our position on the chart. Monica went first and learned to hold the sextant, then marked the measurements and recorded them. Dad forced her to participate even though she felt seasick because she always felt seasick and he had no more sympathy for her.

I was next and found the sun in the scope fairly easily. Lastly, it was Karen's turn. As she sat on deck next to Dad, facing the horizon, she said, "I can't wink."

Dad, surprised and astonished, leaned back away from her and said, "What do you mean you can't wink? Everybody can wink."

To which Karen blinked both eyes closed deliberately long and whimpered, "Not me."

"Well, I have a solution for that. I'll be right back," he said.

He returned with a roll of masking tape and as Karen squirmed and cried, Dad taped her left eye shut. "This will teach you how to wink!"

I felt sorry for Karen. Dad was being brutal to her. Upset by her punishment, Karen went to lie down on her bunk and take a nap, the tape still on. At dinner Dad ripped the tape off Karen's eye while she screamed about her eyebrows and lashes being yanked off.

He yelled, "Wink!" but she couldn't. She cried and whimpered but I didn't feel sorry for her anymore. Monica and I laughed along with Dad. It was a survival-of-the-fittest mentality. One minute everybody felt sorry for you, the next they were pushing you off the cliff. For me, feeling sorry for other members of the family left me vulnerable. I couldn't afford to be vulnerable. I didn't know what Dad had in store for me, and had to focus on keeping my armored shield up and staying alert at all times. It was everyone for themselves.

Monica and I got better at taking our noon shots and figuring out the math below at the navigation station, while Karen's two-eyed shots put her farther and farther away from where we actually were on the chart. "I think you've got us in Texas today, Karen," Dad said a few days later, disgusted. "A first-grader could do better than that!"

Karen ran to her bunk.

"And Leslie, your subtraction today is abhorrent. I could do this when I was in kindergarten! See, you still haven't gotten the knack of subtracting in sixties." He pointed to the place on my computation sheet where I made the mistake.

"You've said before they don't have kindergarten in Norway," I shot back to him.

"Well, *if* they had kindergarten, I'd do better."

"Of course you would," I muttered under my breath as I went topside, glad our navigation lesson was over. I couldn't wait to get back to *The Secret Garden*. I loved reading about a brave young girl who defied the adults in her life and sought out the secret garden and her bed-ridden cousin Collin.

The process of using a sextant and taking a sun shot was fairly easy, as long as we did the computation steps in the correct order and didn't make any "stupid errors." Of course, Dad berated us daily on our dismal math skills, but Monica and I learned how to navigate and plot our course. Karen continued to struggle. Under the scrutiny of Dad's watchful eye, our addition, subtraction, multiplication, and division suffered greatly. According to him we didn't know anything. We froze up under the spotlight he shone on us.

On February 18, our thirteenth day at sea, Monica made a birthday card for Mom. She lay on top of the main cabin with her pencils, writing a long letter and drawing a picture of the boat and the ocean. She worked on the card for hours, having one of her unusually good days aboard. When she was finished she called Karen and I and we added a birthday message. Dad stood in the hatchway and watched as Monica played the guitar and we all sang "Happy Birthday." I couldn't tell whether he was upset or intrigued by our ceremony.

When we were done singing we put her card in a glass jar, yelling "Happy Birthday Mom!" as Karen tossed it into the ocean. We put Mom's address in Canada in the jar, too, believing somebody would find it and send it to her.

We continued our relentless journey across the water, pushing toward the South Pacific. Dad and I sat at the main salon table on day fifteen with the charts and calculations from the afternoon's navigation session around us. Monica napped and Karen stood watch on deck. The building swells came from behind. We were sailing "wing and wing" (with two genoas out on opposite sides) so we were fairly level. Every once in a while the stern of the boat slid one way or the other as a larger-than-normal wave went under us. Dad and I laid our hands and forearms across the books, charts, and papers on the table so they wouldn't slide off.

Dad broke the silence as he put the ruler on the chart to draw our dead reckoning course line. "Let's just eat every other day. We're the only two gaining weight on this voyage. Monica's throwing up all the time, and Karen is so little she hardly eats anything."

"I'm not gaining weight. I'm not fat."

"No, you're not fat, but you're definitely gaining weight. You're not getting any exercise."

All I had to do was gain one ounce and he'd notice. I had a curvy figure and was built like a good Norwegian girl, sturdy and solid, just like him. He had struggled with his weight off and on and knew that healthy quickly turns into heavy—he was obviously worried about that for me, too.

Sometimes he slapped me on the thick part of my thighs, and said words in Norwegian that ended in something like "tre legging," which of course I thought meant that my legs were so fat it was like I had three legs. I begged him to translate it, but he refused, saying, "When you're older I'll tell you." He never did and I never figured it out.

"Do you even think you can go a whole day without food?" he prodded me.

I was ambivalent about fasting every other day. What I really wanted was peace and privacy at any cost. My feelings were hurt that he thought I was fat, but I tried not to care.

After a huge sigh, my hands resting on my forehead, I said, "I don't know, probably not."

But he didn't hear me. He only heard what he wanted to. "I've written it in the logbook, Leslie, so it's law now. We're not eating tomorrow. Okay?"

"Sure, okay," I said.

The following day I thought about food every single moment. I drooled as Karen ate a bowl of Lucky Charms. Before lunch I broke down and ate a peanut butter and jelly sandwich, hiding in the aft cabin, ashamed of myself.

The day after that was an eating day and I ate enough for two days. The next day we were supposed to fast, but by lunchtime I was so hungry I felt nauseous so I ate again in hiding—a chocolate bar, crackers and peanut butter, red licorice, and anything else I could grab on my way through the galley. That afternoon he found me in the aft cabin shoving marshmallows in my mouth, "You have no will-power, Leslie, that's the problem with you."

"Yep, that's me, fat with no willpower," I said. I didn't fast again.

Twelve

As we approached the equator two things happened. First, the weather got nice and warm—even hot on days when the wind was light. And second, for whatever reason, the heat seemed to bring Dad's frustration and anger to a head.

Monica insisted I read *Gulliver's Travels* so we could talk about it, but I wasn't enjoying it much. I much preferred writing stories in the logbook every day. I enjoyed being the storyteller in the family. Sometimes Dad read my stories at dinnertime for entertainment, seemingly proud of the details of our voyage I was documenting. I wrote all the mundane stuff about the day, like when the hook and feather lure we trolled behind the boat continually got bitten off. Dad tried to scare us as he pulled in the empty fishing line. "This line is good for fish as big as one-hundred-sixty-five pounds. Looks like a monster got it." It happened three or four times during the trip, and each time Karen shook and went white whenever Dad announced that another mammoth fish had taken our lure. I could tell Karen imagined a school of sharks following us.

In the logbook I also wrote about the weather, the night sky, the little white bird—all-alone in the world—that landed atop the aft cabin, hitching a ride for a few hours. I wrote about the exotic and strange glass balls we'd find floating in the water, covered in barnacles underneath. *Encyclopedia Britannica* said Japanese fisherman used them to secure their nets. We had a collection of the glass balls in all colors and sizes hanging off the stern railing. I also wrote about the deck full of flying fish we discovered one morning and the mother and baby blue whales we saw—they were more than twice the size of our boat and so majestic, moving in slow-motion to some far off place. I wrote about doing laundry on deck during the rain squalls; the scores for Monopoly and Checkers; the freighters we saw on the horizon, and how we imagined the good meals and fancy desserts they surely had aboard.

I also wrote stories in my diary, swooning about my life back in California. I had named my diary "John," after John De La Cruz. But I didn't tell the brutal truth about my fears because I feared Dad was reading it. It wasn't safe to tell the truth. I shoved down my feelings about Dad's advances, my dread of his visiting the aft cabin, and my indiscretions with Scott. I had secrets, which I hoped would never see the light of day.

Sometimes I had the nagging feeling that someone had moved my diary. I kept it in the little cabinet in my bunk against the hull with my book and a box of Kleenex. I tested my theory by putting a washcloth on top of my diary. When I came back after my watch, the diary was on top of the washcloth.

I could actually feel him stalking me. I had never been able to predict his coming for me. It always just happened, and it always shocked me, like an unexpected swat to the side of the head that knocks you down. But I was fourteen now, and something had shifted.

Dad looked at me strangely sometimes, peering at me and seeming to study me; other times he was fatherly, smiling proudly when I did my calculations right during navigation class. It was confusing. His eyes wandered more obviously, which was probably the thing that was putting me so on guard.

I felt like I was preparing for war. Smiling and being agreeable on the outside when doing my chores or calculations, but wound tight on the inside. It got to the point where the tension felt like I might explode. I had been imagining what I would do if he came into the aft cabin and crawled into bed with me. That was the only scenario I could imagine since I knew he wouldn't try anything in front of Monica and Karen. As I imagined waking up next to him, I also imagined kicking and screaming for my sisters. I had been preparing in my mind since we left San Diego and I began to feel cocky and confident about how I would handle him when he came. I was now at the point of actually egging him on in my mind: *Come on, let's do this thing. I'm tired of waiting for you. I'm pissed now and want you to come. You think you're so strong, well, I'm strong too. I'll show you. I'll fight with every ounce of strength I have. You will not win!*

But the days wore on and nothing happened. We were getting closer to the Marquesas Islands. Our days at sea were coming to an end fast. Maybe the tension I felt wasn't being directed at me. I began to doubt myself. If he was going to make a move, it had to be soon.

I heard the whistle, and then the bell rang five times or more. It was the agreed-upon signal of emergency, indicating a man overboard. I opened my eyes to darkness and felt groggy, like I was in a deep sleep. There was no light out the porthole. The bell rang again: ding, ding, ding. It sounded deliberate and angry, not the sound of a hooked fish. I could hear the wind blowing a constant whir in the vents and knew it was blustery and strong on deck. The boat rocked on the seas. I sat up. I should have jumped out of bed and run up on deck to help. I had been trained to do just that, over and over again. Calm filled my body as a thought came into my head: *This is a hoax.*

The feeling in my body was strong, grounded, composed, assuring me everything was okay on deck, and that this was in fact a fraud. He wants us on deck naked. *Oh, no, you don't mister—not a chance. I'm not playing this game.*

I climbed out of bed and put a T-shirt on over my naked, shivering body, then my underwear, and then my pants, decisively and deliberately. The boat rolled and lurched but my sea legs were solid and I did not fall.

I heard Monica say, "Dad, we're here! What should we do?"

"Where's Leslie?" Dad said loudly.

I stopped dressing for a moment to listen. They stood just outside the aft cabin hatch on deck, by the steering wheel. The wind blew in gusts and they yelled to hear each other.

"I don't know but I'm freezing. Can I go back to bed?" Monica said.

"Yeah, I'm freezing too," Karen said.

"Not until Leslie gets up here," he said.

Dad pounded his fist on the aft cabin hatch. "Leslie! Get up here now!" he yelled.

"Coming!" I yelled back.

I continued dressing. I put on my jacket, my socks, and then my safety harness. The stillness in my heart was solid. Where I would usually jump and nervously rush to his beck and call, I was calm and collected. I climbed the stairs of the aft cabin, sliding the hatch back and opening the small wooden doors. I didn't step out onto the deck, but stayed on the top step.

"Well, look who showed up." He stood about three feet away, leaning against the main cabin, directly in front of me. My heart pounded at the sight of his face. His smug look traveled down my body, studying every piece of clothing on me, "Why did you get dressed?"

I glanced over at my two sisters, standing naked on deck in front of the main cabin hatch, huddled together, arms wrapped around themselves, shivering and cold, the wind blowing their hair. I did not flinch, but looked back at him.

"I knew this was a hoax—you just wanted us on deck naked," I said.

His eyes narrowed and he pursed his lips in a mean pucker, biting the bottom lip a little inside.

"Monica and Karen, you are excused. Go back to bed," Dad commanded, not breaking eye contact with me.

Monica and Karen rushed into the main cabin, closing the door behind them, but just before Monica pulled the hatch closed, she peeked her head out and said, "Lez, are you okay?"

"Go below, Monica!" Dad boomed, but I looked at Monica and nodded just slightly.

Once the hatch was closed he said again, "Why did you get dressed?"

My heart pounded but I yelled into the black night, "I'm on to you! Leave me alone!"

He looked stunned and flinched just slightly at the force of my words. His mouth was open, his eyes wide. He stared at me for what seemed like forever, saying nothing, one eye getting smaller, like he was considering something.

I screamed as loud as I could, my neck craning toward him with every forceful word that came out of my mouth—"Don't ever touch me again!"

Then I shut the doors and pulled the hatch over my head, descending back into the aft cabin.

My heart beat like a gazelle being hunted. I climbed down and leaned back on the steps, alert for any sound. I couldn't hear anything over the gusting wind. I wondered if he would come after me. After ten minutes I flopped down on my bunk fully clothed, with my harness on, still hyper-aware of the sounds on the boat. My mind drifted and I thought about how long I'd waited for him to make his move. We'd been at sea seventeen days. He was like a lion crouching low, studying his prey. The gazelles eventually get worn down. They cannot be on high alert every moment of the day. Nobody can. I was tired of being scared.

After thirty minutes, I knew he wouldn't be coming, the same way I knew the whistle and bell were a hoax. I just knew in my heart and body.

Right then I decided I would never sleep naked again, and I would never shower naked on the foredeck. My body was my own and he would never touch it again. I took off my harness and jacket and laid back down on my bunk fully clothed.

After a long time I fell asleep.

The next morning I woke up sweating from sleeping in my clothes. Outside the portholes was bright sunshine, not the usual weak early morning sun. Karen had not woken me up for my 0700 watch. I wasn't sure what that meant, since she'd never let me sleep in before.

I lay in bed remembering the night before. Maybe Dad had spent the night plotting against me and now I would get my punishment. For a short time I gave into the fear, feeling helpless and weak. Then I saw his face in my memory—the shocked and stunned look after I'd screamed at him. I remembered him flinching and I began to feel better. Even if he makes me pay in some really awful way, I am proud of myself.

I decided to do what I'd learned since I could walk—act as if nothing happened. I was good at it.

Crawling into the main cabin through the engine room, I found Dad working the charts at the navigation station. I passed by him without any acknowledgement or greeting. Karen poured herself a bowl of Grapenuts and I assumed Monica was either on deck doing morning watch, which would have been odd, or she was still in bed. I didn't ask any questions. I was hungry and I needed breakfast. I went to the galley and Karen sat down with her cereal at the table.

"Daddy, you let us sleep in this morning. Thank you. I was tired," Karen said.

"I thought it would be nice for you girls to sleep in. Don't say I don't do anything nice for you," he said with a stern voice.

My back was to him as I dug out a large pot, oatmeal, brown sugar, and cinnamon, "Does anybody want some oatmeal?"

"Yes, I'll have some," Dad said.

He sounded normal, but I was afraid to look at him.

"Are you putting cinnamon and brown sugar in it?" asked Karen.

"Don't I always?"

"I'll have some. Will you take this to the sink?" she said as she handed me the bowl of Grapenuts. "I don't want it anymore."

I took the bowl and called in the direction of the forward bunk, "Monica, are you awake?"

She yelled back, "Yes, but I'm not eating oatmeal anymore. Last time I ate it, I threw it up and it was so nasty. The cinnamon came out my nose."

"Yuck. I'm sorry," I said.

A few minutes later Monica entered the main cabin and sat down next to Karen at the table. Dad stayed at the navigation station a few feet away, working on the charts. I worked in the galley as silence descended. I felt anxious as I listened to each person breathe and move slightly.

"Hey, Dad, what was that drill last night?" Monica said.

"What do you mean?" Dad asked.

"Why did you blow your whistle and ring the bell and make us come on deck? We didn't do a man overboard drill."

"I am always testing you girls. Never relax too much. I want to keep you on your toes," he said, looking at Monica.

I glanced through the pots and pans that hung from the ceiling, but could only see a fraction of Dad's face. He looked serious, business-like.

I didn't know what Monica had heard last night. The wind had howled, and with the closed hatch and the distance to the forward cabin, I felt she was out of earshot. I scanned Karen's face, but couldn't tell if she knew anything either.

"Why did you have all your clothes on last night, Leslie?" Monica prodded. "I thought we were supposed to come immediately when we heard the bell ringing or the whistle blowing. It was freezing out there on deck naked."

I didn't know what to say so I lied. "I misunderstood the bell ringing and got dressed first with my harness." I scooped the oatmeal into the little red pots.

"That's weird," Monica studied me.

"Well, I misunderstood the situation," I said, handing Karen and Dad their pots of oatmeal without making eye contact.

She didn't push me anymore. I breathed a sigh of relief. I took my oatmeal and climbed the stairs out of the cabin to eat alone. It was after 1000 and the day offered sunshine except for a few puffy white clouds on the horizon ahead. The wind blew steady at twelve knots and the boat pushed ahead in her ever-rolling motion.

Monica found me later on the bowsprit and sat with me for a while. When she asked what had really happened, I told her Dad was a creep and I refused to be on deck naked ever again. I said it with such force and finality that she never said anything more about it. I couldn't trust her with my secrets. I couldn't chance her exposing me and my secrets in a heated moment of sisterly competition. I had to keep my fears and secrets to myself at all cost.

Dad ignored me for the entire day, saying nothing to me directly. As I watched him that day, I knew I would be alright. He had backed down. I screamed at him for the first time in my life and he didn't kill me. The darkness of the night had devoured our confrontation, but it was still clear in my mind. By ignoring me all day instead of yelling at me or giving me chores for punishment, I knew he had taken a step back.

That night I crawled into bed in my T-shirt and shorts. I smiled to myself and felt just a little powerful—though I was happy the day was over. *Hopefully, tomorrow will be easier.*

This is the propaganda I wrote on the back of the log sheet:

February 23, 1975 17 days out—8 more to go!

Today was a really pretty day. Dad let us all sleep in cause it was such a nice day. He said the moon was so bright that he took a line of position shot. There were hardly any clouds in the sky when I got up. Dad pulled an alarm warning on us this morning that's where he blows his whistle to see how fast we'd get up to save that person overboard that is blowing the whistle. Well Monica and Karen did fine but it took me 5 min to get dressed. I later found out we weren't supposed to get dressed just come up naked. I'm going to be the first one out of bed next time (I hope). He also rang the bell because if anyone was in the water they could pull on the fishing line and it would ring the bell. He rang it so hard that he broke the macramé string hanging from it. Leslie

P.S. Karen is so bored she always wants someone to play cards, or play Monopoly with her.

Thirteen

In the North Pacific, before crossing the equator into the Southern Hemisphere, the Equatorial Counter Current runs west to east at about three to six knots. We were sailing due south at about six or seven knots, so our forward motion after the current was only about three or four knots with our sideways motion, or crabbing, being the other three knots or so to the east, away from the Marquesas. Dad was uptight about our progress and anxious about the miles the currents stole from us daily. If we could just get over the equator, the South Equatorial Current would actually push us west, much faster to our island destination.

On the second day after our confrontation, and the third day of losing miles, Dad was so angry he actually yelled out from the navigation station, "Damn this current! It has stolen sixty more miles from us!"

The concern was the possibility of bypassing Nuku Hiva, which was only fourteen miles long by eleven miles wide. We had sailed over 2,500 miles of the 3,300-mile journey and if we missed it, Dad would have to recalculate the navigation and try again to make landfall. There was nobody to call on the radio for help and GPS had not been invented yet for sailboats.

As Monica, Karen, and I had learned in the past three weeks, the navigation skills, including corrections for any currents pushing us around, had to be perfect—otherwise we could find our plots on the chart in Europe or China. Of the six or seven steps in the process, each step had to be perfect. The sextant had to be used perfectly in getting a shot of the sun, moon, or stars. The calculations had to be

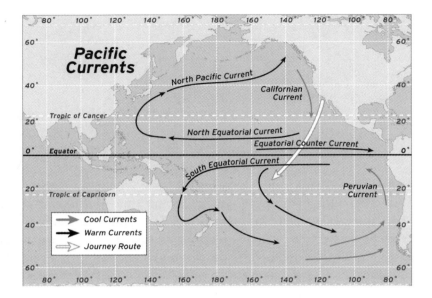

textbook, and of course, the plotting on the chart had to be flawless. If any step was incorrect, even in the slightest, our location would be wrong.

In his frustration with the navigation and the current, Dad enlisted my help by having me duplicate all of his solar shots, his computations and estimations (dead reckonings) on the charts so we could cross-check each other. I had become consistent and reliable with my navigation, and working together gave us a common goal and created a safe dialogue from which to begin some semblance of a new relationship. I made sure I didn't act too self-satisfied in my perceived victory, but I also didn't want to continue to act like nothing had happened. It was a shaky tight rope to walk. I tiptoed around him, muting my normal sarcastic personality in favor of an "all business" first mate attitude.

For eighteen days straight we rode the conveyor belt of wind and current from San Diego, and then at the equator everything just stopped. The wind stopped, the current stopped, and the ocean played dead. We had hit the doldrums—that no-man's land between the two hemispheres where sailboats without engines have languished for weeks. Dad didn't want to start our engine right away because we only had so much fuel. So he let us bob around for a day or so hoping the wind would find us. There was no forward motion whatsoever.

Every hour aboard the silently bobbing boat felt uneasy. I had grown accustomed to the constant motion of *Aegir* plowing through the waves. I now knew what it meant to have "sea legs." My body still rolled and pitched as if we were sailing, though we were hardly moving. It felt awkward dangling my legs over the side of the boat as I usually did to dip my toes in the water but I couldn't reach the water with the boat sitting level. And during my watch, there was nothing to watch—no sails full of wind, no dolphins jumping around, no compass course to check. The sails hung motionless from their halyards like emptied balloons, shriveled and lifeless. There was no place to hide when the boat stood like a picture on painted water. The stillness served to magnify Dad's impatience with the current, and his navigation.

The hours of that day burned away slowly one by one, as the fireball in the sky climbed higher and higher. Without wind, we were like ants under a magnifying glass, and life on the sailboat was empty.

Animated and herself again now that we were level and still, the person trapped inside Monica for the past eighteen days finally came out in a burst so ecstatic it shocked me. She made beef stew for breakfast, pancakes for lunch and she baked brownies in the heat for all of us. Her light brown eyes were once again clear and bright.

We bobbed around for ten hours or so, until the middle of the afternoon. "It's so hot, let's go for a swim," Karen said to Monica and I as we all sat on deck, staring at the vacant horizon.

"Dad, can we go swimming? Pleeeaaaase?" Monica pleaded.

Dad came up on deck and said, "Yes, you girls swim, I'll watch the boat."

"But come with us, Daddy, I want you to swim, too," Karen said. Her fears about sharks were ever-present and I knew she wanted to hold on to Dad's neck while she swam.

"It's silly to be afraid of sharks here, Karen. We're small specks of nothing in a great big ocean, like a dot of pepper in a huge punch bowl," Dad said.

"Let's not talk about sharks now, okay?" I said.

Karen stood ready to jump in but backed away from the edge. Monica did a cannon ball from the main cabin and was treading water beside the boat. "Oh, can we talk about the barracudas then, huh, Lez?" Monica teased, remembering my fear of barracudas when we were in the Bahamas.

I got on top of the main cabin and faked like I would jump right on top of her as punishment. "Shut up, Monica!" I yelled, and jumped in the water right next to her while Dad shook his head and rolled his eyes. It was good to have Monica back again.

Up on deck Dad yelled down to us, "We can't all go swimming at the same time because somebody needs to stay on the boat in case the wind picks up. What if the boat sails away without us—what will we do then?"

None of us had an answer to that, and none of us wanted to think about it.

"Okay then, Monica and Leslie swim first, and then you and I will go," Karen said. Dad agreed.

We swam for an hour, first with snorkels and masks, chasing each other under the boat and watching the sun's rays shoot down through the cobalt sea into the black depths below. Without a ripple on its surface, the ocean—unbelievably clean and clear—felt like a private swimming pool. We floated on our backs holding hands, staring up into the deep blue sky in complete silence as the ocean filled our ears with strange echoing sounds. Monica and I raced around the boat, bow to bow, with Karen as referee. Monica won, of course. In my defense I reasoned that she was full of food, which converted itself to energy and left me at a disadvantage. Monica was a fierce competitor on land and I had spent my entire life trying to be athletic enough to beat her in a race. Clearly the old Monica was back.

"Ha, ha, Leslie, I win," she said. She floated on her back, breathing hard.

"Monica won by a mile," Karen said, looking down on us from the deck of the boat.

"Okay, you don't have to rub it in, Karen. Why don't you come down here and race me, and then we'll see who's the loser?"

"No, Daddy and I are swimming after you."

"Hey girls!" Dad yelled. "Why don't you scrub the bottom a little for me while you're just hanging out doing nothing, okay?"

"Dad! No!" Monica yelled and dove deep into the water so she couldn't hear him protest.

"Here, Leslie, grab these brushes and you girls get to work, okay?"

"Dad, we were just getting out of the water. We're done swimming. It's yours and Karen's turn. You two can scrub the bottom." My first attempt at a little teasing and sarcasm left me feeling uneasy.

"Oh, I see," Dad said, "you guys are too tired to scrub, is that right?"

I relaxed a bit. He was playful. "Yeah, something like that. She just beat me at a race and I'm exhausted."

Glad the ice had been broken, I admonished myself not to act too cavalier or confident. I didn't want my relationship with Dad returning to the same tension of before our confrontation.

Monica climbed up the swim steps with me right behind her. She ran to the bow, climbed up on the bowsprit, and dove into the ocean in a semi-elegant swan dive. I followed her exactly.

Once we were in the water again, Dad yelled, "Hey! Grab these brushes." He threw two plastic brushes into the water after us. But Monica's head didn't come up where the brushes had landed—she swam under water until she reached the swim steps, and climbed out completely unaware that Dad had thrown the brushes in the water. When I surfaced and saw the brushes I joined Monica in swimming straight for the steps.

In his first good mood in days, Dad said, "Damn it," with a smile. "Karen, I guess it's our turn to swim."

Cat Stevens's album *Tea for the Tillerman* blared out from the deck speakers while Monica and I munched peanut brittle pieces, lying on the rough non-skid deck. Every ten minutes or so we scooped up a bucket of water and dumped it on ourselves to cool off. The temperature must have been over one hundred degrees.

I startled awake when Karen wrung her hair out on my back and Dad stood over Monica, dripping water on her back.

"You and Monica can scrub the other half of the hull once we anchor in Nuku Hiva," Dad said.

The water felt clean and refreshing. It brought me back to life, "Okay, okay, we'll scrub the other half," I said.

"Who's cooking din din?" Dad said.

"I will," Monica said, "Let's have breakfast for dinner, okay?" She licked her lips and slurped a bit when she said, "How about corned beef hash and eggs with toast and strawberry jam?"

"I want orange marmalade jam," Dad said.

As the evening turned into night, a light wind rippled across the water. Dad got impatient and turned on the engine (the "iron wind," as he called it), so we moved forward at four knots until after midnight.

As we left the doldrums and the equator behind, unstable weather descended on us in the form of a squall. It was hard to believe that just twelve hours earlier we were roasting under the one-hundred-degree sun and now the wind had whipped up four- to six-foot swells and poured a warm tropical rain on us during breakfast. It was short-lived, as squalls usually are, but we rinsed our hair on deck in the fresh water falling from the sky and were sunning ourselves again by 11:00 a.m. The wind started light and then picked up until *Aegir* plowed through the water in the familiar roll and lurch motion we had become accustomed to.

The sails once again filling, we said good-bye to the Northern Hemisphere with high hopes in our hearts for the exotic Southern Hemisphere. We were all anxious to get to our first South Pacific anchorage. I hoped for peace in my relationship with Dad, and that I had endured the last of his advances.

On my watch that night, I wrote John a letter. It was the third letter I set adrift to him since we left San Diego. Instead of it being another teenage love letter, I wrote more truth than I intended. I told John how I had stood up for myself when Dad pulled the fake man overboard drill. I scribbled down all my worries and fears—it felt good to unload the heavy truth of it all. After I finished, I felt guilty and exposed and was afraid to sign the letter. It was easy to write everything out, knowing the odds of John ever getting it were zero. But a vision flashed through my mind of someone finding the letter, identifying *Aegir* and our family, and giving it to Dad in some huge on-camera ceremony. I guess our whole televised departure made a bigger impression on me than I realized. So I didn't sign the letter or name anybody aboard the boat so it couldn't be traced. I quickly stuffed the pages into an empty pickle jar and tossed it overboard when nobody was looking.

Writing out the truth and throwing it overboard made me feel even closer to the ocean than I already felt after being at sea twenty days. She expressed affections in the form of good weather, clean waters, abundant fish, steady winds, and clear skies. I returned the affections by allowing her to become my confidante, my friend, and hopefully my protector. A deeper affinity and love grew between us as my secrets floated on her surface in a pickle jar.

As the days disappeared and landfall became imminent, the excitement I felt was almost unbearable. We hit the Southern Equatorial Current and sailed an incredible one hundred sixty miles in twenty-four hours. Monica, Karen, and I dreamed of walking on land and wondered what the native people would be like. Dad told us to read from the ancient history of the islands even though we all objected loudly. I didn't care how the islands were then, I wanted to see them now. But Dad insisted, so we took turns reading pages from the *Encyclopedia Britannica* out loud on deck after dinner. We read how the Marquesas Islands were discovered two thousand years ago. We learned that Nuku Hiva was part of French Polynesia, which included the Marquesas Islands (Nuku Hiva, Ua Huka, Hiva Oa, and Fatu Hiva), the Tuamotu Islands (which were really atolls and not islands at all), and the Society Islands (Tahiti, Moorea, Bora Bora, and Huahine).

The encyclopedia had a frightening picture of a group of dark-skinned men with large carved wooden swords and disturbing masks, standing on a beach in loincloths. There was also a small picture of a bare-breasted young woman. I wasn't sure what to expect when we arrived.

We also read articles about the Marquesas in *Cruising* and *Sailing*. The sailors who had visited said the natives were very friendly people who enjoyed American things for trade, but they didn't speak any English.

Monica and I made secret plans to go ashore in the dinghy and hike and climb all over the island. Just thinking of seeing a tree or grabbing a handful of dirt seemed almost alien. Our eyes had been saturated with images of the empty horizon and the vast barren ocean for too long. I desperately hoped for friendly native girls or other cruising families with girls my age.

On the evening of Thursday, February 27, 1975, my sisters and I sat around the table in the main salon, anxious to hear the verdict on our position from Dad. As the minutes ticked away, and Dad scribbled figures and looked up declination schedules in the navigation books, we moved from the table to hovering over the navigation station until we stole all of his light and air and he yelled at us, "Move away, girls! Go sit down!"

After a few more minutes of silence, he spoke: "Okay, we're getting close—only today and tomorrow left on this journey. I'm a little worried about navigating around Clark Bank, but I think it'll be fine."

"What's Clark Bank?" I said.

"It's a coral and sand shoal—not quite an island because it hasn't cleared the top of the water yet—but it's not that far down either, maybe a little more than a fathom."

"How much is a fathom?" Karen asked.

He let out a big sigh, like she was bugging him. "Six feet. And *Aegir* draws about seven-and-a-half feet of depth."

"Oh, that's close," I said.

"Where is it?" Monica said.

"That's the million-dollar question," Dad said, and stared at the chart on the navigation station desk. "If the current hasn't moved us too far from my estimation, we should pass it on our starboard side tomorrow morning."

"But when will we walk on land again?" Monica whined.

"Soon, Monica. On the second morning we should see Nuku Hiva off our starboard bow at first light."

From the Hourly Logbook, February, 28, 1975. 22 days at sea.

0800 Heading 175. Nice—warm. No wind. Used iron wind for 7 ½ hours. Noon to Noon we made 114.8 miles. Landfall tomorrow is certainly foremost on my mind. I know my navigation is good, but the growing fear that something has gone wrong keeps entering my mind. What will I do then? Cry a lot I guess and then re-check my navigation. To explain to the girls shall be worst. I also have Clark Bank to navigate around. It was reported to have depths of 1 ¼ fathoms in 1950. That's not at all deep enough for me.

Sun is right on top of us and I wonder about my noon shots. Big dark clouds all around and once in a while it sprinkles a little. Tropical, nice and warm. Hope for a good last noon shot before sighting land tomorrow morning sometime. The girls are impatient to reach Nuku Hiva. The promise of it all seems to be too exciting. My mind is also on a correct landfall always occupied with it. The sails are slamming and we are making 4 knots on the iron wind. BJ

Dad stayed up the entire night, confirming and reconfirming our location, afraid his calculations were off, but he announced the next morning that we had passed Clark Bank without incident. "That's good, Dad," Karen said as we ate our cereal. Nobody breathed a bigger sigh of relief than he did.

The wind died and, unwilling to bob around the ocean and let the sails flap when land was just across the horizon, we motored most of the day. We celebrated by each picking something special from the food stores. I picked a can of fruit cocktail and split it with Karen. Dad decided on some saltine crackers with butter, and Monica picked beef stew. We hadn't had fresh fish in over a week, and everybody was tired of the remaining canned meats, except Monica.

That night I had a hard time falling asleep as the excitement of landfall and new friends filled my mind. I woke up early and could see the beginnings of daybreak out the porthole of the aft cabin. I got up and poked my head out the hatch to see if there was land.

My stomach flip-flopped. The sky was painted in reds and pinks against the night of dark blues and blacks still filled with millions of stars. It was 6:00 a.m. and Karen was on watch, sitting on the aft cabin cushion, dressed in a cute little sundress I hadn't seen in weeks, staring forward to the horizon.

"Do you see anything?" I asked.

"Yes, on the port side there's an island."

"No way! You're full of it, Karen. Dad said we would see Nuku Hiva on the starboard side."

She pointed to the port side horizon and described a blackness that wasn't the night sky. I climbed out on deck and walked to the bow of the boat and squinted. There was no wind and the engine churned. The boat was level and the seas flat. I looked and there it was, smaller than I expected, but definitely there. I screamed, "Land Ho!" and jumped up and down and hooted. I walked back to Karen who was smiling broadly. "I told you. That's Ua Huka," she said. "We should see Nuku Hiva as soon as the sun comes up a little more."

Dad had overcompensated for missing Clark Bank and we had entered the channel between the two islands on the left side, so we saw Ua Huka first.

I stood in front of the main cabin hatch looking down at Dad as he sat at the navigation station pouring over the charts. All of the lights in the main cabin were on and Dad yelled up, "Yep, I did it!"

"Yes, you did. You navigated us all the way from San Diego to a tiny little island in the middle of nowhere. You did it, Dad," I said.

I had mixed feelings about my dad in that moment. I'd spent years looking up to him, thinking he was a god or something. He knew everything and always had the right answer. He fostered that belief in me. But I was older and wiser now. He had betrayed my trust. I had been abused by him on traumatic occasions; the rest of the time had been sprinkled with leers and picture taking. I was proud of him, but reservedly so.

"Yeah, Dad, you did it," Karen said.

I turned to Karen and said, "Let's wake up Monica and go up on the bowsprit together until we all see Nuku Hiva."

Soon all three of us sat on the bowsprit staring into the early morning sky, waiting. Within thirty minutes, Nuku Hiva was visible. We all laughed and screamed for joy. Dad stood on the foredeck smiling, legs spread apart, hands on his hips like the King of Siam, watching the islands rise out of the sea before us.

Leslie and the boys of Nuku Hiva

Fourteen

*W*e anchored *Aegir* in the northeast corner of Taiohae Bay, the farthest boat from shore. Seven similarly sized sailboats between us and the shore flew flags from the United Kingdom, Switzerland, France, Canada, and the U.S. As we anchored, the people waved and bid us, "Ahoy!"

After inflating the dinghy and putting on the Evinrude motor, Dad disappeared with our passports while Monica, Karen, and I waited impatiently on deck like abandoned puppies, pacing back and forth, staring longingly toward the beach.

Nuku Hiva's jagged peaks and velvety mountains loomed mossy green, not lush and tropical as I had imagined. There were neither natives with swords nor bare-breasted women waiting for us on the beach. In fact, the island looked empty, uninhabited and deserted. Dad told us later that the island had a population of only a few thousand.

An enormous grove of trees lined the beach and disappeared around the curve of the bay into a valley. I felt the flutter of adventure. How far inland did the grove of trees go? How high was the mountain in front of us? Could I climb it? Memories of hiking our ranch in Paradise flooded my mind as I waited for Dad to return.

Two hours later I was jolted back from my daydreams as he drove up in the dinghy. "The French Polynesian Customs and Immigration Officers are all business and not very friendly, but we got our six-month visa."

I didn't care about the officials, their friendliness, or a visa.

Bouncing up and down, shuffling my feet, I whined, "Can we go now? Please can we go and look around?"

"Yes, go and have fun. Be back before dark," Dad said.

Monica, Karen, and I piled into the dinghy as Dad talked to our nearest neighbor about sharing a cold beer. "Take some money and get us some fresh bread if you see a bakery," Dad said. He gave the money to Monica and we sped away from *Aegir*. Within five or six minutes we docked on the cement quay near a hut draped with fishing nets and spears.

"I hope they're friendly," Karen said as we grabbed our flip-flops from the bottom of the Zodiac and began walking. To fight the heat and humidity we had our hair up in ponytails—mine pulled to the side like Marsha from *The Brady Bunch*.

I thought my first steps on land would be phenomenal and that I would drop to the ground and kiss it, or run and do a cartwheel. I waited to see what Monica and Karen did, but they didn't run screaming down the road. I think we all felt a little self-conscious, smiling and looking around at the old wrinkled men dressed in small floral loin cloths, the toddlers playing naked on the beach while their mothers pounded fabric on a big stone near the water spigot. It felt like we had stepped back in time. Some of the men pushed the trays of dried coconut we later learned was called *copra* around with a handmade rake.

As we walked toward the dirt road that led to the village, I noticed the locals stopped what they were doing and stared at us. I'm sure we were a spectacle, three teenaged white girls with long blonde hair. Too bad Dad couldn't see their reaction. He'd have loved it, and to be honest, I kind of loved it, too. I was definitely happy to walk on the ground. The solid earth beneath my feet was wondrous but the island felt tribal and I was a bit leery. We weren't in California anymore.

We walked side-by-side down the single-lane dirt road into the thick grove of fruit trees until houses lined either side. Some of the houses had concrete floors and walls, with thatched roofs and corrugated metal siding over the thatching. The metal roof was rust-red from the rain. But most houses were not as sturdy. The natives used misshapen or leftover pieces of plywood haphazardly nailed together for the walls, leaving holes wherever the wood didn't fit. For doors some of the houses simply had a piece of fabric hanging, while others had plywood doors. We glanced inside a few of the houses whose doors hung open, or whose fabric hung to the sides. We could see they were scantly furnished but clean.

After walking inland about ten minutes, we found a school where a soccer game was in progress. It felt almost normal. Here were families sitting on blankets with little kids running around watching two teams of boys kick a ball across a grass field. The same scene played out all over the world.

We stood under a palm tree at a distance, scared to insert ourselves into a crowd of strangers. We sat down and watched the game, but really I watched the families. The mothers sat in groups and watched the game and talked. The young girls sat close by with the smaller children, dressed in pareos tied crisscross around their necks like all the tropical pictures of Hawaiian girls we'd often seen in California. They really did wear the pareos—it wasn't a gimmick to sell the mainlanders on tropical wear. I could see girls my age, but they sat with their mothers.

A group of boys standing apart from the families stared at us. Before too long they came over and said, "Hello." We answered them but when Monica asked, "Is this your school?" they just looked at us and shrugged their shoulders. It quickly became obvious that "hello" was the only English word they knew. They spoke what we guessed was Marquesan, the local language. Even though we couldn't speak we certainly communicated in the same bashful, interested, and golly-gee-whiz body language. They kicked the dirt, giggled, pushed each other, smiled at us, pointed at their families, giggled a little more and then sat down next to us. Monica grabbed an extra soccer ball and started kicking it around. The boys joined in and soon they were laughing and kicking the ball back and forth. Karen and I watched as Monica soaked in the affections of six or eight twelve- or thirteen-year-old Marquesan boys half her size.

The men I'd hoped to meet were mature, handsome, and muscled, with bright eyes and big white smiles. What we got instead were scrawny young boys.

The soccer game ended and we walked back to the beach, followed closely by the gang of boys. All three of us kept swatting our legs and arms. I felt as though I was being bitten, but I could never see any bugs. One of the boys said, "no-no's," and then imitated us swatting and scratching where the invisible little pests had bitten us. I was already seeing raised bumps on my legs and arms. I swatted my arm again and said, "no-no?" to one of the boys. He nodded and laughed. "I guess that's what's biting us," Monica said. "No-no's."

We walked past a church with a cross on the top. It was the nicest building we'd seen in the village. There was only one bakery, which looked like a house from the outside. We saw a couple leaving with bread in their hands, so we stopped and bought some fresh baguette and round rolls with seeds on top for sandwiches. The dirt road was shrouded in lime, breadfruit, banana, mango, papaya, and coconut trees. The smell of fruit was pungent and sweet as we walked back to the bay. The trees didn't grow in neat rows like in California—they were haphazardly planted around the huts and houses. Little children played near the road in front of their houses with sticks and tennis-sized balls that looked and sounded like rocks when hit. Old weathered women sat in front of their huts watching the children and weaving what looked like palm fronds. We smiled at them, and they smiled back, some of them toothless.

We stopped at the only convenience store in the village to see what they had. It was a thatched-roof hut that sat in front of a family home, on the edge of the road. A large window swung open where the owner could hand out groceries and conduct business like the old surf huts on Highway 1 in California. There was also a small door on the side to enter the shop. Inside we found bags of rice, a few canned goods, shelves of cigarettes, beer, candy, and soda. There was salt and various spices, plus C&H sugar, a familiar brand. As we stopped to look around, the boys bumped into us and laughed. The store was only big enough for maybe three people. The boys held the door open, saying something I didn't understand to the shop owner. We didn't buy anything.

We smiled and left, saying thanks as the boys followed closely and watched every move we made. They hovered over us while we loaded into the Zodiac and waved and smiled at us as we motored back to the boat. "Bye!" Karen yelled as she turned around to wave once last time.

"Please don't encourage them, Karen," I said. The last thing I wanted was to be followed by those boys every time we came ashore.

We settled into anchored life and quickly became a curiosity for the other cruising couples and families because we were sailing around the world without a mother. We became a bit famous in the village for the same reason. We were unique, and an anomaly to the other sailors anchored in the bay, which was just the way Dad seemed to like it.

The only other teenager in the anchorage, Susie Corley had white blonde hair, a cute round face with a pug nose, and rich brown skin. She and her parents were from Santa Cruz, California, and had sailed their boat *Evening Star* by way of Hawaii. They had been in Taiohae Bay for three weeks and knew the routine ashore. She was our guide in all things Nuku Hiva. She explained the cool reception Dad had received. "Having eight boats anchored in their bay is a lot of white people in their village asking questions, disrupting their lives. Don't take it personally. If you stay longer you will meet people in the village and become friends."

Her comments opened my eyes—our families were intruders on the island, rather than welcomed visitors. Now I knew why Dad had told us to "step lightly" when going to the village. I was even more tentative in my actions ashore, smiling and nodding, making sure I didn't offend.

Early in our stay we heard there was a cinema in the village that was showing an old "Cowboys and Indians" movie. Several of the sailing couples recommended the experience, saying it was fun to see a John Wayne movie in Nuku Hiva. It was the first time Dad decided we all should go together for some family fun off the boat. As we loaded into the dinghy with Susie in tow, I reminisced about movie popcorn, which made all of us remember the butter and salt and crunchy kernels, which seemed a million miles away. "I want popcorn and a Snicker's bar." Monica said.

We walked around in the dark for a half-hour, trying not to point our flashlights into too many homes while looking for the theater. Without streetlights or the moon to light our way, we couldn't find it and finally gave up, feeling like we were intruding in the village. Quite by accident we stumbled on the one and only restaurant, hidden at the end of a small driveway and run by an older couple. Dad had heard about the restaurant from the other sailors who said it was pretty good. They had a menu hand-written in partial English, hoping to entice some cruisers, I'm sure. The husband happened to be on the road with a torch picking up coconuts when we walked past. He wore a traditional blue pareo wrapped around his waist, and rubber sandals. He had a small round belly and kind eyes, and he waved us in with a smile and grand gestures.

Dad said we should eat, so we sat at their kitchen table on a dirt floor and watched the woman cook for us. She served us fried fish, rice, and fruit. The woman was grandmotherly and dressed in traditional fabrics with her hair up in a bun on the top of her head with a shiny pearl colored pick in the bun. She put a big bowl of purple jiggly stuff on the table. Dad told us it was called poi and was made from a root, and then indicated with his eyes that we should all try it. I scooped a very small amount of the paste-like stuff on my plate. It reminded me of papier-mâché projects from first grade where I rubbed glue over paper. The slimy and slick consistency turned my stomach, making it hard not to shudder just from the look of it wiggling in the bowl. We drank warm Coke because that's all they had to offer and ate in silence. I was scared that if I said anything it might come off as a complaint, and that it wouldn't be nice. I smiled at the woman cooking us dinner and she smiled back, exposing her missing teeth. The meal cost Dad 6.60 French francs for the five of us, (maybe $11.00 USD) which Dad thought was expensive. We thanked the mother for the food.

"Everything's expensive here," Dad complained as we walked shoulder-to-shoulder back to the dinghy, the single beam of light from Dad's flashlight leading the way. And then he added as an after-thought, "Except fruit and baguette. Fruit and bread are cheap."

The village boys we had met at the soccer game had boundless energy and on weekends or after school, they waited on the beach until they saw one of us on deck. Then they'd swim out to the boat—sometimes five or more of them—with bags of fruit as gifts, treading water and calling our names with their funny Marquesan accents. They said "Mooonica" like they were cows, and "Corrrron" with rolled R's and O's instead of A's, then "Lezzzzzlie," like the elementary school kids teased me. But instead of making me mad, it was cute and made me laugh. They called our names and swam until we invited them aboard. Dad loved to watch us squirm as he made us sit close to them while he took pictures.

These weren't dating-age young men. They were "wannabe men" in my eyes, and probably in Dad's eyes as well. I thought of John and felt far more mature than these young boys. That said, they smoked and drank like grown men. They swam from shore with bottles of beer in fishing net bags and cigarettes tucked in plastic bags tied with twine to the top of one of their heads. Dad let them drink and smoke, even though he forbade us to.

"It's their culture and we must respect their ways," he said when we questioned him after they left. I guessed it was like being European, which I still didn't want to be.

We never knew their names, and the group of boys changed as the weeks went by, some rotating out and others rotating into the group that would swim out and visit us.

Music was a common denominator, so we sat on the main cabin in the shade of our awning and played guitar and sang James Taylor, Cat Stevens, and Carole King songs to them. They loved it, watching with eager faces which guitar chords we played and listening intensely to our words. After Monica and I played a few songs, the boys would take the guitar and sing Marquesan songs to us as some of the other boys kept the beat by clapping on their legs.

Eventually Dad got irritated when the boys continued to show up, taking up the entire deck, and we girls felt like we had to entertain them. It became more convenient to go ashore and play guitar on the beach with the boys in the late afternoons. Lying under the coconut and mango trees, we sang songs, sometimes swimming and searching for shells nearby. Susie had her own guitar and played mostly Beatles songs, which we all knew the words to and were fun to dance and sing to. I learned the chords to all of Susie's Beatles songs while Monica harmonized.

Once we sat under the trees and sang songs well into the evening. Dad had lost track of time drinking wine with the other sailors. His big booming voice usually echoed off the water at sunset and that meant an end to our fun for the day. But that night we sat on the beach in the dark. The full moon rose and hung over the island, making me feel sure Nuku Hiva was the center of the universe. It could only be shining on Taiohae Bay. It was my moon and tonight it was watching out for me. The clear and sparkly path of light on the water lined up down the center of the bay and made it seem like I could walk straight up to it and cup it in my hands. Once again the moon was following the Johansen family, confirming our specialness.

The second week after we arrived, Susie's parents, Bill and Pat, told us of the abandoned villages in the interior of the island. Susie offered to show us so we hiked to the ancient ruins in the middle of the island as a farewell celebration—she and her family were leaving the following day to continue their sailing adventure. The boys played hooky from school in order to hike with us that day, which made Dad comfortable about not going with us. In French Polynesia the school system followed the French school year, beginning in late August and ending in June, with a break for Christmas, which is right smack dab in the middle of summer in the Southern Hemisphere.

As we hiked five or six miles to the inner part of the island, we told Susie about the stories we'd read in the *Encyclopedia Britannica*. At one point back in the 1500s there were a hundred thousand people living on the island, but the majority died from diseases after the Spanish explorers arrived. The deserted overgrown villages were evidence of huge townships, surrounded by what the natives thought would bring protection: tikis and totems carved out of volcanic rock. It was sad that their religious beliefs in the tiki gods failed them when the outside world descended on their island so long ago.

The interior of the island was hot, dry, and swarming with bugs. The paths were so overgrown, the boys had to use their machetes to hack a path through the vegetation. When we found the abandoned villages, we saw huge stone structures, some of which had fallen over, and what looked like one of the main squares of the village. We ate our lunch amongst the tikis and totems at the edge of the village in the shade of the big coral trees, swatting away big biting flies, sweating profusely, and wishing we were swimming at the beach. When it was time to hike back, we ran the entire way as visions of water filled our minds. At the beach, we dropped our bags and clothes and dove in, wading and floating in the cool liquid. It was the perfect end to our hot hike.

The Corley Family said good-bye to us aboard *Evening Star* that night. We promised to meet up again in a few weeks on Fatu Hiva, the southernmost island in the Marquesas.

Anchored life meant chores and Dad loved to keep us busy scrubbing *Aegir*'s bottom and keeping the decks clean. I hated it, but there was always something he wanted done. I avoided him as much as possible and went to shore whenever he let me. Once a week Monica, Karen, and I did the laundry—which mostly consisted of towels and shorts—ashore in fresh water. It was hot and muggy most days so we lived in our bathing suits unless we went to town. Then we wore shirts. It was such a treat to have fresh water, we always squeezed in a hair-washing session, too, using lots of conditioner to get out all the tangles. The fresh water drained from a mountain river and was captured in a craggy old cement tub. It reminded us of the polliwog-infested cement bathtub back on the ranch, but there were no polliwogs in Nuku Hiva. We scrubbed our clothes on rocks and beat them with sticks, just like the native women standing beside us. It was a great way to get out our aggressions toward Dad for thinking up chores and working us all the time. That's where we met a young mom named Mohea.

Mohea showed us how to grind the clothes on the smooth rock with the soap she made from coconut. Beautiful in a very Polynesian way, with long black hair tied up in a knot atop her head, she had mahogany skin, big brown eyes, and a flat nose. Mohea wanted to try our Ivory soap, so we gave her a bar. In turn, she gave us half a coconut shell filled with her soap, which looked like white paste. The soap worked very well and smelled like plumeria—much better than the Ivory soap smell, I thought. Mohea seemed to like our Ivory soap, smiling as she scrubbed. She was married to Maxim, and they had three daughters—ages five, seven, and eight. They ran around the washtub on wash day, chasing each other and playing in the sun and sand.

An instant friendship ensued when Dad met Maxim one day when we were doing laundry with Mohea and her kids. They became close and showed their affections in traditionally masculine ways, like hand shaking and bowing. Dad was usually stoic and pretty passive when meeting new people, never animated and eager to please, especially after the cool reception he'd received in the village that first day. So I watched in astonishment as he waved his hands, acted out words, and made funny faces while trying to explain how he could help Maxim fix a leaky roof. Maxim was equally silly as he hopped and wiggled trying to act like a fish. They slapped each other on the back and laughed at each other's pantomime actions. Neither one spoke the other's language, but they didn't have any trouble communicating about fishing or sailing. Dad loved Maxim's outrigger canoe with a sail on it and they disappeared for hours, learning to fish with a net, out at the head of the bay. Maxim taught him which fish were poisonous and which were safe to eat. Maxim distracted Dad from focusing on Monica, Karen, and me all the time—we loved him for that. And just like Susie had predicted, we had made friends with the locals. Generous and kind, Maxim sent fruit, bread, and fish to the boat regularly.

By the end of March, a mere three weeks after arriving, we had become the elder statesmen in the anchorage at Taiohae Bay. One by one, all of the other the sailors anchored in the harbor moved on in their cruising journeys and new boats from other exotic locations replaced them. We moved *Aegir* closer to shore, to the most desirable anchorage in the bay, leaving the new sailors the outer bay. We removed the motor from the dinghy, and simply rowed to shore. The heat was intense. The boys from the village taught us how to spear fish, and how to dive deep for conchs and other shellfish, which were a delicacy. Swimming was our only relief from the bugs. We were being eaten alive by the no-no's, which Dad called "no-see-ums." They were so small and silent it was impossible to catch them biting. The islanders were resistant to the no-no's, having built up immunity.

I scratched myself raw from the bites on my body. The worst time was at night when I scratched in my sleep and woke up with bleeding sores. I had one particularly bad spot on my shin that itched like crazy and eventually opened into a sore.

Dad was covered with bites everywhere, but the bites on his back were so plentiful they covered almost his entire torso. His back was left exposed to the bugs as he worked on the boat, snorkeled for dinner, or walked around without a shirt every day. He scratched at the bumps with anything he could get his hands on—a pair of scissors or a long metal stick from the engine room. The only place free from the no-no's was in the water, but the warm water contained micro-organisms that got inside the open sores and infected them.

One morning just before sunrise, Dad yelled from the main cabin, "Leslie! Bring the first-aid kit."

I got the kit and found Dad lying on his stomach on the main cabin cushion. The thirty or forty sores on his back were oozing white pus and looked like they had merged into one giant sore. Monica and Karen woke up and we all stood over Dad, examining his back.

"How do you feel?" I said, making a face at the infection.

"Hot." His cheeks were flushed and his body was pink all over. Sweat dripped from his face and neck.

"Should we try to clean your sores out?" I asked, cringing because they were so gross.

When he didn't reply, we used the thermometer and found he had a 103-degree fever. "God, he's burning up! He needs medicine," Karen said.

"Sit up, Dad, and take these three aspirins," I said.

Karen got him a glass of water and he sat up and took the aspirins.

"Do we have any antibiotics in the first aid kit?" Monica asked.

"I'm scared, Daddy," Karen said. "What's wrong with you?"

Dad didn't answer. He faded in and out, closing and opening his eyes at varying intervals.

I whispered to Karen, "It's going to be okay. Dad's going to be fine."

But I was scared, too.

Dad opened his eyes and whispered, "Girls, take me to the hospital now."

Fifteen

The village hospital was a rustic outdoor medical clinic run by native women and one man who sometimes wore a white coat and a stethoscope—most of the time he checked on patients shirtless, a pareo wrapped around his lower half. None of them spoke English, only French and Marquesan. When we'd seen the hospital a few weeks earlier, Dad joked about never getting sick in Nuku Hiva because he might not make it out of that hospital alive.

"It really isn't much of a hospital, Dad," Monica said.

"Take me now!" he commanded in a tone of voice we all knew well. We jumped to help Dad stand up.

We loaded Dad into the dinghy carefully, helping him navigate the ladder hanging on the side of the boat. He sat leaning forward over Monica's lap for the ride to the shore. I rowed as fast as I could. A pinkish glow filled the bay as the sun rose in the eastern sky. The wind was calm, guaranteeing another sticky and sweltering day.

At six-feet tall and two hundred pounds, Dad needed all three of us to help him walk the half-mile to the hospital. As we walked into the thick grove, it became darker and darker. The sunlight had not reached high enough in the sky to light our way very well. Monica and I stood on either side of Dad, arms wrapped around his waist, careful to stay away from the sores higher up on his back. His arms were draped over our shoulders for support. His head hung forward and his feet shuffled down the road. Karen walked backwards in front of us, talking to Dad and kicking rocks out of the road so he wouldn't trip. "Come on Dad, just a little bit further," she said, "We're almost there, Daddy, keep walking."

As we approached the hospital, a few of the women saw us coming and ran to help. They relieved Monica and me and almost lifted Dad up as they ushered him into a hospital bed. Once they saw his back, they knew immediately what was wrong and the doctor hooked him up to an IV of antibiotics.

The hospital had about ten rooms. Each room had three beds. The beds were made with the softest white sheets, which surprised all of us. The rooms had doorways but no doors. The wind blew through the hospital, and chickens clucked up and down the hallway. Pigs slept in the shade of the front porch and goats grazed on the shrubs below the windows.

Dad had a bed against one wall in his own private three-bed room. After an hour of watching him fade in and out, he seemed to fall asleep. The nurse and doctor had not come back since they put the IV into his arm. While Dad slept we snuck back to the boat for breakfast.

"What are we going to do?" Karen asked, as we ate our cereal. "I'm scared."

"The doctor seemed to know what was wrong with him," I said. "We'll go back as soon as we're done eating, okay?"

When we arrived back at the hospital only ninety minutes later, we couldn't find the nurses or doctor. The place was vacant except for patients resting in chairs by their beds, or staring off into space. I hadn't really noticed the other patients earlier, but now I wondered how I could have missed them. One woman had legs the size of pillars, with folds of flesh covering her feet. Large bumps grew over the eye of one man and part of his nose was missing. As we walked down the hallway side-by-side, Monica, Karen, and I grabbed each other's hands and arms, holding on to each other, trying not to stare or make a spectacle of ourselves. We had read about the elephantiasis and leprosy prevalent in the islands from the books on *Aegir*. We were scared and intimidated by the condition of the other patients. It was especially upsetting not to find any nurses around.

When we got to Dad's room I found a chicken in the corner on a towel. We stood around Dad's bed looking down on him.

"Hi, Dad," I said quietly. His eyes fluttered open and after a few seconds he focused on us and smiled just slightly. The IV still pumped medicine into his body but a trail of ants had crawled up the leg of the bed and up Dad's arm and was circling around the entrance of the needle. Karen screamed, "Leslie, get them off!"

I looked around for a cloth or towel and cursed the chicken. As all three of us realized there was nothing clean to use, Monica took off her shirt and brushed the ants away gently from the needle area, leaving her in just a bikini top and white cotton walking shorts. Karen stomped on the trail of ants coming through the doorway. Dad's eyes were focused far off like he wasn't really with us in the room.

"Where's the nurse?" I said, looking at Karen. "Can you find the nurse? We need help."

Karen left and the chicken followed her, clucking. I stared at the brown egg on the towel in disbelief. Monica and I continued to wipe the ants away from Dad's arm and the bed but they landed on the floor and crawled up our legs. "Get them off me!" Monica yelled.

"They're crawling up my legs too!" We ran to the hallway and jumped and squirmed and swiped the ants away from our flip-flops and legs.

Karen came back shortly, "I can't find the nurses, but I found a broom of sorts." She held up a short stick with palm fronds tied to it.

We swept the room, each other's legs, and our shoes, getting poked by the fronds with every swipe. Bent over like an old woman, I swept the ants back to the dirt. Dad's eyes were closed.

"They aren't even taking care of him," Monica said.

"I know. What are we going to do?" Karen said.

Dad loved testing us, and even though he seemed semi-conscious this could still be a test. It would be just like him to give us a problem we had never talked about before. With his unannounced man overboard drills, and difficult navigation problems, he pushed us every day to rise to the next level. Without time to be scared or hysterical, we had to get into action and solve the problem. At the moment Dad could be asleep or unconscious, none of us knew.

"We should look for a nurse and get help from Maxim and Mohea," I said.

"I'll go to Maxim's house," Monica said.

"I'll go with you," said Karen. "I don't want to stay here. This place scares me."

"Oh fine, just leave me here alone with all these weird people, and Dad unconscious. I'll be fine. Just go."

"Don't be such a spaz, Lez, we need help," Monica said.

"Can't Karen stay with me?"

"Okay, I'll stay with you."

"Give me your shirt, Leslie," Monica said. "I can't go into the village with just my bathing suit top."

I stood and stared at Monica, about ready to protest when she said, "And don't tell me to wear that shirt over there on the floor. It's filthy now, covered in dead ants."

I took my shirt off and gave it to her, leaving me in my bikini top and pair of frayed cut-offs. Monica ran out of the hospital to find Maxim.

I peeked outside the door of Dad's room, gazing down the hallway in both directions and saw only chickens.

"Hello?" I yelled. "Is anybody there?"

Nobody answered.

"Go look for somebody. I'll stay here with Dad," Karen said, holding Dad's hand. "But don't go far, okay?" The carved wooden club chair she sat in swallowed her, making her appear even smaller than she actually was.

"I won't go far, don't worry." I inched out of the room and turned right. My mind's eye saw the lady with the pillar-sized legs. I didn't want to see anybody else with elephantiasis so I avoided looking into the rooms. I walked to the end of the hall and turned left, yelling, "Helloooo?" but nobody answered.

At the back of the hospital I heard voices and saw a small white house. "Hello?" I repeated as I walked toward it. Laughter, singing, and clapping filled the air. I approached the doorway, which was covered by a dark blue flowered fabric, "Hello?" I said. A woman pushed the curtain aside. She had a pretty Polynesian face with big almond-shaped eyes. Beyond her, I saw a cake with candles, a plate of fruit, and three women sitting around a table. The woman holding the fabric smiled at me. "*Bonjour,*" she said.

"My father is very sick. Can you come?" I scooped the air in a motion for her to follow me and walked back the way I came. She did follow, and when we entered the room I showed her where the ants had been. I pointed to the bed legs and imitated an ant walking with my two fingers, circling around the IV site. She nodded and smiled. I wasn't sure she understood. It didn't matter now. I wanted her to look at Dad and adjust his medication or something.

"He's sick. Can't you help him?" Karen said as she stroked Dad's forehead.

The nurse nodded, raised one finger, and left the room.

"Karen, you follow her and see where she goes."

"Why me?"

"Why not you? I found her. So you follow her."

Irritated, Karen scrunched up her face at me but followed the nurse out of sight. Still asleep or unconscious, Dad hadn't moved. I touched his forehead and found his fever down but not gone completely. I remembered a supply room I had seen earlier, ran there, and grabbed a small towel. I got it wet and ran back to Dad's room.

Here was the most powerful man in my world lying helpless. His face was calm, peaceful, even kind-looking. The pinkish glow of his skin from the fever gave him an almost rosy look. The laugh lines by his closed eyes were deep and in my mind I saw him laughing one of his great big, embarrassingly loud belly laughs where he laced his fingers behind his head and leaned all the way back.

A few weeks ago I definitely hated him and would have loved to have seen him unconscious, writhing in all sorts of pain. I'd have reveled in his agony and punched him hard if I could. But now, it was different. The itty-bitty no-no bugs had beaten my commanding father. No matter how much pain he'd caused me, I didn't want him to die in this hospital in Nuku Hiva. I would not have hurt him, nor inflicted more pain on him, for anything in the world. I laid the towel across his forehead, spreading it out over his bald head.

He opened his indigo eyes and looked at me, "That feels good."

Surprised he was alert enough to respond, I stood over him and adjusted the towel again. "I think your fever's down, but not gone yet."

He glanced around the room, "Where are your sisters?" His voice was soft but clear and stable.

I told him the plan to get Maxim and the nurse. He smiled, "Good job taking care of things, Leslie. You're a good daughter."

My eyes flew open in surprise, "What?"

"You heard me, you're a good daughter and I love you."

My face turned red and I looked away. The silence in the room was unbearable. The chicken clucked outside. In the distance a pig snorted and in my flustered state I blurted out the only thing I could find in my mind: "A chicken laid an egg in that corner." I pointed to the far corner. Dad took my hand and kissed the open palm.

"Help me sit up," he said.

I felt warm inside and proud of myself. "Let's wait for the nurse to come back, or Maxim to arrive," I said with authority.

"I want to sit up now!" His voice hardened to a demand.

The gooeyness hardened and I remembered who was in charge and jumped into action, pulling on his outstretched arms until he was in a sitting position. The tenderness was gone.

As he sat up I could see his back was covered in red liquid and the sheet of gauze underneath him was stuck to his back.

"Pull that gauze off," he said. I grabbed a corner of it and it slid off his back and landed on the bed.

"They did clean you up! We thought they were ignoring you."

"No, they're not ignoring me."

"What's all the red stuff?"

"An antiseptic, Mercurochrome. We have it on the boat."

A few minutes later Monica arrived with Maxim, and Karen arrived with the nurse who had a mosquito net. Maxim helped put the mosquito net over Dad so he could sleep without being attacked by the no-no's that night. Maxim squeezed Dad's foot lightly and smiled at him as he made his way around the end of the bed, adjusting the netting. Dad smiled back at him and mouthed "thank you."

We showed Maxim the ant trail that was already coming back. He nodded and pointed back toward the village and then he disappeared.

The nurse wiped Dad's face and head with the towel. She checked his sores and changed the large piece of gauze, "*Bon*," she said nodding and smiling.

"That means good, doesn't it?" I asked.

"*Oui, il va bien,*" she said as she smiled and patted Dad's shoulder.

"I think that means Dad is doing well," I said.

I was relieved, realizing the lack of care was a fluke due to a birthday party and not neglect. Monica, Karen, and I stood outside the mosquito net at the foot of Dad's bed watching the nurse. I felt love surge in me for the nurse and Dad. He lay on his side to give his back a chance to breathe. The nurse adjusted his pillow and wiped his head one more time and then smiled at us and left.

We stood by Dad's bed for a short time telling him stories of seeing all the strange patients in the hospital, and about the ants, and the missing nurses. He tried to pay attention, but his eyes closed for long periods. He finally fell asleep again. We left to go back to the boat and eat.

As we walked down the road toward the turquoise water, I relived that special moment again. I was a good daughter and he loved me! I'd sometimes wondered if Dad loved me. I guessed he did, but at times I was convinced he really didn't. It was confusing. He hardly ever told me in an honest way. He'd joke about it, or yell it as I left the room, "Love ya," but he never said it in a tender, genuine moment. Maybe it took the delirium to break down the walls so that genuine affection could escape. I wondered if he'd remember saying it.

We got back to the boat around 6:00 p.m. and Monica made fish sandwiches from leftovers.

"Did you see the guy covered in big bumps?" Monica said, taking a bite of her sandwich.

"Do we have to talk about this while we eat?" I said.

After a short pause, Karen said, "How long does Dad have to stay there?"

I shrugged and said, "We should ask the nurse next time we see her."

"She's nice. I like her," Karen said.

"We should take our French/English dictionary, don't you guys think?" Monica asked.

"That's a great idea. Get the book, and I'll pack some food. Let's go see him again before it's dark," I said.

When we arrived back at the hospital for the third time that day, Dad was sitting up with a plate of fish, rice, and poi in front of him. Mohea and Maxim stood by him. Maxim showed us the homemade brown sticky stuff he'd placed all around the doorway and windows to stop the ants. Monica, Karen, and I thanked him.

The nurse lit the only source of light in Dad's room: a small white candle on a piece of teak wood. After he finished eating, we stood around looking at him, not knowing what to say. His eyes drifted closed for a few long seconds, and then they'd open again trying to focus on us. I had never seen my father so tired and it sunk in just how sick he must be. We stood in silence for a few moments with Maxim and Mohea. Dad drifted off again and, exhausted, we left for the evening, rowing back to the boat in the dark to spend our first night aboard alone.

In bed, I thought about Mom. I missed her gentle touch and knew Dad needed her nursing. I wished we were a family again. Karen could use her comfort and maybe Monica and me, too. But having her with us wouldn't help in the long run. The hospital had nurses, and they were qualified. Mom and Dad were not compatible. Mom withered into her addictions in Dad's presence. She always said about being with Dad: "It's hard to shine when you're standing next to the sun." Boy, I sure knew that was true. Longing for a sober, normal Mom was fine, but the reality of it was different than the wishes in my heart. We were on our own now, more than five thousand miles away, and would have to face this challenge alone.

That night I was proud to be his daughter, and to be self-sufficient enough to live alone with my sisters anchored in the South Pacific while he was in the hospital. I felt grown up and important. I knew in my heart I wasn't the weak "stupid little girl" he'd called me since I could remember.

Over the next three days, my overdeveloped sense of purpose kept me doing my normal chores instead of loafing and enjoying some free time while Dad recovered. We visited him in the hospital two or three times a day. He improved each time until he could walk by himself around the entirety of the hospital grounds and visit with the chickens and pigs. He told us stories of the cockroaches that came out at night. I laughed and looked above to the ceiling but I couldn't see any hanging there. He had hooked me again and I wanted to please him, hoping against hope that he would notice I was a good girl and praise me when he returned.

His praise came as sporadically as wind in the doldrums. On several occasions over the years he'd say, "Don't expect me to praise you every time you do a good job. The only time you'll hear from me is when you've made a mistake." It was so deflating.

His game operated like this: I worked at my chores for a long, long time, taking criticism and correction for years sometimes, and then when I least expected it, when I was sure it would never happen again, when I'd promised myself I didn't care if he said anything because it had been just too goddamn long, he'd say it: "Good job!" and kiss my cheek or run the back of his fingers up my cheek with that glow of pride and love in his blue eyes. And of course I melted, like I did that day in the hospital. I felt important and worthy and I didn't want to do anything to mess that up. I carried that warm mushy feeling inside—that I was loved—for as long as I could. I compartmentalized his genuine love. It was pure and I kept it separate from the hatred I felt for him for touching me.

On the fourth morning, Dad stood on the front porch of the hospital as we made our way down the road. He leaned against the wall, watching us as we walked. He wore his cut-offs and flip-flops and no shirt, just like we brought him into the hospital. He looked much better with bandages and gauze that went around his chest.

"Can you come home today?" Monica yelled as we approached him.

"Yes. Where have you girls been?"

"It's only eight o'clock, Dad. We're here now," I said.

"I have to talk to the doctor and then we can go. Wait here while I find him."

We rolled our eyes at each other at the familiar stress and tension oozing from Dad. He got his pills for the infection, and we said good-bye and thanked the doctor and the nurses. As planned, we'd brought gifts of perfume, soaps, and lotions for the nurses. They were overjoyed and thanked us profusely. American items were always such a big hit.

Even though the experience of a primitive hospital was horrifying and very different from the hospitals in California, I had to admit they saved his life. We were all grateful—for about thirty minutes. Yes, Dad was back alright, doling out chores and jobs, demanding meals, and generally being his king-like self. In retrospect, we should have enjoyed the peace and quiet aboard the boat and taken it easy, saving up our energy.

Two days after Dad arrived home from the hospital I collapsed on the floor. The giant sore on my right shin had grown to the diameter of a plum. It was large and swollen with white pus and had a black bump in the nucleus that went deep into my leg. I called out in pain and Dad came running, "My God Leslie, when did this happen?"

"I don't know. It's been hurting for a few days now."

"It needs to be drained. Let's get you to the hospital."

"No! No! I don't want to go there. Please, Dad, you clean it. I don't want to go there."

I could see the huge machete in my head they would use to cut open the sore on my leg and panicked. Dad got the first aid kit and took my temperature. It was 102.

"You need to be in the hospital. Let's go."

"Dad! Please! No!" I cried.

Monica and Karen shrieked when they looked my leg.

"That looks horrible!" Monica said.

"I don't want to go to that hospital! There are weird people there. Please, I don't want to go there by myself."

"Stop it now, Leslie. Just stop it," Dad said. "They saved me, didn't they?"

"I don't care. I don't want to go there," I cried. I felt weak, like I would pass out. Fighting with Dad was pointless. I leaned back and closed my eyes.

"Let's get her to the hospital now. Get the dinghy ready."

When we arrived at the hospital, I got the middle bed in a room without any other patients. I was happy not to share a room with leprosy or elephantiasis patients.

Dad and the doctor spoke in broken English and French, with Dad referring to the dictionary every few sentences. The nurses wiped my legs with Mercurochrome and took out a small shiny blade with a fine tip.

"Please don't cut me open. *Please!*" I screamed and bawled and became hysterical. I hyperventilated and couldn't stop my tears. I grabbed the sides of the bed and thrashed back and forth so they couldn't use the knife on my leg. The nurses gathered at the doorway.

"Typical drama and overreaction by Leslie," Dad said.

I looked away from him, feeling weak and dizzy and embarrassed. I had gone from being the powerful one when Dad was in the hospital, to the weak and sick one. I hated it.

Dad grabbed me by the waist and put his face right up to mine. "Leslie! Stop it!"

Unexpectedly he let go of me and fell back into the chair. He leaned over and grabbed his head. One of the nurses felt his forehead. I silently stared at him. It was obvious that he hadn't regained enough strength after his hospital stay and the exertion was too much for him. Monica and Karen rushed to him. Dad lay down on a bed and talked to the nurses and had his own temperature taken.

I grabbed Karen's hand and whispered, "Stay with me here, please?"

"Okay, I'll stay with you. I can sleep right here in the bed next to you."

"Oh, thank you. I'm so scared to stay here alone."

I held Karen's hand and asked Dad if she could stay. Dad and the nurses agreed to let Karen sleep in the bed next to me after I let them lance my wound. I rolled over and looked down on the floor but I didn't see any ants. Three baby chicks huddled in the corner of the room, but there were no ants, thank God.

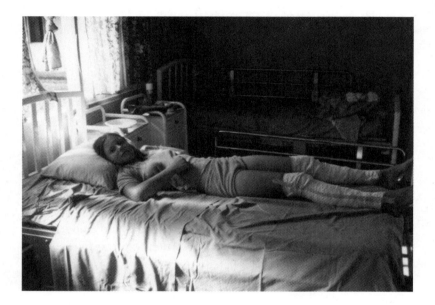

Sixteen

I stayed in the hospital for two days. Karen stayed with me and we made a game of counting the number of cockroaches we saw: seventy-one. They were as big as two fingers and almost as long. They came out in the evenings and stayed until dawn. Dad said we could ride them if we had saddles. He'd named several of them when he was in the hospital. "Did you see Kurt and Katie?" he asked. "They always travel together."

"Dad, stop. Don't say that," I begged. Dad laughed, thinking it was funny to scare us. We tried to ignore him. We made sure our sheets never hung on the ground, and we checked each other's beds for cockroaches and ants each morning.

I couldn't wait to go back to the boat. I missed the aft cabin, my chores, and even Dad yelling at me. The doctor told me not to swim for a week until the sores on my legs healed. They doused me in Mercurochrome and wrapped my legs in white bandages from my ankles to my knees. I didn't want to swim, hike or move at all. The fever and infection robbed me of all energy and enthusiasm. I wanted time in bed to sleep, read, and eat, but I didn't get more than a few days before Dad announced it was time to weigh anchor and head to Hiva Oa, a long one-day sail away.

Before we left Nuku Hiva, Maxim paddled out to the boat and delivered several spectacular, intricately hand-carved swords and masks to remind us of our time on Nuku Hiva. Mohea had made each of us girls a shell and nut necklace. Dad almost cried when he said good-bye, hugging Maxim like a brother. We gave Maxim gifts for Mohea and the kids—lotions and soaps and small inexpensive toys, which seemed so worthless compared to the handmade gifts Maxim had carved, but Maxim expressed such love for us and gratitude for the gifts, it almost made me cry. We never saw them again.

Difficult and cranky since he returned from the hospital, Dad's demeanor turned impossible as we prepared the boat for departure, stowing items and readying our bunks for sailing. The night before we left, he paced on deck, and grumbled to himself while studying the charts and tides at the navigation station.

Dad woke us up at 5:00 a.m. on my third day out of the hospital. It was still dark outside when we began to prepare *Aegir* for the ninety-mile sail to Hiva Oa. Karen and Dad took down the awning, folding and storing the poles below deck as the lights from the cabin shone up through the hatch, filling the dark morning. The black heavens began to turn deep purple and blue. With stars flickering in the early morning light, Monica and I uncovered the main sail, unbagged the genoa, and hanked it onto the forestay. The stillness of the morning made every sound carry across the bay and bounce off the mountains. Dad kept his orders to a whisper or if we were far away, a whisper-yell, as he doled out commands from the captain's chair. Monica and I were stationed on the foredeck, ready to bring up the anchor. Karen sat next to Dad because she was too small to contribute much muscle power.

"Pull up the chain and let me know when there's no slack," he whispered loudly.

Always tied up to a dock, we had never anchored in California, and never practiced bringing up the chain. Monica stood near the very tip of the bow, bent over the handle of the windlass, the machine that pulled the chain and anchor up. I was behind her, feeding the chain through a hole on deck and into a special locker below. It wasn't difficult to pump the windlass handle as the chain lay on spokes for traction. We took turns cranking the windlass handle, occasionally looking over the lifeline where the chain disappeared into the dark water below. During daylight hours, the water was turquoise, but in the early morning darkness, we couldn't see anything below the murky surface. I expected to see the anchor come up any minute.

"Every link you see with red paint marks twenty-five feet of chain," Dad whisper-yelled as he stood up and leaned toward us. "And don't slam the chain down on the deck. Feed it into the hole gently."

After counting two red links, the windlass wouldn't budge. The chain was taut.

"Let's try it together," Monica said under her breath. I stepped forward, to show Dad that we were trying our best. He continually accused us of doing the bare minimum, of being weak, silly girls, and not giving it our all. I looked back at Dad to make sure he was watching as we both grabbed the handle and pumped, but nothing moved.

"It's stuck. No more chain will come up," I said in a subdued shout. To the east, oranges and yellows burst into the sky as the sun prepared to peek over the horizon.

Dad started the engine and drove the boat slowly forward over the chain to see if he could yank the anchor loose from the sandy, muddy bottom. No luck. It was buried deep. We tried again to pump the windlass, but nothing. I turned around and shook my head at Dad.

"Goddamn it!" he said in a voice that echoed over the entire bay. I cringed at the sound. Monica and I tried to pump the handle again as he walked to the bow, but the chain did not budge. The sun now glanced above the horizon, blazing a stream of yellow light directly at us.

"The anchor's stuck in the mud. You'll have to dive down and dig it out," Dad said.

Monica and I looked at him with furrowed brows. "Dive down? Dig it out?" I said.

"Yes, you can do it together."

"But I'm not supposed to swim. My sores haven't healed all the way," I said.

"I can't do it alone," Monica said.

He looked at my leg. "Let me see."

I hoisted the leg with the huge infected sore on it onto the mound of genoa sail piled on deck next to me. He peeled the gauze and tape back, looking briefly at the sore. "You can swim. Get your gear."

Disappointment descended heavily, and dread filled my heart at being forced into the water before I felt ready. I didn't feel as strong as usual, but there was nothing I could do except hope it would be okay. Visions of the hospital flashed through my head. I didn't want to go back there for anything in the world.

Monica and I went below to change into our suits and grab our dive gear, "I don't want to dive down. I don't feel well," I whispered to Monica as we put our suits on.

"I don't want to dive down either. It's so dark."

Adrenaline began to pump as I envisioned the dark, unfriendly water swimming with all those microorganisms that had made me sick in the first place.

"Should we refuse?" I asked.

"No way. He'd kill us," she whispered.

I let out a chest full of air. "Let's go then, and get it over with."

We came back up on deck. Karen smirked. I squinted at her and stuck out my tongue. I hated her for being the little one—for getting out of this.

Without making any noise or splashes, we lowered ourselves into the cool morning water from the swim steps. The adrenaline and excitement left us panting as we swam forward to the chain. We hung onto it as we put our fins on. Dad and Karen watched from above.

"It's deep, Dad, I don't know if I can dive that far," Monica said as she struggled to get one fin on.

"It's only twelve or thirteen feet, Monica. You should be able to dive that deep," Dad said. "Don't be pathetic, girls."

We both put our dive masks on, staring at each other through the lenses. The unspoken words leapt from her eyes into my eyes: *I'm scared. I don't want to do this.*

"Get going!" he yelled. All pretense of keeping voices low was gone. My eyes shot around to the other boats. I didn't see anybody on deck yet. We each drew in a big breath and dived down together, Monica on one side of the chain, me on the other, kicking our fins and pulling ourselves down the chain to the bottom. The mask was useless in the darkness. I felt my way like a blind person, touching Monica's arm, she holding on to my shoulder. I felt her hand searching the sand as my hand overlapped hers. We felt where the chain disappeared into the sandy mud and both scooped a few handfuls out and then raced to the top for air. I took a deep breath and felt prickly adrenaline pump through my body. Then it drained away and I felt weak.

"What does it look like down there?" Dad asked.

"We can't see anything. It's dark and it feels like the anchor's buried pretty deep. Do you have a tool we could use?" I said.

Dad passed us a small hand shovel.

"You go first, I need to catch my breath," I said to Monica. Dad stood over us watching and listening. Karen stood beside Dad.

Her eyes sending arrows at me, Monica dived down with the hand shovel while I hung onto the chain, laying my head against it, closing my eyes and resting. She returned to the top. I took my turn, pulling myself down into the blackness once again. I felt my strength drain with each kick of my fin. I'd dug at the anchor a few times when something brushed against my thigh. I shuddered and scrambled to the top for air.

"Something touched me down there!" I yelled.

"Quit being a baby. It was probably just a sleeping sting ray."

The spikes of fear under my skin ramped up my breathing. All I could see in my mind was a shark. I hyperventilated. Oblivious to my reactions, Dad pumped the windlass handle to see if the anchor was loose, but it was still stuck. The adrenaline waned again and I felt like I would faint. I lay on my back, and looked up into the morning sky.

"I don't want to go down there, Dad, if there are sting rays," Monica said. We both clung to the chain kicking our fins hard to keep the creatures away.

"You big babies, nothing will get you, I promise. Now get going, Monica. It's your turn."

Monica's teeth chattered and her mouth strained against the frown as she dived down. She was only gone thirty seconds when she returned to the top. It was obvious to me she hadn't gone down all the way, but I didn't say anything.

Dad yelled, "Why haven't you dug it free yet? Come on girls, don't be pitiful."

When I looked across the bay, the sun had climbed two fingers above the horizon and other sailors were now coming on deck with their morning coffee.

"It's not that easy, Dad, it's buried deep and every time we scoop, the hole just fills in again," I said.

"Are you pulling on the chain at the same time you're digging?"

"No," we both said simultaneously, still kicking furiously. "You didn't say to pull and dig," I added.

"What a bunch of weaklings and scaredy-cats. Get out of the water. I'll do it myself."

Grateful, Monica and I hauled ourselves out of the water. We stood on deck dripping as Dad dove in, making a noisy splash. I looked around and saw people on boats watching us. A few waved, and I shyly waved back. When he came up from the dive Dad recited his favorite mantra: "If you want something done right, do it yourself."

So do it yourself, you bastard! I thought.

Dad angrily kicked his feet, yanking and pulling the mask over his face in an almost violent way. He swam to the chain and grabbed ahold. "You girls stay on the bow and every time I come up you try to crank the handle." He paused, looking up at us to make sure he had eye contact with Monica and me before adding, with heavy sarcasm, "Do you think you can do that?"

He disappeared below and Monica mimicked him perfectly, "Do you think you can do that?" she said, and I laughed out loud.

I sat down on the deck feeling weak and drawn. I wanted to lie back on the deck but knew that wasn't possible while Dad was diving. I had to be alert. My waterlogged bandages hung off my legs. The sores looked shriveled and white; I tried to pull up the bandages with my puckered fingers to cover them again.

"You guys better not make fun of Dad. You'll get in trouble," Karen said.

"Shut up, Karen," I whispered. After a glance at Monica, I added, "And go away."

Making fun of Dad at any time was dangerous. But making fun of him when he was struggling was sure suicide. Knowing all of that, mocking him felt exciting, like living on the razor's edge, and

Monica and I stood together holding hands on that edge. We giggled as Karen walked back toward the captain's chair.

Dad surfaced and we put on serious expressions and pumped the handle, but nothing happened. He dove down again. We burst out laughing as we peered over the side of the boat to where he disappeared. "Did you see how intent he looked?" Monica said.

"Yes. It's life or death," I said. We now had the giggles and anything could happen. "I bet it takes him ten times to dig that thing out," I said with a laugh.

"I bet it's more than ten, unless he gets eaten by a shark," Monica laughed uncontrollably.

Dad surfaced and we got serious again fast, pumping the windlass. "It's buried down at least two feet," he said.

Monica pumped the handle, but the chain still didn't move. I kept on my funeral face. Dad dove down again.

"Maybe he'll get stung by that sleeping ray," I said.

"What's the bet?" Monica said, unable to stop the giggles from escaping.

"Galley duties for the day," I said with a huge grin.

"Ughhhh, I hate the galley."

"I know, which is why I always get stuck cooking for everybody."

Monica pushed me with both hands and said, "Okay, and if I win, you have to give Dad a big hug and tell him what a strong swimmer he is when he gets back on deck."

"You're crazy, I can't do that. He'll know I'm lying."

"I know," she said, laughing, holding out her hand, "Shake on it."

Dad had returned to the surface. His lips were white and his penetrating eyes stared up at us. "Are you girls paying attention? Pump the handle, Goddamn it!" Monica pumped the handle again, but the anchor didn't budge. He dove down again.

"Did you see his eyes? He's pissed," I said, giggling. I finally let myself relax a little. I lay back on the genoa and rested. I stared at the now blue sky, and said to Monica, "Maybe we won't be able to leave Nuku Hiva and we'll be stuck here forever."

Having inched her way back from the captain's chair, Karen said, "You're mean."

"Get out of here," I whisper-yelled. She crept away with her head low.

"Do we have a bet?" Monica said. I nodded as we shook on it.

"Okay, okay, how many times has he gone down already?"

"Six times," Monica said.

"No way, José! It's only been four times," I said.

"Let's agree on five, and start counting now," Monica said.

Karen yelled from the captain's chair, "You guys are going to get in big trouble!"

Monica and I turned together and full on yelled, "Shut up!"

Each time Dad came up and went back down, we yelled out the count. Six. Seven. We burst out laughing each time, pushing and shoving each other. It felt good to have the upper hand and see him struggle for once, but I also knew we were playing with fire. He came up again and again—eight times, nine times—and each time he looked paler and paler, with white lips and fading eyes. I started to feel bad for laughing at him.

The anchor finally came loose on ten. It had been more than thirty minutes since he'd begun digging. When he came back on deck he collapsed on the main cabin cushion looking weak and spent. Our good humor evaporated as Monica and I stood and watched him. Karen brought him water and a croissant and after a few minutes Dad sat up and began eating and drinking.

As soon as I realized he would be fine and that I had won the bet I punched Monica in the thigh with a protruding middle knuckle and gave her a Charlie horse. She screamed out and punched me back in the arm yelling, "Dork!"

"Stop fooling around you two and get that anchor on deck!" Dad yelled.

We cranked the handle and brought the anchor up. Monica whispered, "I'll get you for that."

Thank God I hadn't lost the bet. I would have died if I'd had to hug Dad right then and pay him a compliment.

As he got his strength back, Dad berated us. "You girls should have been able to do it. I'm disappointed you aren't stronger divers."

"I just got out the hospital two days ago," I said.

With a sour look on his face, he whined back at me, "You just got out of the hospital, huh? Well, tough. You look fine to me."

While I was concerned about the water and my sores, Dad wasn't concerned for either one of us. He hadn't listened to the doctor when he told him not to go in the water for a week. He'd been in the water almost every day since his release. There wasn't anything any of us could say because nobody had the guts to question him. He had been a deep-sea diver in Norway before he left. I'm sure he felt he knew his own body and felt more than adequately equipped to dive in French Polynesia.

Once the anchor was up we had no choice but to head out and hope we made Hiva Oa by nightfall. Dad made his way over to the captain's chair and sat down in his position of authority over us, "Now that we've lost almost two hours, let's get moving. Raise the main sail."

Monica and I hoisted the main and we motor-sailed out of Taiohae Bay, making sure the sail wasn't luffing.

"Now raise the genoa," he ordered.

Half a boat length away, Monica mimicked Dad's earlier sarcastic tone of voice, "Do you think you can do that?" We raised the genoa, giggling, and then stood on deck, she rubbing her thigh and me rubbing my arm from the punches that had followed.

Dad yelled, "Stop laughing!" and Monica punched me in the arm again. It hurt so bad I thought I would cry. Laughter turned to anger and I pushed her in retaliation. She stumbled back against the lifeline and I quickly grabbed her hand so she wouldn't fall overboard.

"Girls! Stop it now!"

We went to our corners in a truce, Monica atop the main cabin and me on the stern, watching and waving to the boats we were leaving behind. The quiet and serene bay was alive and awake now at almost 7:00 a.m., having watched the Johansen family's morning show. We left Nuku Hiva in a flurry of shouts and giggles.

The wind blew a steady fifteen knots and we made good time. The day was cloudless, the waves were small, and *Aegir* resumed her familiar seaward motion. Dad had stopped writing in the logbooks the day he went into the hospital. In fact, he never wrote again in either the red leather-bound Logbook or the Daily Log Sheet we used to enter hourly information about heading and wind speed. He studied the charts below as Monica, Karen, and I lay on deck sunning ourselves. We listened to the Beatles on the big outside speakers, adjusting the sails as Dad called out orders. "Trim the main sail, she's luffing."

Monica turned greener and greener as the day progressed. She moaned and groaned as her stomach turned inside out until finally she hung herself over the side and retched.

When it came time for lunch, I just couldn't make her go below. Plus, I was worried she'd throw up all over our food, so I made chicken salad sandwiches for everybody. Keeping to himself, Dad refused his sandwich. I could tell something was wrong. He was brooding, or feverish, or something. He slept below for a few hours, telling us to keep watch for him.

I stayed as far away from him as possible, sitting on the bowsprit, and eventually curling under the bowsprit, where I stared at the water. Hiva Oa rose out of the sea as a brown bump on the horizon, but as we got closer the mountains loomed over us and we had to strain our necks to see them. As we approached Ta-a Oa Bay, Monica, Karen, and I sat on the bow checking out the other anchored boats, hoping to see somebody familiar.

"I hope Susie's here," I said to Monica. But we didn't see *Evening Star* among the boats.

We anchored at sunset and by the time our chores on deck were done, it was nine o'clock and dark and Dad was asleep again in the main salon.

We were all exhausted and hungry. Monica went below and grabbed a jar of peanut butter, a knife, and two baguettes. We sat quietly on the bow eating and dangling our legs over the edge, watching the sky populate with stars.

"This isn't dinner from the bet," I said to Monica.

"Oh, come on. It's dinnertime, and I got it from below."

"No way. You make breakfast, lunch, *and* dinner tomorrow," I said firmly.

She looked away and I knew she agreed.

As we lay on deck eating our dinner we heard quiet, indiscernible talk float across the water and saw lights glimmering below deck on the other boats anchored in the bay. We hadn't met any of them, just waved our hellos when we anchored. Tomorrow we would meet them all and we hoped there were kids on some of the boats.

Seventeen

*N*o other kids were aboard any of the other seven boats anchored at Hiva Oa. We were told that Susie Corley and her family had left a few days earlier. I was bummed—Monica, Karen, and I were stuck together alone again.

Digging the anchor out in Nuku Hiva had zapped Dad's energy, but after a couple days of rest he recovered. Most evenings he rowed to the other boats to visit and drink wine, leaving us alone aboard *Aegir*. It was heavenly to have time to ourselves to do what we wanted in the evening. I wrote in my journal, read, and played games with Monica and Karen. We wrestled with each other in the forward berth, and reminisced about our friends back in California.

"I miss John. I wonder what he's doing right now, this very instant," I said, lying on my back on the big trapezoid-shaped forward bunk, looking out the hatch above us to a vast sky filled with billions of stars.

"I miss Bill," Monica said, laying her head down next to mine so we could both look up into the sky through the square-shaped hatch.

Karen tickled my feet and teased both of us. "You two are boy-crazy."

Dad always came back a little drunk, and I worried about him coming into the aft cabin after me. But he never did. He stayed away and slept in the main cabin.

During the evenings he spent aboard other boats, he must have bragged about sailing with his daughters, telling stories of our ocean crossing to the other cruisers sailing the world, because they always asked us questions whenever we saw them onshore.

"You really know how to navigate with a sextant?" or "We heard the story of how fast you can retrieve a man overboard cushion, and we're all very impressed."

It was nice to know Dad bragged about us to strangers—oddly enough, it made me feel good to know that he was proud of us, even if he couldn't tell us.

Dad had us in the water daily, trying to increase our stamina for holding our breath and swimming. We dove to the anchor fifteen feet down and practiced digging it out as Dad watched from the deck. Monica and I had competitions to see who could hold their breath the longest. Karen joined in and was a worthy competitor. I felt stronger each day as I built strength in my lungs underwater. My sores had all healed. I had a big scar—an indentation from the huge sore on my right shin. Dad called it my battle scar. "You will tell your children stories one day about how you got that scar." He was right.

Dad still worked us on the boat, too. We put another coat of oil on the teak railings and we learned to splice ropes together. None of us were excited to go hiking inland because of the no-no's, but we braved them one day and hiked to a gorgeous three-tiered waterfall in a rainforest because all the other boaters had raved about it. We swam in the pool at the base of the waterfall all afternoon and napped in the shade of thick breadfruit, banana, and mango trees. It was gorgeous, but the no-no's really bothered us so we headed back to the boat earlier than we might have otherwise.

One evening we had shark steaks for dinner in a multi-boat barbecue on the beach after Dad and several other men set nets at the head of the bay and caught two juvenile sharks. Shark steaks were one of my favorite dinners. The fish was firm, tender, and very flavorful, especially with butter, salt, and pepper. Dad was particularly uplifted that night. He talked and drank a lot of wine with the other adults, laughing and telling sea stories. He looked happier than I had seen him in a long time.

Monica paid her debt from our bet and cooked three meals for all of us and I secretly enjoyed each and every bite of food she prepared. She cooked French toast one morning after one of the native women gave us six eggs. She heated two cans of clam chowder and served it with a baguette we got ashore, and it was delicious. Dinner was leftover shark steaks, papaya, and rice. Dad was completely unaware of the bet between us, and I made sure he wasn't going to find out by reminding Karen to keep her mouth shut.

After ten days, we said good-bye to all the people anchored at Hiva Oa, knowing we would run into them again at other island stops along our way. The flow of boats was predictable in French Polynesia, as everybody who came to the Marquesas Islands started in Nuku Hiva because of the French Customs and Immigration Office. We all had to check in and get our visas and permission to sail the other islands. From Nuku Hiva, the flow of boats went to the other Marquesas Islands (Hiva Oa, Ua Pu, Ua Huka and Fatu Hiva). The boats then headed further south to the Tuamotu Archipelago, and then to the Society Islands of Tahiti and Bora Bora. Seeing friends was just a matter of being lucky enough to catch them anchored where you were stopping, unless plans were made ahead of time to rendezvous in a specific place on a certain date. Plus, we all had VHF radios and could communicate as long as we were close enough. So far in our journey Dad had not made specific plans with anybody. Much to my disappointment, our casual plans with Susie Corley's family didn't pan out. Not many kids sailed with their families, but I kept hope alive that we would meet a family and make friends with them.

We headed to Fatu Hiva, the southernmost island in the Marquesas. While underway with clear skies, ten-knot winds, and a pod of whales traveling on both sides of the boat, Dad explained the main anchoring spot, Hanavave Bay. "It's also known as the Bay of Virgins," he laughed. "I wonder how many virgins we'll meet on Fatu Hiva?"

Embarrassed to hear him talk so openly about anything sexual, I fake-laughed to appease him. But after he said it again, probably hoping for a bigger response from us girls, I just bowed my head and ignored him. Monica and Karen thought it was funny, too, at first, but after Dad said it a hundred times, it got old and they stopped laughing as well.

Fatu Hiva was a visually imposing island. Unlike the more rounded mountains on Nuku Hiva and Hiva Oa, the mountains on Fatu Hiva shot straight up from the ocean, into the clouds and were covered in green moss. "This island looks like the fjords back in Norway, girls. We'll have to go there sometime."

After all the virgin comments from Dad the entire day, I hated him again and didn't want him to speak to me. My inner dialogue was sarcastic and snippy—*Sure, anything you say, Dad.*

Covered in emerald vegetation, the sheer-sided mountains looked formidable. The small bit of beach sand in Hanavave Bay was black and coarse, made up entirely of crushed volcanic rock. The bay was small, compared to the other islands we had stayed on, with only room for about five boats. We anchored right next to a yacht named *Resolve* from Cleveland, Ohio. Aboard was a family: Sy and Vicki Carkhuff and their seven-year-old son, David. Sy was Dad's age, about forty, but taller and thinner than Dad, with short dark hair and kind brown eyes. His skin was pockmarked from teenage acne, making him look very rugged. Vicki was tall and thin as well, with long straight blonde hair. She had beautiful blue eyes and a smile that showed perfectly straight white teeth. Dressed in her white shorts and red and white striped tank top, she looked like she belonged in a fancy yacht club. *Resolve* was sleek and trim just like Vicki, and I thought of them as racers and us as slowpoke cruisers.

While Dad drank wine and ate cheese with Sy and Vicki, we had to play Monopoly and cards with David, who whined and cried if he lost. David looked like his mom, with straight blonde hair that was practically white. Also like his mother, he had beautifully straight teeth. They had sailed to the South Pacific from the east coast of the

United States, going through the Panama Canal. Dad showed special attention to David, taking him under his wing, treating him as a respected member of the crew instead of as a child. He showed him how to tie a bowline knot and how to splice two lines together. One evening when Dad visited *Resolve*, Monica, Karen, and I ate dinner alone on *Aegir*.

"Dad wants a son so badly he's adopted David," Monica said.

"Yeah, we're a big disappointment to him. We're girls, weak and soft, huh?" Karen said.

"I'm not weak and soft. I'll beat David up and then we'll see who's crying," Monica said.

"Yeah, that'd prove a lot. A fifteen-year-old beating up a seven-year-old kid," I said.

"Well, he's a pain in the ass, a whiner, and he bugs the crap out of me," Monica said.

We tried our hardest to do everything right—to make Dad proud—but we would never be boys.

It seemed Vicki wanted a daughter as much as Dad wanted a son. Vicki and Karen were two peas in a pod and Vicki spent hours teaching Karen how to do needlepoint. Monica and I were invited but politely declined, opting instead for some privacy aboard *Aegir* to play backgammon and read our books. Much to Monica's excitement, I was finally reading *Treasure Island* and couldn't put it down. She'd been wanting to talk about the book with somebody, and couldn't wait for me to finish it.

We stayed on Fatu Hiva for about two weeks, spending time with the Carkhuff family, hiking to the interior of the island where a village sat on a plateau in the rain forest. We traded our American gifts for fruit and copra, and the locals were friendly and generous. Dad even traded some sailing gear for a handmade spear gun.

Every day, we swam with the Carkhuffs in the bay and dove for shells and fish. Sy had a book showing all the French Polynesian fish and we had exciting times finding them all in the coral reefs surrounding the bay. Dad dove constantly while we were in Fatu Hiva, snorkeling and trying to spear fish with Sy and David each day. We began to call Dad, Sy, and David "the boys" because they were always together. They sometimes caught dinner, and some-times not. As the days ticked on, I became bored of my sisters, swimming, snorkeling, and reading. I wanted to see other people and a big city. My heart ached for John and I thought about how he'd kissed me on the jetty. I also had darker thoughts, like how Scott had tricked me into intimacy with him. I stopped writing in my diary because I knew Dad was reading it. There wasn't any place to write that was safe. I stayed busy with baking cakes and cookies. I made fruit salads and I played the guitar for hours on end until I was sick of it. I longed to be off the boat, back in California with my friends. I was getting restless.

"What will Papeete be like, Dad?" I asked one evening as he sat on deck straining to read a book in the fading light. "Is it a big city with lots of restaurants and people?"

He folded the book onto his chest. "It's the capital, so I imagine it's big with bustling city streets. Why?"

"I don't know. I want to explore a big island and meet other kids."

"If you're bored I can find some chores for you, or maybe I should fly you back to your mother in Canada," he said sternly.

"No, I'm not bored, I was just thinking about being in a city," I lied. I certainly didn't want to go to Windsor to be with Mom.

On the third day, Dad had no appetite for dinner and was increas-ingly angry and cranky again without any warning. I was used to his unpredictable behavior, so when he decided hastily that we would leave Fatu Hiva and continue our journey to the Tuamotu Archipelago I was excited. I couldn't wait to get to Tahiti.

The day before we left, Dad talked about the history of the Tuamotu and we took turns reading from the books aboard. We learned that the Tuamotu Archipelago was nicknamed the "Dangerous Islands," and was comprised of hundreds of atolls with the highest point being a coconut tree. There were no mountains, no volcanoes, and no warnings when the water got shallow. An atoll is shaped like a bagel, hollow in the middle where the pristine, inner lagoon is pro-tected from the open ocean. But because there were no mountains to see, accurate navigation was a must. Hundreds of ships that hadn't navigated properly littered the coral reef atolls.

Resolve was skipping the Tuamotu and sailing directly to Tahiti. Dad made plans to meet Sy, Vicki, and David in Papeete in ten days.

We left Fatu Hiva for Rangiroa, the largest atoll in the Tuamotu, and *Aegir* plowed through the water at seven knots.

During the day, the water was spectacularly turquoise and merged with the cloudless sky at the horizon, creating the illusion of a blue bubble around us. But at night the top of the bubble turned black. The stars got dimmer each night as the moon, waxing full, swallowed up the night sky.

We had fresh fish aboard, caught by "the boys" on Fatu Hiva, along with fresh baguettes from the village bakery, and a large bunch of bananas hanging off the stern. It swayed back and forth with the motion of the boat, the ones on the bottom beginning to yellow. We also had mangoes, papayas, star fruit, and pamplemousse (a type of grapefruit) aboard.

After sailing for five days, with landfall expected the following day, I was unexpectedly awoken by Karen in the early morning hours. "Wake up! Dad's really sick and we have to take his watch," she said, shaking me. As I opened my eyes she explained that she heard a weird noise from the main cabin when she got up to go to the bathroom.

"Okay, let's go check on him," I muttered, half asleep. The boat lurched forward as I sat up. The clock over my bunk read 0300.

I followed Karen, crawling through the engine room tunnel. Dad was lying on the main salon couch on his back. I touched his forehead—he was burning up. His eyes were closed, his skin pink and glowing, and he shook slightly. He looked like he had that first day in the hospital.

My mind began to work through the many problems we faced. The boat was plowing through the water at seven knots and we were surrounded by "dangerous" atolls. It was the middle of the night and I didn't know how long Dad had been unresponsive. Had it been fifteen minutes, or four hours?

I yelled, "Monica, wake up! Get the first aid kit and bring it to the main salon."

She groaned from the forward cabin.

"I'm going on deck to stand watch," Karen said, as she went topside.

Our big daytime voices awoke Dad briefly—his eyes drifted open and then closed again. Sweat beads sat on his bald head as he lay shirtless on a sheet, wearing only his cut-off jean shorts.

"Can you tell me what's wrong?" I asked.

He didn't answer, so I shook him lightly. "Dad, wake up! Tell me what's wrong." But he didn't respond.

Monica stood nearby in her oversized T-shirt and underwear. I looked into her plate-sized brown eyes just as she hunched over, clutching her stomach, holding the first aid kit in one hand. Her long blonde hair hung in her face. She handed me the first aid kit the best she could while doubled over, looking like she was about to retch.

"His fever is back. We need to get some aspirin into him," I said.

Karen stuck her head down through the main hatch. The moon lit up the deck almost like it was daytime. She wore a tank top and shorts and I could see her hair blow in the breeze. "What's wrong with him?"

"I don't know yet. He's got a fever and won't talk," I said frantically. "Watch for ships and listen for waves crashing. Yell down if you see or hear either."

I had no idea how long ago Dad was on deck or the last time he checked our position. My mind saw all the dangerous scenarios: the reefs, water coming in, *Aegir* sunk or stranded on an atoll. I imagined all the freighters that might be out there and feared they wouldn't see us.

"What do you think about trying to get Sy and Vicki on the radio?" I asked Monica hurriedly.

"I doubt they're awake, but I can try."

"Are you going to throw up?"

"I don't think so. Let me try with the radio," she said. "This is *Aegir* calling the vessel *Resolve*—Sy and Vicki, are you there?"

Nothing. No response. Her words disappeared into the black night.

I stood over Dad with three aspirin in my hand as I tried to get him to swallow the pills. He was drifting in and out of consciousness. "Dad, you have to take these pills. I think your infection is back."

Nothing.

"Dad!" I practically yelled. The slits of his eyes opened and he tried to say something. With his mouth open, I stuck the aspirins in. I poured water in, but it ran over his cheeks and down onto the sofa. He swallowed and coughed a little. I couldn't tell if he'd swallowed the pills or not. He was unresponsive again.

Monica continued on the radio—her calls sounding more and more frantic—but there was no answer.

"Monica, stop calling. It's no use. Let's get our safety harnesses on and stop the boat."

"What's wrong with Dad?" Karen whimpered again from deck.

Panicking inside, I said too loudly, "I think his infection's back."

"Oh," Karen said quietly with her head lowered. "Did you check his back?"

"No. Not yet."

I knew she was scared, but there was nothing I could do or say. I was scared, too.

"Let's get the sails down and stop the boat for now."

I took the boat off autopilot and Karen manned the helm and brought *Aegir* into the wind. Monica rallied and seemed to forget her seasickness for the ten minutes it took us to drop the sails. Once the sails were on deck, we had virtual silence around us. We did not hear any waves crashing or water rushing. I knew from previous conversations with Dad that big freighters could see us on their radar screens because we had an aluminum mast. And sailboats like us hopefully had somebody on watch like we did, especially in the Tuamotu. The moon lit up the ocean and it sparkled in the night. The seas were flat and calm. We were dead in the water.

Karen

Eighteen

On deck, Monica and I sat on either side of Karen, who was at the helm in the big white captain's chair. Two of her could have fit in that chair, but she placed herself in the middle, with her feet on the steering wheel, her arms resting on top of the wheel in the position of power—and she looked good. Brave. Her brown freckled face looked earnest as she sat focusing forward. The boat had stopped moving. We silently stared over the bow of the boat into the night sky.

I struggled with whether we should stop the boat or not, but I didn't discuss it with Monica or Karen. I don't remember why. Probably because I thought they'd agree with me. I was pretty sure Dad would object to stopping the boat if he were awake. He would say, "Keep going, we need to push on." But moving through the water at seven knots in the dark felt like we were careening blindly into no man's land. I couldn't get my bearings in the dark and it accentuated everything scary about our situation.

I searched behind us for any hint of sunlight. There wasn't any. "Somebody should check on Dad," I said. Nobody said anything. Nobody moved. We just continued staring ahead.

I didn't want to go below because I didn't know what to do for Dad. Keeping the boat on course toward Rangiroa seemed an easier task than taking care of him. Where I felt strong in my abilities as a deck hand, almost at Dad's level at times, I had never sailed the boat without him being available for questions.

The warm tropical breeze caressed my arms and neck. It was like having an arm wrapped around my shoulders saying, "It's going to be okay. You'll be fine. You know what to do." The ocean, my friend and confidante, would guide us. The full moon seared a path in the water, reminding me that nothing bad could happen to us because we were special. All of the elements worked together to make me feel safe.

Karen finally spoke. "I'm scared. What are we going to do?"

"It's going to be fine. The sun's coming up soon and then we'll be able to see where we are." I reached below Karen's feet and turned the key to start the engine. "Let's turn on the engine and do circles in the ocean so we can stay where we are in case we're close to any atolls."

"Okay" she said.

"Doing tight, slow circles will give us a chance to figure stuff out."

Karen smiled slightly, and even though it was an awkward position because she sat higher than me in the captain's chair, she laid her head on my shoulder. I pushed the hair out of her eyes. Monica sat on the other side of Karen and grabbed Karen's knee in solidarity.

There weren't many moments when I comforted my little sister. At twelve years old, Karen was a capable helmsman.

"You steer circles, okay?" I said trying for tenderness.

She nodded, her head still lying on my shoulder. Then she sat up and turned the wheel with her feet, pushing the spokes around and around like we used to do in Oceanside when we had to steer the boat into the harbor and felt cavalier and confident. The boat began a big slow motion circle. It was more difficult to hear anything when the engine ran.

I prayed for the sunrise. Monica went below and checked on Dad. She announced the time when she came topside again, "It's 0345 What are we going to do?"

"I don't know yet. Let's think," I said.

"Dad's the same. I put a wet rag on his forehead and he moved slightly but didn't open his eyes," Monica said.

"How much longer until sunrise?" Karen asked.

"I'm not exactly sure, but around 0600 I said.

We sat quietly on deck together, nibbling on bananas. We studied the horizon in every direction for lights from other boats or islands. We listened for waves crashing on the coral reefs, and we took turns checking on Dad. The minutes ticked away slowly.

After thirty minutes I left Monica and Karen on deck and went below to the navigation station, turned on the overhead light, and looked for the chart Dad had been using when plotting our course the day before.

Five days earlier, before we left Fatu Hiva, Dad had shared the sailing plan with all of us, which was unusual. Normally we just followed orders and did our watches, cleaning, and cooking aboard the boat as told. We were never included in the planning portion. I remembered him saying that the land was really just a coral reef that had grown above the waterline. He had told us that Rangiroa was the largest atoll and that it meant, "vast sky," in Tuamotuan. Besides impressing upon us how dangerous sailing in the Tuamotu could be, I remembered him saying how important it was to arrive at Rangiroa at slack tide—the time between high and low tides. I really liked that term "slack tide" and it stuck in my head. He said that entering the lagoon at slack tide was crucial because the water rushes through the opening at an incredible five-knot velocity with the incoming and outgoing tides. Fish and sea creatures are swept in and out of the lagoon through the opening. Huge numbers of sharks gather at the opening during the changing of the tides to gobble up the fish being swept through.

Over the past five days, he'd also read to us about the geography of Rangiroa. I pulled the book down from the shelf and sat at the navigation table re-reading the important sections. I found that the opening we were aiming for was called Tiputa Pass, which was more than thirty feet wide. Visibility was easily one hundred feet with white sand on the bottom, making it appear much shallower. The book said that, inside in the protected water of the inner lagoon, Rangiroa was forty-two miles long and sixteen miles wide, with an average depth of one hundred fifteen feet, making it the second largest atoll in the world.

At 0500 before going topside to see Monica and Karen, I checked on Dad. He was completely unresponsive. His eyes fluttered open when

I changed the cool rag on his forehead. I tried to get more water into him, but it spilled all over.

I poked my head up to check on my sisters. They had traded places and Monica was now at the helm. Karen was half asleep, leaning her head on the captain's chair. Monica held the wheel with her feet and leaned back in the chair half asleep herself but both woke up instantly when I appeared. The black night sky began to turn dark purple, then light purple, and blue. The sun was coming up. Under power, the boat moved slowly in tight circles through the water at two knots. It was mesmerizing and dizzying, the slow motion movement around and around. It made me sleepy after a few circles.

"Can we stop the engine now and make a plan? It's so loud," Monica yelled. "It's light enough to see we're not in danger of running aground."

"Yes, go ahead and kill the engine," I said, and returned to the chart.

We were sailors at heart, always wishing the sound and smell of the engine would go away. Glorious silence swept over the boat as the engine stopped. I looked at Dad as he lay on the main salon cushion, still unconscious. *Aegir* was dead in the water again. We desperately needed a plan.

Monica sat on the steps leading into the cabin, while Karen stood over her on deck. "Do you remember all the stuff Dad told us about before we left Fatu Hiva?" I asked them. They looked at me with blank stares. "Oh, come on you guys, please tell me you paid attention."

"Yes, I paid attention . . . sort of," Monica said.

"Me too," Karen said. "Kind of."

I felt sick to my stomach with nerves.

I found the atolls, Manihi and Ahe, on the chart, along with the dead reckoning course line drawn by Dad—a straight line from Fatu Hiva to Rangiroa. I just didn't know where we were on that line. Back out on deck, Manihi and Ahe, if those were the right atolls, were located a little ahead of us. It made sense since we'd slowed down and done circles for a few hours that we'd be behind schedule.

"Monica, do you remember Dad saying that we needed to hit Rangiroa at slack tide, around 11:30 a.m.?"

Monica shrugged her shoulders. When I looked at Karen she looked away.

"Well, we need to get going. We wasted a few hours circling last night, so we have to make up some miles."

Based on the chart and my hopes of reading it properly, I confidently announced our location to my sisters. "I think we are only forty-five miles from Rangiroa."

We started up the stink pot engine again, put up the sails, and began making good time. I used the binoculars and studied the horizon in every direction, sure those atolls were in fact Manihe and Ahe. They were barely a bump on the horizon, as flat as a pancake. Everything looked okay, except for Dad.

He was pale and still shaking. I put a blanket over him, thinking he was cold, even though his temperature was still about 102 degrees and the temperature outside was 85. The pills I'd given him earlier were probably still in his mouth, but maybe they had dissolved. I silently hoped Rangiroa had a hospital. I couldn't worry about that because the most important thing was getting us safely anchored inside the lagoon.

We motor-sailed for close to five hours, checking on Dad frequently. By 10:30 a.m. we could clearly see Rangiroa straight ahead. It was huge and lay barely above the horizon, just like Dad had said. It was in the right location based on the charts, and I was almost certain we had reached the right atoll. As we approached, the binoculars helped me scan for the Tiputa entrance, and within thirty minutes we could see it straight ahead. We were right on time—it was 11:15 a.m.

Dad had plotted our course on the chart going directly for the opening, and I was so grateful. We followed the heading laid out on the chart precisely. We took the sails down and reduced speed to three knots. With Monica at the helm, we continued to approach Rangiroa until I could see white sand and palm trees on our port side, through the binoculars.

"Let me see through the binoculars," Karen said. I handed them to her and she studied the atoll ahead of us. She gave them back and I offered them to Monica, but she declined.

"I'm turning on the depth finder so we can monitor how close those coral reefs are under the boat," I said. The depth finder said 115 feet, which was good news because we had plenty of room between the bottom of the boat and the bottom of the ocean. I went to the bow and saw Tiputa entrance straight ahead.

"Karen, I need you to call out the depth every time it changes, okay?" I yelled back to Karen, next to Monica at the helm. We needed to make sure we entered the opening straight down the middle. I didn't want to hit anything on either side of the opening, like a jutting coral reef or something else I might be unaware of.

I walked halfway back to the helm so Monica could hear me. "Let's make a pass by the opening and then turn around and come back."

Monica nodded her understanding. She turned the boat and we moved parallel to the land.

I could see everything, studying the opening with the binoculars and without them. There were no other boats around. I could clearly see the inner lagoon and it was breathtakingly gorgeous. The light blue water, white sand, and coconut trees were inviting. Through the binoculars, I could see masts at the far end of the inner lagoon. Monica maneuvered the boat alongside the Tiputa entrance and then turned around and headed back toward the opening again.

We were probably one hundred feet from shore. Through the binoculars everything looked calm. I wished my heart were calm, too, but it wouldn't stop beating in my throat. My palms were moist—I had a sudden crisis of confidence. I hoped we were doing the right thing by bringing *Aegir* into the lagoon. I thought I remembered everything Dad had said, but I hadn't really been paying close attention. We had no choice about going through the opening, but if *Aegir* landed on a coral reef I knew Dad would kill me. The boat was his baby and he would absolutely hang me if I grounded her, I was sure of it.

A few minutes later, as we passed the opening, at about 1145 I said, "Let's do it. Let's go through the opening. Are you ready, Karen?"

"Yes, I'm ready. The depth is 150 feet."

On the bowsprit I watched for anything that could hinder our passage through the opening. We approached Tiputa Pass slowly, straight down the middle. Monica did a fantastic job of aiming us through the opening. Everything looked good. At noon, the water flowing through the channel didn't have whitecaps and was relatively calm.

"Okay, let's motor up to the entrance slowly!" I yelled.

My nerves were raw. The charts told us that the water was about fifty feet deep through the entrance, so I was prepared when Karen yelled out, "Fifty feet!"

As I looked down at the crystal clear water, I could see the white sand bottom. I could see orange and red coral reefs well below the surface and schools of fish all around them.

Karen yelled out, "Twenty-five feet!"

Monica steered the boat straight down the middle of the channel and I held my breath. We were through the opening in a matter of three minutes. I was so happy we hadn't hit anything I yelled out, "Yes!"

I looked back at Monica who gave me thumbs up, and then Karen raised her thumb too. I turned around and realized we still had a way to go before we were safe. We'd had success so far, but it wasn't time to breathe a sigh of relief yet. We needed to motor over to the other boats and anchor by ourselves for the first time ever. I wished Dad had taught us anchoring techniques, including how to pick a location to drop an anchor around other boats. At least the water would be shallow, and it sure was clear enough to see the anchor at the bottom.

"Keep calling out the depths until we get to the anchorage. I'll watch the bottom from up here," I yelled to Monica and Karen.

Monica turned the boat and we slowly headed for the other anchored boats near the village of Kia Ora, a community of several hundred. Schools of orange and blue fish swam under the boat. The lagoon was breathtakingly beautiful, calm and serene and so beautifully turquoise. The fish were easy to spot against the white, white sand. A manta ray swam under the boat.

Karen yelled out, "Twenty feet!"

"Are we going to anchor by ourselves?" Monica said.

"We don't have a choice. We have to get a doctor for Dad as soon as possible."

"Karen, check on Dad really quick," I said.

Two minutes later Karen came up on deck. "He's still out of it and burning up."

We continued motoring and I searched the binoculars for any boat familiar to us. How I would have loved to have seen *Evening Star* and the Corley family. But no luck. I didn't recognize anybody. A pod of dolphins swam just off the starboard bow.

"Monica, bring us around to the port side of the boats. We'll drop anchor there, far away from everybody since we don't know what we're doing." And then I added, "Karen, we need the depth every thirty seconds."

As we approached the sailboats, Monica slowed the engine and we barely crawled forward. We took in the surroundings. There were six other boats anchored in crystal clear water. Karen yelled, "Eighteen feet!"

The boat inched forward. I saw a few of the other sailors on deck greeting us. I waved a hello to them from the bow.

Karen yelled, "Sixteen feet!" and I yelled to Monica, "Neutral!" The boat continued forward for a few seconds and then slowed to a stop. I hit the button that released the anchor and line of chain into the water. I watched the anchor travel down and hit the soft, white sand.

"Fourteen feet!" Karen yelled. And I answered, "Reverse."

Monica put the engine in reverse and we backed up slowly. I watched as the anchor buried itself in the sand and disappeared from sight just as it was supposed to. I let out another one hundred feet of chain and watched it lay on the bottom. The clearness and stillness of the water was unnerving. I felt like I could reach down and scoop up a handful of sand in fourteen feet of water. I gave the thumbs up to Monica and Karen.

We were safe. We were anchored. We did it!

I looked up and found the other sailors watching us. Monica killed the engine and she and Karen came to the bow of the boat. Monica waved, "Hello!" Several couples aboard different boats smiled and waved back tentatively.

I yelled out, "Our father is very sick! Is anybody a doctor?"

A man and his wife from the closest boat got into their dinghy and rowed over to us. Their names were Rick and Ann and they sailed aboard a ketch named *Aotea*. Rick was not a doctor but had sailed for many years and knew about island diseases and sicknesses. He brought a doctor-type leather bag with him and took out some antibiotics.

"Is there a hospital here?" Karen asked.

"No. There's a medicine man in the village. That's it," Ann said.

As he covered Dad's entire body with cold, wet towels and his face with a wash cloth, we told them our story about Dad getting sick in Nuku Hiva and then again the night before.

"You girls sailed this boat all night and navigated all the way here to this anchorage by yourselves?" Rick said, as he got Dad to swallow two antibiotic pills dunked in honey.

"Yes," I said.

"Well, you three should be on the cover of *Cruising World Magazine*, I swear!" Ann said with a smile. "I have never met any children like you before. Your Dad will be so proud of you."

I looked at Monica and Karen. Karen shrugged and Monica averted her eyes. *Would he be proud of us?*

Nineteen

Dad began his slow recovery aboard *Aegir* with the help of Rick and Ann. The other boaters consulted, too, and even the medicine man in the village offered a black root for Dad to chew on. Within twenty-four hours he had improved immensely. He seemed embarrassed by all the attention from the other cruisers. They sent gifts of food and handwritten notes expressing their concern and offering help. In his mind being sick equaled weakness, so he was irritable and grumpy.

Four days after our arrival, when he was well enough to sit up and focus, he asked for the details of the night we sailed the boat alone. It was time for the debriefing, and the time-honored Johansen tradition of picking apart everything we'd done.

Sitting around the table in the main cabin munching on popcorn, we began. Monica, Karen, and I told Dad the story like we used to tell him stories of adventures we had in the redwood forest at Henrik Ibsen Park—talking at the same time, finishing each other's sentences, and ratting each other out.

"They didn't remember anything you said about Rangiroa—not even one danger," I said proudly.

"And you did? You remembered all the dangers?" Dad asked in a challenging tone.

"I remembered more than Monica and Karen. Besides, we made it safely, so I must have remembered the right dangers, like coming through the opening at slack tide."

Dad smiled and seemed pleased.

Monica jumped in. "Leslie turned on the engine and burned more than two hours of fuel making *Aegir* go in circles around and around until the sun came up."

"What? Why would you do that? That was a mistake."

I wasn't shocked at his criticism, but I was by Monica's. "If you didn't agree, Monica, then you should have said something at the time," I said.

Dad jumped in. "Well, in this case, I agree with Monica. I don't think you should have stopped the boat. You had the skill to continue sailing."

"But it was dark and the boat was moving so fast and I didn't know where we were or how long you'd been passed out."

"It was dark and we were sailing fast, huh?" Dad said sarcastically. "We sail fast in the dark all the time, Leslie."

He always honed in on the weak thing and exploited it. "I know we sail in the dark, but not through the Tuamotu, where boats are littered on every reef you see."

Dad changed the subject at that point and said he needed a sandwich and some Tang. I stared at Monica angrily. "It's your turn to make Dad lunch."

I went to the aft cabin to get away from them. The discussion was over and we never spoke about the incident again. Once again I was left with the feeling I didn't do it "right," and that I didn't measure up.

While Dad regained his strength, Monica, Karen, and I ventured ashore to walk on the beach and collect shells. We saw four local teenage boys at the water's edge, wading out onto the reef to deeper water. They carried a huge net and in unison threw it out over the water. The net hovered in the air, spread out into a perfect circle, and then landed gently on the water and sunk quickly. We watched as they hauled in a net full of little fish with every throw. In turn they watched us.

A few days later we saw three other boys carving a downed tree into a canoe. It had a defined bow and stern and a recognizable passenger hold almost completely carved out of the middle of the tree. The older boy waved and smiled at us. The younger boys just watched. That's how we met sixteen-year-old Hitti and his two younger brothers.

Hitti was tall with defined muscles. He wore an old stretched-out Speedo and had warm brown skin, short brown hair, and the trademark flat nose of the Polynesians. His smile was a little crooked and his chin jutted out a bit. His smile was bashful as he sized us up—three American girls standing on the beach. His eyes landed on Monica and stuck there. She wore shorts and a tank top, her long legs and athletic body golden brown from the sun, her long blonde hair blowing in the wind. The focus of his attention was too much for Monica—she took off running down the shore, tossing a coconut in the air like a ball. Hitti followed her with his eyes, mesmerized. Karen and I watched Hitti run down the beach near Monica, drop his machete on the sand and promptly scramble up a one-hundred-foot coconut tree with the ease of a leopard. Hitti's muscles rippled in his legs and back. He cut down a fresh coconut and came back down the tree just as easily as he had gone up. He sliced the top off and offered it to Monica without a word.

She waved for us, so Karen and I joined her and drank some of the milk. Clear and thick, the liquid had a pungent sweet taste. As we each finished our gulp, Monica having several and wiping the excess off her face, Hitti gently took the coconut from Monica's hand, put it down on a rock, and sliced it open with the machete. He offered it to Monica first, both hands cupping the coconut like a love offering. Monica smiled and blushed, taking the coconut and averting her eyes. Only then did Hitti split the other half in two and give a piece each to Karen and me with barely a glance. While peeling coconut meat away from the shell and eating in silence, I watched Hitti and Monica avoid each other's eyes.

My big sister soaked up the attention one minute and the next she looked like a bug under a microscope, anxious to get away. Karen and I looked at each other, discreetly making faces, puzzled by this turn of events, smiling and trying not to stare at the two of them. After a few bites of coconut, I put it down. Karen followed beside me as we wandered to the water.

Monica had long, skinny arms and legs and at five foot nine

inches, she was tall for a girl, and had a goofy smile. Hitt's attentions made me jealous. I was still mad at her for ratting me out to Dad a few days earlier about stopping the boat and doing circles. I wanted to get back at her.

"Lunchtime!" Dad broke my train of thought when he yelled from the bow of the boat, anchored just off the beach.

Perhaps Dad had been watching the entire scene unfold. I'd been unaware of my surroundings as I watched my sister with child-like fascination. I turned and walked down the beach toward the boat. Karen followed.

"Did you see that?" I asked Karen.

"Yes, I think Monica's in love."

A few minutes later Monica caught up to us as we loaded into the dinghy. She sat on the bow of the dinghy and waved to Hitti, who was still standing on the beach holding the coconut shell, staring after us.

The next day Monica couldn't wait to go ashore. We all headed into the village for some bread and to show Dad around. Monica, Karen, and I swam ashore from the boat, while Dad rowed the dingy containing our towels and dry clothes. In the heat, we often took turns snorkeling to shore with our masks and fins. It gave us the opportunity to cool off and see the vibrantly colored fish—yellow and black, red and blue—against the reddish-orange coral reefs.

As we walked toward the village, we found Hitti hiding behind a coconut tree along with his two brothers, ages ten and twelve. Through charade-type motions Hitti invited us to his canoe to show us his hand-made spear. He pointed out to the lagoon.

"Dad, can we go fishing with Hitti and his brothers?" Monica asked.

After a short silence, as Dad sized them up, he said, "Yes, follow them in our dinghy."

Dad continued on to the village, eventually going back to the boat alone, swimming out to *Aegir* with whatever goods he found in the village. Up the beach in the shade of the coconut trees stood two girls who looked to be about our age. They were dressed in traditional

Polynesian fabric, wrapped around them as dresses. I only noticed them because one of them yelled something to Hitti, who waved the girl off, ignoring her.

While Hitti loaded the outrigger with the extra spear gun his brother had gotten from the village, I heard one of the girls begin to shout and walk toward us. The other girl followed behind. The one yelling was hefty with long black hair wrapped in a bunch on her head. We stood in shin-deep water next to the canoe, waiting for Hitti, who was standing next to his outrigger a few feet away. The girl stared directly at Monica with sharp eyes, pointing her finger at Monica, yelling something in Tuamotuan.

We didn't need to speak her language to understand.

Hitti bowed his head and walked over to her, putting his arm around her and attempting to turn her and walk her away from us. But she was angry and turned away from Hitti, running back toward where we stood in the water.

She walked up to Monica while shouting and pointing at Hitti. Monica flinched at the force of her yelling. I stood near the back of the dinghy, scared the girl might punch Monica. But suddenly she stopped yelling. She looked down to her feet, bent over, and quickly grabbed something out of the water. Then she turned and ran to the beach, splashing water as if she were being chased. I looked down into the water, wondering what predator was lurking.

She stopped on the sand and turned to us and only then did we see what she was holding: a baby octopus. It squirmed in her hand, its tentacles wrapping around her wrist. It was white and small, the body no bigger than her hand. We watched in complete astonishment as the girl slammed the octopus down on the rocks, furiously glaring at Monica while yelling. The baby octopus bounced a little and squirted black ink onto her leg and the sand. I grabbed Monica's arm. Without taking her eyes off Monica, the girl picked the octopus up again and slammed it down harder, still yelling words that matched her crazy eyes. Speechless and mesmerized, we stared at her.

The dead octopus lay splayed out on the rock. Both girls scowled at us, and then the angry girl picked up the octopus, turned sharply, and marched away. The octopus dangled lifeless from her hand.

The brothers awkwardly smiled and Hitti looked sheepish, shrugging his shoulders. Clearly he didn't want to linger on the reef. He pushed the canoe out into the lagoon and waved for us to follow. We watched the girls disappear into the trees, and climbed into the dinghy, still stunned. Karen rowed our dinghy, following Hitti. The whole scene suddenly struck me as incredibly funny.

"Hey, you man stealer, did you get that subtle message?" I giggled.

"Yeah, geez, that was pretty violent. I thought she was going to hit me." Monica said.

"Stay away from her man, or you could be the octopus," Karen said.

"I don't want her man," Monica said, her voice trailing off. After a moment of thought she added with a smile, "I don't think."

I laughed. "Yes, you could stay here and marry Hitti, fighting the girl in a village ceremony for him. You could have his babies and build a thatched hut."

"And we could come and visit you. You could build us a guest-house down the beach from your house. It could be really fun," Karen added, with a smile.

"Shut up! Just shut up," Monica said.

Monica switched with Karen and rowed in the noon heat out into the lagoon.

"Do you even think Hitti's cute? Because he obviously thinks you're pretty," I asked.

"I don't know," she said. "He's not cute like Bill Smith is cute."

Bill Smith was tall and rail thin, his face full of pimples, and had braces. If she thought Bill Smith was cuter than this rippled guy taking us spear fishing, she was crazy. But Monica and I never had the same taste in men. I was always drawn to the good-looking bad boys, while Monica was attracted to the Poindexter, nerd types. I decided right then and there that I would try to win Hitti's affections away from Monica to get her back for ratting me out to Dad. It would make the next few days or weeks we were anchored here interesting and fun. The lagoon was sparkling and Karen hung over the bow, dragging her fingers in the water. "I can't believe how many fish they have here and how clear it is. Look! There's a dolphin."

We stopped ten minutes offshore. Hitti dove off the bow of their outrigger in a graceful way with a handmade rope made of woven palm fronds in one hand. We leaned over the edge of the Zodiac to watch him dive down into the crystal pure waters and hook the rope around the coral reef. He swam around without a mask or fins as if he had gills and flippers. After three or four long minutes, he came up, grabbed his spear, and waved us to follow. The spear had a sharp arrow on the end and was crafted of a hollow wooden tube with a rubber bungee that was pulled back to a full stretch right before shooting it. His brothers had spears of their own and jumped into the water less gracefully to join him.

"Let's go," Monica said.

"So go then," I said. "Go be with your man."

"Lez, stop it," Monica said seriously. Then her tone softened. "Come with me, you guys. I don't want to go alone."

The lagoon was flat and calm. The sun beat down on us, making the water look cool and inviting. Land was maybe a mile and a half away. We dropped our small anchor in the water, but the line wasn't long enough to reach the bottom. I looked over the side and saw the anchor dangling midway down to the bottom, swinging back and forth. One of the brothers saw our dilemma and swam the anchor up to the surface and put it into their canoe. Now our boats were connected.

Hitti came up shortly, looking impatient for us to join him. In one hand, he held two fish by the gills while his spear gun was in the other. He threw the fish into the bottom of his outrigger and dove down again. His brothers came to the surface and threw more fish into the canoe. Monica, Karen, and I put our masks and snorkels on and followed them.

Monica took off first and I dove after her, but only made it ten or twelve feet down until my ears started to feel the pressure and I had to return to the top. Monica swam faster and deeper, trying to catch up with Hitti and his brothers. It was a competition, and Monica needed to prove she could swim as deep. I wanted Hitti to notice me, so I dove back down and touched the top of the coral, but the fish were down near the white-sand bottom, another five or seven feet below.

I looked up and saw Karen treading water, hanging onto the boat, her legs kicking in a frog-like motion. I went up for air.

"I can't dive that deep," said Karen.

"I know. I can't get down to the bottom either."

Monica came up for air, exhilarated and sputtering water as she spoke, "Did you see the shark?"

"What? A shark?" I said.

"Yes, a shark! Hitti just poked it with his spear and the shark swam off," Monica said excitedly. "I'm going back down."

Just then Hitti and his brothers brought up another load of fish they had speared. They threw the fish into the bottom of the canoe, smiled, waved us down into the water, and disappeared again. I made sure Hitti saw me smile very big at him.

"I'm going to check it out. I'll be back in a sec," I told Karen and dove down. I didn't see the sharks, but a huge eagle ray swam by.

Hitti and his brothers were not bothered in the least by the shark's presence. Monica followed them, copying their calm, quiet attitude. Karen, who should have been scared to death and crying, imitated Hitti and Monica and stayed calm. I couldn't be the only one freaking out about the sharks, so I acted like they were no big deal either. Dad had told us numerous times since we'd landed in the islands: "When in Rome, do as the Romans do."

Hitti brought another fish to the top and I hung on the outrigger, smiling and pointing to the boatload of fish in the bottom. Hitti just smiled politely and dove back down. My womanly wiles weren't working on him. Exhausted, I joined Karen in the dinghy for a rest.

I pulled our dinghy alongside the canoe. "Check out all the fish they're catching."

Karen's eyes popped as she saw the bottom of the canoe covered with more than twenty fish. There were big ones and little ones; purple, red, and blue ones; and some were rainbow-colored. There was a fish with a mouth like a beak that we later learned was a parrotfish. The colors of the fish faded as they died, until they looked mostly grey and brown.

"Do you think we should stay out of the water because of the sharks?" Karen asked.

"I don't know. I think Hitti and his brothers know what they're doing and if we stick with them and listen to them, we'll be fine."

Monica came to the surface and threw a fish in the bottom of our boat. "I got one! I got one!" She was breathing heavy. "Man, this isn't easy. If only I could breathe underwater," she gasped, hanging on the boat. Hitti had given Monica his spear and stayed by her until she found a fish to shoot. There was no need for instruction on the spear—it was as basic as a can opener to us once we saw the boys use it.

"Hitti seems to breathe like a fish," I said. "And you're his mermaid girlfriend." I wasn't surprised that Monica could master something as athletic as spear fishing on her first try.

If I wanted to change Hitti's opinion about me, then I better try again.

"Come on, Lez. You can get your first fish, too. Here's the spear gun," Monica said.

We headed back down and were swimming side by side near a small inlet in the coral reef when Monica hit my arm and pointed to two sharks swimming near the bottom, scanning from side to side. They looked to be about five feet long. Hitti swam from around the coral reef, and then his two brothers appeared behind him. They were right next to the two grey reef sharks. The sharks turned and swam toward Hitti, who had a dead fish in one hand and his brother's spear in the other. As the sharks approached, he reached out with his arm fully extended and poked one of them in the nose. The shark shuddered slightly at the touch, skin rippling from nose to tail, then turned sharply and swam away. The other shark followed and then we all surfaced for air.

"The sharks are hanging around awfully close," I said.

"Yes, too close."

Hitti listened to us, shook his head, and dove back down. We didn't know what he was doing.

"I'm done, Monica. I'm so tired."

"Okay, I'm going to try again." She took off after Hitti.

I hauled myself into the boat, gasping for breath. After a minute I leaned over the side of the boat with Karen and we looked through our masks, just under the surface of the water. We saw Monica near the bottom with a fish on the end of the spear. She had caught another one. I had to admit Monica was pretty impressive. We watched her pull the small blue fish off the spear and begin swimming to the surface.

"Here she comes," I said.

"And here comes the shark!" Karen yelled.

"Oh God, he's coming after the fish in her hand. She doesn't even see him." I said anxiously.

I slapped the water as Monica got closer and closer, which only made the water ripple so we couldn't see anything. Monica surfaced just as Karen grabbed the fish out of her hand and yelled, "Shark!"

Monica jumped into the boat like she had wings, barely escaping the shark. It was tracking the fish in her hand and as soon as the fish came out of the water, the shark turned sharply and headed back down. Hitti surfaced and laughed, acting out the motion of poking the shark in the nose with the spear.

Monica shook her head. "No. I'm not going to poke the shark."

But she would eventually poke the sharks in the snout and so would I. We swam with the lemon sharks and grey sharks for the next few weeks, trying to become local girls. Like anything done repeatedly, it became ho-hum to swim with the sharks and push them away by poking them in the snouts. Monica led the way and I struggled to keep up with her both in fish count and boy count. After diving with Hittie and his brothers several more times, I finally got my first fish and celebrated loudly.

Dad got used to us bringing home fresh fish for dinner and declared it our job to provide dinner. Soon, a fun and competitive way to spend the afternoon became a daily chore, which we came to resent.

After resting in Rangiroa for more than three weeks, Dad said it was time to leave to meet Sy and Vicki in Papeete, the capital city of Tahiti. On our last day we went ashore to find Hitti and his brothers to thank them with some American gifts. As we walked down the beach headed into the village, Hitti's youngest brother came running up to us out of breath, pointing up the beach. "Hitti pico pico!" he yelled.

We walked at first, and then ran after him. He repeated it again, pointing to Hitti, who was lying in the shade of a breadfruit tree like he was passed out. The tree was heavy with the strange green bumpy fruit. The brother said again, "Hitti, pico, pico," but this time he put his palms together like in prayer, and laying them aside his cheeks, closed his eyes.

Monica got the charade instantly and teased, "Hitti pico pico." Hitti sat up and smiled at Monica, nodding yes. We all laughed and Hitti jumped up and bowed to Monica. We gave Hitti our gifts of a baseball, some lotion for his girlfriend, and a Frisbee which Dad had found aboard. We thanked them over and over as we acted out spear fishing. Hitti gazed at Monica with a faraway stare, and Monica blushed on cue. The energy between them never diminished and never progressed passed those awkward stares.

Clearly my attempt to woo Hitti away didn't work. He only had eyes for Monica, who was stronger and healthier than I had seen her in a long time. I could tell she was sad to leave Hitti, but she knew she wasn't meant to stay with him. Dad didn't seem bothered at all by Monica's affection for Hitti, he almost seemed proud as he watched them awkwardly say good-bye.

Downtown Papeete

Twenty

*W*e approached Tahiti after a short, uneventful three-day sail from Rangiroa. Behind schedule because of Dad's recovery time, we worried about missing Sy and Vicki.

On May 10th, while in Rangiroa Dad had turned forty and I can't remember doing anything special. Even after he was feeling better he just wasn't in the mood for anything fun. But now that we were at sea again, his most favorite thing in the world, and on our way to meet friends and see a big city, he was in an excellent mood, as evidenced by the fact that he sang out loud with the 8-track tape of *My Fair Lady* the entire time.

For three whole days, Dad sang every word to every song as he worked on various projects and we sailed toward the Society Islands. Sometimes the outside speakers blared, sometimes the cabin speakers blared. Laughing, dancing, and singing in a way I had not seen him do since we were back in Oceanside, he pretended to be Rex Harrison to some invisible Audrey Hepburn. It was a silly singing game we all eventually joined in, dancing and mouthing the words, singing outrageously, twirling each other on the deck. Acting out the songs was an opportunity to have a little fun with Dad, and although we knew his mood could change as fast as the wind, we were swept up in the frivolity.

As we approached Far Ute Point on Tahiti, Monica, Karen, and I took up our now familiar spot on the bowsprit, just as the mermaid figureheads did on the old ships, studying and inspecting the new island.

Dad yelled, "Can't wait to get to the big city girls, and see if some of our friends are here! Heck, maybe we'll even run into Marlon Brando! Wouldn't that be exciting?"

We knew well that Marlon Brando had bought the atoll of Tetiaroa, very close to Tahiti. Dad adored Marlon Brando and his irreverent, showy ways.

As we approached, clouds hid the tops of lush green mossy mountains, obscuring their true height. Tahiti was a massive island compared to our previous stops. The French flag flew next to the French Polynesian flag at the entrance of Papeete harbor. We rounded a large sea wall built on the natural coral reef that protected the harbor. The enormity of it was exciting. In the harbor, as we motored toward the other sailboats, I saw tourists unloading from a cruise ship and two large freighters unloading pallets. I longed for masses of people, other kids who spoke English to hang out with, familiar foods—hamburger or, perchance, a steak—pay phones to call home, a post office to actually buy a stamp and mail a letter, and possibly even some cute American or Australian boys. I couldn't have been happier.

We motored into the harbor where about twenty other boats were tied up to the cement seawall everybody called "the quay." Four-story brick and mortar buildings rose from the concrete streets on the waterfront. Cars and buses packed with people rushed past. Everything seemed sped up and nobody noticed us. In the outer islands, our arrival usually brought curiosity from the islanders, but here we were invisible. A family of five drove past us, all piled on a minuscule moped, the mother holding a palm-tree woven bag of groceries on her head with one hand and cradling an infant in a front pouch with the other. The two older kids, maybe eight and ten years old, held on with nonchalant attitudes. Horns honked and people talked loudly enough for us to hear, though we couldn't make out what they were saying. Shirtless men unloaded trucks of coconuts, copra, and boxes of fish into shops. Stray dogs, skinny and scared, darted between the cars and the markets on the hunt for food. Monica wistfully said to Karen and me, "I want to keep all those dogs. I wish I could take them to the ranch right now." She spoke of the ranch lovingly, like we still owned the property in Paradise. Later when she voiced her desire to Dad about the dogs, he forbad us to go near them, telling us they were feral and probably rabid.

Sy called us on the VHF radio as we neared the quay and said he had an empty spot for *Aegir* next to *Resolve*. As we set our anchor and backed in, Sy caught our dock line calling out, "Glad to finally see the Norwegian and his daughters. We were beginning to worry."

Vicki waved and greeted us warmly while Sy dragged a wooden plank over to connect the stern of the boat to the quay so we could disembark. Silly jokes about "walking the plank" were irresistible. David poked his head out of the cabin and waved hello.

"I'll catch you up on the news and why we're so late, but we're happy to be in the capital city. We're ready for some action!" Dad yelled to Sy.

Finally tied to solid ground, we found ourselves directly in front of the main two-lane paved road, which we later found skirted the entire island. Separated only by a sidewalk and a row of hibiscus trees that lined the main boulevard, I watched, mesmerized, as people scurried around like cockroaches in the morning light. It was odd to see the Tahitian women in western clothes like shorts and T-shirts, since the women in the outer islands all wore traditional island pareo. The pungent odor of exhaust from diesel trucks and roasting meats filled my nose. Natural sounds, like birds or the ocean slapping against the hull, were drowned out by the open-air market, which stood only about a block away from us, directly across the street from The Bank of Tahiti. The natives in the outer islands lived a slower more peaceful life compared to this disorder and I wondered if they yearned to visit the big city of Papeete like Americans from small towns dreamt of visiting New York. I couldn't have been more eager to walk amongst the Tahitians. I silently hoped Dad would give us money so we could shop in their stores.

But Dad didn't want to give us money for "frivolous things," as he called them. I didn't think dresses and new clothes were frivolous. He even refused to buy fish every day, which he had gotten used to getting for free when Monica and I spearfished for dinner each night.

"The big city is expensive! We'll only buy necessities."

His idea of necessity and mine were completely different. After some discussion, we finally compromised and bought fresh fruit and baguette—and beef and lamb sometimes—while eating from the canned food aboard *Aegir* as we had done on the other islands. We found real milk like we had back in the States, and stopped drinking the powdered stuff immediately. It tasted familiarly creamy and heavenly and I would have loved to have it on Fruit Loops, but we had run out of them a few weeks earlier. Instead I had the milk on my morning bowl of noisy, crunchy Grapenuts, the only cereal we had left. Dad bought more of it than anything else because Grapenuts were his favorite.

The next day, Dad visited the Customs and Immigration office to announce our official arrival. Monica, Karen, and I wandered the streets near the boat, taking in the wonders of big city chaos. In a parking lot down the street from the boat, cruising people gathered around a food truck selling kabobs and sandwiches that smelled heavenly. Of course we begged Dad to join the other boaters at the trucks and try the meat sandwiches. It was all Monica and I could talk about. We hadn't had beef in months and we all craved a steak or some roasted chicken. He gave in after Sy and Vicki applied some good old-fashioned peer pressure on our behalf.

That night we all headed down to the end of the quay. The two trucks selling food were small and looked to be family-run. Sy and Vicki placed our order as they were regular customers and knew the best food. Dad chatted with Sy and Vicki while David, my sisters, and I hovered nearby waiting impatiently for our order. The smell of meat and onions filled the air, and hunger pains churned in my belly. When the sandwiches finally came, partially wrapped in white paper, they were piled high with thinly sliced meat on a soft, warm French baguette. A white sauce dripped from the sandwiches, and the scent of grilled onions wafted through the air. My mouth watered as Monica's big brown eyes stared into mine in anticipation. We huddled around a cement post used to tie up cruise ships, but big enough to be used as a dinner table. Dad handed each of us a sandwich. "They're pretty small, I think I want two," Monica said.

I anxiously took my sandwich and pulled the paper back. The baguette was soft and smooshy next to the meat, yet crispy on the outside. I took a great big bite. The heavenly mixture reminded me of a French Dip. Monica's eyes actually rolled back inside her head on her first bite. I stood directly in front of her, still savoring my mouthful, when Dad said, "This dog meat is good, isn't it?"

Monica stopped chewing mid-bite and dropped her sandwich immediately—it hit the ground with a thud. We all stared at it, then took a step backward. Tears filled her eyes faster than I would have believed possible, and I thought she would burst out crying. Dad began laughing. She looked around for the stray dogs we had seen earlier. They were nowhere to be seen.

Karen and I held on to our sandwiches to see if he was teasing. Dad could be so mean sometimes, always striking just where he knew it would hurt us most. Sy and Vicki burst into laughter but continued eating. Apparently they thought Dad's sense of humor was hilarious. David chomped on his brisket-type meat, acting like he didn't even hear my father. Dad's small, shifty blue eyes were impossible to read. I searched his face earnestly, trying to find the joke, but I couldn't tell if he was kidding or not. His trademark smirk didn't appear. He continued to eat, and I absolutely hated him in that moment.

"Dad! Are you telling the truth?" I begged. We imploringly searched Sy and Vicki's face, "Come on, tell us!" But nobody answered. They just kept on eating. Dad finished his sandwich and motioned to take mine out of my hands. I took another bite, believing in my heart they were all just teasing us, but that sandwich never tasted as good again. Vicki tried to assure us they weren't dog, but the idea had been planted and grew quickly in our minds as we watched the wild dogs around the city.

By the end of our first week in downtown Papeete, it was clear there were no other kids our age aboard the twenty or so sailboats docked with us. Only one of the other families we met had girls our age, and they left shortly after we arrived.

During that first week I became aware of the effect I had on some of the males aboard other boats. In the months since we had left the States, I must have matured outwardly, as older men looked at me in a new and different way. My skin glowed like a sunset and I could feel a real flame growing in me. I learned why people called romance a cat and mouse game, as I experienced firsthand the looking and then not look-ing at the young men who cruised on the other sailboats. In the past, young men had never so much as glanced my direction, but now they were enthralled, openly gawking when I walked past their boats. Crew on other boats, surfers just passing through, travelers, and vagabonds were not immune. If I was running to the store alone, they whistled and hummed to get my attention and then smiled and waved, eager and attentive. The sailors three, five, or even ten boats away were interesting to watch and they were all close. As I walked past them on the quay we were all tied up to, I wondered how many would follow me if I wore just my bikini. When I was with my sisters, they were more discreet, mostly hiding their attentions. Monica dressed like a tomboy, wearing men's T-shirts and oversized shorts, hiding her skinny straight body.

I did what any fourteen-and-a-half-year-old would do when trying to act older: I dressed up a little, wearing what I thought were adult-looking, maybe even risqué, clothes. Since I didn't have much of a wardrobe, I rolled up my halter tops and short shorts to show even more skin. I cut a piece of blue Tahitian flower fabric in a big square, folded it diagonally and tied it around me as a handkerchief shirt which exposed my stomach, sides, and back. Being coy kept my mind preoccupied. It was fun to be noticed by cute men—a hobby to keep me busy. Life was pretty boring in downtown Papeete because Dad denied us permission to explore the island without him, refus-ing to let us take the dinghy by ourselves, or even leave the boat for any length of time. We weren't allowed to immerse ourselves in the city because Dad felt it was unsafe. There were just too many bars and men, so we were kept as spectators on the sidelines.

We had impromptu get-togethers with the other sailors on the quay or at the nearby beach. While Dad visited with the other adults on the sailboats, my sisters and I hung in the background, wading out in the water to look at the reef just for something to do. These "get-togethers" were a place for me to test my newly discovered effect on men. How many would stare at me during a sunset get-together? It was fun to count as I walked past them. One evening three of the men followed me out on the reef in knee-deep water. I think Dad noticed these men watching me, but there wasn't anything he could do because I played like I didn't know what was happening. Maybe he said something to the men, I don't know. He never said anything to me. I felt powerful and untouchable. I wanted to see how far I could push it.

We had been in Papeete about three weeks when Bill Anderson and his crew full of young surfer men brought the beautiful seventy-foot wooden schooner, *Summer Wind,* into Papeete. Maybe in his late twenties, Bill had suntanned skin with blond hair that curled around his chiseled face. His eyes were set far apart and were brown, like mine, and I would catch him looking at me with such intensity. When our eyes met his lips opened just slightly and he smiled slyly.

The third day I saw Bill on the quay, I walked by his boat to go to the store for some bread. Dad had gone someplace with Sy to do some banking or something—I didn't know and didn't care. It was another hot and humid day and I wore a cropped white halter top with a flower on the front, no bra, of course, since Dad still forbade us from wearing bras, and a pair of frayed cut-off jean shorts that barely covered my backside. My bare brown stomach showed in front and my long blonde hair flowed down the back. He rushed down his plank and stood right in front of me, blocking my way. He wasn't wearing a shirt, and had a nice strong body.

"Hello, pretty lady," he said, and winked at me. "Where are you off to?"

"The store," I said, flashing my big brown eyes at him, smiling a little and twisting my body just slightly. He smelled like teak oil and salt water.

"How about some lunch? I'm about ready to head to the hotel. I'm starving."

"Sure, that sounds great," I said more boldly than I thought capable. *What am I doing? Dad's going to kill me.*

"Let me grab a shirt and change into another pair of shorts. You are looking beautiful today," he said, smiling as he went aboard his boat. The brief time he was gone gave me time to wonder how stupid I was to accept the invitation of a complete stranger for lunch. In a nervous jitter, I untangled my hair from one of the turquoise and sterling silver dangling earrings Raine and her mother had given me before we left. Those earrings made me feel twenty years old, and I played make believe with myself that I was old enough for Bill.

Before I knew it, he was back on the quay, smiling and touching my arm in an oddly familiar way, soft and yet rough, his hand calloused from boat work.

We walked side-by-side in the direction of the store as he made small talk and I answered yes or no, staring straight ahead. *What am I doing?*

About half a mile down the road, we entered a lush resort full of Australian and French families on holiday. The sweet scents of red and yellow hibiscus, brilliant orange birds of paradise, and delicate pink and yellow plumeria engulfed us. There was a plantation feel to the overgrown lobby as ferns and banana trees filled the courtyard. The employees rushed around us, wearing matching red and white hibiscus-printed pareos.

Bill led me to the restaurant by the arm like he'd been there many times. The heat of him surrounded me. We moved closely together in unison as if we were a couple, like an invisible thread connected us. His eyes were dark and intense and I wondered what it would be like to kiss him. We were given a poolside table and I stared out at the beautiful ocean and watched couples and kids play in the pool. I looked at anything but him. He made me nervous.

"How would you like to try something Tahitian and something French today?" Bill asked.

"Sure, what is it?"

"One's called *poisson cru* and the other's called *escargot*."

"Okay, sure," I said quietly. I had no idea what *escargot* was, but I would probably have eaten live octopus if Bill had offered it to me.

The waiter came and Bill ordered lunch for both of us, which felt sophisticated. He also ordered mango margaritas and my mind leapt into fear. I'd never had hard liquor before, just beer and wine back in Oceanside. The only sip of margarita I had tried was the day we left Oceanside when Dad handed me that carafe from La Beaner's filled with the lime-green slush. I wondered what a mango margarita would taste like. I wanted it. I liked being treated as an adult. My stomach churned and flopped over. I tried not to hyperventilate. I wasn't the least bit hungry.

As we waited for the *escargot* and margaritas, Bill touched my forearm again. I could tell he was trying hard to please me. I stared out at the pool and realized everyone accepted me in this role as Bill's girlfriend, his equal. Nobody said, "Hey you, girl! You're too young to be here. Go home." As long as I didn't go screaming out of the restaurant, laughing and giggling at the sham I had perpetrated, people went along. This was the moment when I learned how to "act as if." It was an important discovery and one I would use over and over again as I grew up. Not speaking too much seemed to be working, so I stared out at the ocean where the waves curled to shore.

I couldn't look into his eager eyes. *What if he starts touching me?* I felt like somebody else—some older version of myself—a million miles away. *I don't want him to touch me. Yes, I do want him to touch me. Touch my leg!* The turquoise water sparkled, while the French women swimming topless and the families splashed in the water idyllically. Bill continued to stare at me with soft eyes and a knowing curvy smile.

"You're very pretty. Do you know that?"

I shook my head shyly.

"Well, you are. How old are you?"

And there it was. Now I would have to lie. My face felt hot and I began to sweat. Luckily, the waiter brought our food and margaritas and saved me from answering. I took a long sip of the slushy orange-colored drink and tried to think of what to do. *Yum, this drink is good!* Shocked, I stared at the plate of snail shells on the table swimming in melted butter. Escargot *are snails!* The garlic smell helped. *Act normal. You can do it. Look away from the snails!* A familiar dish to me, the *poisson cru* sat in a colorful red and blue bowl. It consisted of small pieces of tuna soaking in coconut milk, laced with cucumbers, ginger, onion, lime juice. It smelled fantastic.

Bill picked up a strange-looking utensil and squeezed it, pinching one of the snails. I tried to remain calm, knowing a snail would soon be in my stomach. I took another large gulp of my margarita.

He smiled at me and then took a miniature fork and extracted the dripping meat and offered it to me. I leaned over the table, closed my eyes, opened my mouth, and let him put the *escargot* in. It was warm, buttery and garlicky and yummy. I quickly took another sip of my drink and helped myself to the *poisson cru*. The alcohol spread out in my stomach in a warm rush. I felt myself relaxing. I loved the way it made me feel.

"I have to get back soon. Do you know my father?" Images of Dad yelling at me, veins popping out of his neck, suddenly filled my head.

"No, I don't think I've met your father," he said, eating the remaining escargot. "We just pulled in a few days ago and we're leaving tomorrow."

I took another sip of my margarita. Bill pulled the baguette apart and offered me a hunk, I took the bread and dipped it in the melted butter.

"Where are you going?"

"Australia, to deliver this boat." He looked at me closely and said, "Want to come?"

I giggled nervously. I need to get out of here. I was in the deep end of the pool that was for sure. "Can we go?"

"Yes, let me get the check," he said, as he searched for the waitress. "Can I see you again before I leave?"

"No, I don't think so. I have to get back now. My family will be missing me."

He got the bill. "Your family will miss you? How old are you?"

The waitress came and stood by the table as Bill finished pulling out money. We rose and I walked out of the resort ahead of him. I couldn't wait to get away from him and tell somebody—anybody— what I had just done. But I knew I wouldn't be able to tell anybody. It would have to be my secret.

I walked faster until he was trailing behind me. "How old are you?"

I turned my head. "Probably not old enough to have lunch with you. But thank you, it was delicious."

When we arrived in front of *Summer Wind*, Bill said good-bye. I felt loose and warm and friendly from the alcohol as I ran off.

He called, "Come see me when you're five years older, okay? Promise?"

I turned around and smiled, "Sure."

Down the quay I could see Dad watching me say good-bye to Bill. I quickly walked back to *Aegir*.

"Who was that?"

"Oh, nobody. He just needed to know where the market was, so I showed him," I said, as nonchalantly as I could. I ran up the plank and went into my aft cabin where I screamed into my pillow for five minutes.

A little while later he lowered his head into the aft cabin hatch. I was reading. "How do you know that man?"

"I don't know him, I just showed him where the store was," I said without looking up from my book.

He left the aft cabin without another word.

He's jealous, I thought.

The next morning at breakfast, Dad reasserted his strict rules about taking off alone to explore, or even going to the store. We had to stay on the boat. Bored, I retreated to reading my days away after a book swap spontaneously happened on the quay. All the sailors brought books out to trade and I found lots of interesting ones. Dad didn't monitor which books we picked from the pile. I think he was just happy that we were reading. The first one I read was *Catcher In the Rye*. I related to Holden's youthful angst because the small storm brewing inside me was getting bigger. I handed it off to Monica, who gave me the book she'd just finished, *Coffee, Tea or Me,* about a young girl who becomes a stewardess. I could see myself as a stewardess—after all, I cooked and served food to my family all the time.

The raciest book I snagged at the swap was *Valley of the Dolls.* It was thick, fascinating, and held my attention for more than a few weeks. The word "doll" was code for pills, and also for the beautiful women in the book. I wanted to be Anne Welles so badly I insisted everybody call me Anne from then on. My family looked at me strangely, but it made sense, sort of, because my middle name was Ann. Dad, Monica, and Karen hadn't read the book and didn't understand. The mere size of it, 442 pages, made Monica squish up her nose like it was sour milk. She preferred adventure books and wasn't drawn to read about life and fashion in New York City.

These books were more adult than anything I'd read before. They opened a whole new world to me, and not one Dad would have approved of. But he didn't know, and that made me happy; I loved getting away with things right under his nose. If he'd known how much sex and drugs were in *Valley of the Dolls,* he would have ripped it from my bloody fingers and burned it. I was drawn into the seedy side of life—drugs, sex with gorgeous men, and fast city living—and it was like no other world I'd ever read about. I lost myself in the characters, imagining the woman I would become someday. Physically, my body sat on a boat in Tahiti, but my mind and heart were in New York, learning the sophistication of toying with handsome men.

Dad picked up some work on other boats and was gone most mornings. He returned to *Aegir* one afternoon and found Monica, Karen, and I in our bunks, hibernating away from the hot sun reading. He yelled out for someone to make him lunch, which meant me, of course. I made everybody cheese sandwiches on baguettes and we read our books while we sat at the table and ate. I looked up to find Dad staring at us.

"It's time you girls enrolled in school," he announced. We'd discussed attending school in previous weeks. It was only a matter of time before the fateful day arrived. He had always talked about enrolling us in schools in as many cultures as he could while we sailed the world. And since he'd found work, it looked like we'd be staying in Tahiti for a while.

"That sounds good," Monica said. "I'm bored all day. Can we learn to speak French?"

I didn't want to get up early, and be gone until late, but Dad insisted. He had apparently been making plans and setting it all up without telling us, which was just like him.

"You girls will start school on Monday."

"What? You mean like in three days?" I said.

"Yes, in three days." He looked at Karen, who was sitting quietly. "What do you think about school?"

"I guess it'll be okay. I'm bored on the boat all day."

I couldn't read *Valley of the Dolls* fast enough. The sex scenes were captivating and so was the drug use. I stayed up late into the night, reading and re-reading passages I loved. I considered it a personal challenge to read as many pages as I could before we started school, knowing my unrestricted free time had just evaporated.

A few days later Dad took us to the local school, filled with Tahitian children our age, and left us there. Every day we attended math, science, history, and canoe making, all taught in French. And in the English class we helped the teacher when she needed it, which wasn't very often.

We went to school each day by ourselves in *le truck*, an open-air Mercedes truck with benches and a roof. They had brightly painted wooden passenger compartments in red, blue, and yellow mounted on the back. We rode with other students, and workers headed into the city. On the roof, passengers could store luggage and barrels of fish, or other cargo. All the locals got around the island in *les trucks* which stopped anywhere along the road if you caught the driver's attention, and gave him a few francs for the ride. We boarded each morning in front of the boat quay and rode inland on a dirt road thickly bordered with Plumeria trees and hibiscus bushes as high as houses.

The classes were divided up roughly by age, but mostly by gender. Monica and I were in the same classroom with all the teenage girls. The teenage boys sat in another classroom on the other side of the school, completely separated. We even had separate recesses and lunch periods, making it impossible to check out the boys. Karen was horrified to find she was with what she called "the little girls" at the other end of the school. Although she was with other eleven and twelve year olds, she hated it. She begged to be near Monica and me, but the teachers said no.

Even though the classes were segregated by gender, I discovered one of the strangest things about the girls' class—a few students were boys dressed as girls. Nobody acknowledged them as different or paid any attention to them in any negative way. They acted like girls and seemed to like cooking, sewing, and child rearing. The only way I knew they were boys was because they had fuzz on their faces. We discovered that in the Tahitian culture at that time, the eldest boy in a family was raised as a girl—called a Mahu. Women were very important in the Tahitian culture, and having a first-born daughter meant she would help with the younger siblings and around the home with cooking and traditionally female roles while the boys fished and tended the family's fields. The Mahu were not only treated with respect and kindness, they were revered as special, in that they possessed the secrets of both men and women. They were a special member of the family, accepted by all. The same held true at school. These Mahus were proud to be leading their family and were genuine yet feminine in their mannerisms. It wasn't long until I forgot about them being different and treated them like any other girl in the class.

Sitting and listening to a foreign language six hours a day was excruciating. I learned some French but mostly I fantasized and zoned out, dreaming about *Valley of Dolls*, waiting to get home so I could read about sex and drugs. Soon, I started sneaking my book to class and reading it on my lap. Even the English class was boring because the teacher didn't teach American English, she taught British English. She must have been uncomfortable and irritated about American teenagers being foisted on her because she never called on Monica or me in class. When I did offer to explain a word or idea, I was told to sit down and be quiet as she taught us words in British English.

One day she told me to pick up a crumpled up piece of paper and "put the rubbish in the rubbish bin." I figured out what she meant but it took me a long moment while everybody stared.

Thank goodness Dad listened to our complaints about going to school. After five weeks, he decided we should move away from the big bad city of Papeete and sail around the coast of Tahiti to find a quiet anchorage elsewhere. Tired of the traffic noise and the bar fights at night across the street, he wanted a quieter, more idyllic scene to anchor in. On our last day of school, Dad came and took a picture. The photograph shows Monica holding her chin up with her hand, and Karen and I staring at the ground. We're interspersed with the rest of the Tahitian girls in front of the school, bored and completely unaware that we're getting our picture taken. Dad must have taken a long time to set up the camera because only one or two of the twenty people in the picture bothered to look at the camera.

Part 3

The Return

Twenty-One

*W*e moved *Aegir* to the west side of Tahiti, near the village of Puna'auia, which was like the villages we'd encountered in the outer islands. Dad brought us to this less-populated part of the island, I figured, because having three teenage daughters coming of age was more difficult than he'd thought it would be when he planned the trip. Maybe he was being protective. Maybe he didn't trust me. But whatever his motive, we arrived in what soon felt like solitary confinement. We were the only boat in the inner lagoon until a week later when Sy and Vicki brought their boat over.

Puna'auia Bay was like the *Undersea World of Jacques Cousteau* with its crystal clear turquoise water jam-packed with fish, manta rays, and dolphins swimming over sparkling white sand. Anchored in fifteen feet of water, shallow enough to watch the undersea life swimming all around us, we were only fifty yards from shore. The palm tree-lined coastline disappeared into gorgeous white sand beaches. Half a mile away on the outer coral reef, the waves broke sometimes ten or twelve feet high, but the peaceful inner lagoon of our anchorage lay serene and still.

It was late June, the beginning of winter in the Southern Hemisphere, but it was unlike any winter I had experienced. Windsor in the winter meant ice, slush, and snow up to our eyeballs. The cold nearly broke our bones as we pushed through snow to the school bus stop. Oceanside in the winter sometimes had violent rain and windstorms, though the temperature never dropped below the forties. Tahiti in the winter was like Oceanside in the summer: eighty-five degrees every day. The humidity was the only difference, but it wasn't unbearable because the dazzling water beckoned us in to cool off. The mornings in Tahiti could be chilly to the point where we needed a light jacket or blanket to stay warm. But as the sun rose higher, the heat descended on us and before breakfast was over we were in our bikinis.

We erected our white awning which kept the cabins shaded and protected us from the searing sun. All portholes were open, along with the forward hatch over Monica and Karen's bunk. I still slept in the aft cabin alone, while Dad continued to sleep in the main cabin on the couch. We hated to turn on the stove or oven during midday or afternoon heat, so Dad mounted a Hibachi grill on the stern and we grilled everything we ate.

The beautiful isolation of our anchorage left me feeling terribly homesick. I wished every day I was back in Oceanside with my friends, writing papers in English class, taking typing on those clunky typewriters, or going to Black's Beach with Raine again. I relived moments from the previous years over and over again in my mind, writing about them in my diary. I especially missed John. Imagining us together, I wrote poems and songs, using somebody else's music and changing the words to fit my needs. Every day I wrote, sometimes several times a day, describing my boring life in paradise.

We went ashore with Dad at times to sightsee, eat out, grocery shop, or visit his new friend, Pilar, who lived in a cute little house on Tahiti-iti, a smaller island connected to Tahiti. Pilar was stunning, with long straight thick black hair, a half-French and half-Tahitian woman in her late twenties or early thirties. She made couscous for Monica, Karen, and me one day when we visited. I watched in awe from the living room as she made us dinner. She intimidated me with her easy style, free way of being, and obvious affection for my father. Dad doted on her, drinking wine and laughing too loud and big. He told us they were business partners, but that's not what it looked like to me.

As usual, Dad delineated the rules after we moved the boat to our idyllic jail. Along with the old rules of always staying together and never going ashore alone, he added the rule I hated the most: if he was gone with the dinghy ashore, we had to stay on the boat until he returned. No swimming ashore to collect shells on the beach or go to the store half a mile away by ourselves, even to get an ice cream. He was working very hard to keep us from interacting with anybody when he wasn't around.

A few days after arriving at our new anchorage at Puna'auia, we woke up to find a note from Dad: "Gone to town. Be back by dinner." Karen read the note aloud and then threw it across the cabin. It floated in slow motion to the ground and Monica stomped on it as she made her way to the galley. I groaned and moaned, flopping down on the couch, screaming, "We're prisoners! What are we going to do all day?"

"The same thing we do every day—read and write and play games," Monica said.

"We could bake cookies," Karen said. "Dad and I got butter when we went to the store last night."

"Oh, butter! Let's have baguette, butter, and jam for breakfast. We have to get some of the jam before Dad eats it all," I said.

We got out all the ingredients and sat on deck in the shade of the huge white awning breaking off chunks of bread, piling on slabs of butter and scooping generous amounts of Smucker's Strawberry Jam out of our last jar. That day, like every day, was hot and sunny with the occasional squall, which left as quickly as it had arrived.

During the morning rain shower we ran to the bow and stood in our bikinis as the large drops of precious water were carelessly tossed from the heavens. Fresh water was a true blessing, especially due to our long, thick hair. Dad still insisted we have long hair—none of us had the courage to ask for a haircut for fear of his reaction. I preferred the cooler showers in the mornings over the warmer showers in the afternoon. There were times when we tried to wash our hair on the foredeck in an afternoon squall, but the water falling from the sky was so hot it made for an uncomfortable shower.

That morning, as we stood on the bow soaking ourselves, Karen said, "Let's make a chocolate cake."

"Not me. It's too hot to fire up the oven," I said.

"But you love chocolate cake," Karen urged. "Come on."

"You can. I'm going to read, then write in my diary, then play the guitar, and then maybe take a nap," I said. I was still reading *Valley of the Dolls,* hoping it would never end, but the final pages thinned every day.

Karen looked at Monica with a questioning face.

"Not me. I'm re-reading *Gulliver's Travels* and I'm at a good part," Monica said.

The rain shower ended too soon—I didn't even get my hair wet all the way through, but I did get the salt off my skin. I brushed out my hair and curled up with *Valley of the Dolls* in the shade on the deck cushion.

Karen gave up on baking and began drawing. She'd become quite the artist, sketching and painting the fish we saw with watercolors, along with scenes of the islands and cruising life.

A few hours later, when the heat became too much, I looked at the water longingly.

"Let's go snorkeling and cool off," I prompted. "Dad won't be back until tonight, so he'll never know."

"Yeah, we haven't been snorkeling in weeks," Monica said.

"I'm so hot. Let's go!" Karen agreed.

We left the boat and swam along the edge of the coral reef. The cool, clear water slid off my arms as my snorkel and mask dangled from my upper arm. I swam the breaststroke at a slow easy pace next to Karen, Monica's fierce freestyle had left us behind. The white wash from waves breaking on the outer reef filled my sight.

We arrived at the reef, about two hundred yards from the boat, and I put on my mask. Millions of silver fish—all with bright yellow stripes and a black dot on the tail—swam in synchronicity, confusing predator and human alike; it was hard to see which end was the front or the back. Other fish the size of butter plates were bright neon blue on top and sparkly yellow on the lower half. A shockingly bright orange fish with a thick black stripe down its side darted between two rocks to avoid us. We saw schools of black fish with electric blue Magic Marker swipes on their sides. From the new book we'd acquired in Papeete, *Tropical Fishes of the South Pacific*, I identified a parrotfish with its teeth-filled beak and rainbow colors. Parrotfish were big enough to eat, but the book said they were poisonous in parts of the South Pacific because their diet consisted of toxic coral.

There were no predators hunting humans in the inner lagoon, just manta rays, giant turtles, and eels hiding in rocky holes and caves. No sharks, thank goodness. Swimming with the sharks in Rangiroa seemed like a lifetime away. We were bold then, but I wasn't sure Monica and I could keep up the nonchalant way of dealing with the sharks without Hitti and his brothers to protect us.

We dove down, struggling to reach the fifteen-foot depths we so easily swam to on Rangiroa just two months earlier.

"It's amazing how fast my lungs got weak," Monica said.

We didn't have the dinghy, so we had to tread water while catching our breath. I'd sometimes joked that Monica had grown webs between her fingers. She had always been a better athlete than me and Karen, which didn't bother me very much. But I did try to keep up with Monica because competition was what kept our relationship fun and exciting, which meant we both left Karen behind.

"Hey you guys! What about me?" Karen asked, when we came up for air.

"Keep up, lil' sis," I said, as Monica kicked away from us.

I followed Monica, feeling outmatched and out-swum. Karen began to scream, "Don't leave me again! Don't leave me!"

"Oh, God!" I said, resigned to the fact that I'd have to stay. I swam back to Karen, tired and ready for lunch. "Let's go back," I said.

We yelled for Monica but she'd swum around a bend and disappeared into a small cove. "We're supposed to stick together. Come on, let's get Monica."

Karen and I swam side-by-side to the cove and found Monica. I yelled to her as she came up for air, "It's getting late, and we're hungry. Let's go back."

She shook her head. "I want to swim some more. I want my spear."

"Your spear is back on the boat. Karen and I want to go back," I added emphatically.

"Alright," Monica conceded, disappointed, but then yelled, "Let's race!" She took off, kicking water into our faces, swimming freestyle. Karen and I followed, both swimming the breaststroke—our "go to" stroke because we could swim all day without much effort.

We got back to the boat to find Dad sitting in the captain's chair, feet up on the wheel, arms spread out and fingers laced together behind his head. It was a familiar position to me, one of confidence and foreboding. Every time he sat like that he was right and we were wrong. I knew we were in trouble.

We climbed up the swim ladder one at a time. My heart pounded. He waited until all three of us were standing on deck, dripping wet in front of him.

"Where the hell have you girls been?" he yelled.

"We went for a swim. It was hot," I said ready for battle.

It had become natural for me to do the talking. Monica and Karen didn't seem to mind, and I kind of enjoyed the power. I'd taken on a pretty cavalier attitude, wondering what he could do to me if I was too sassy. Maybe it came from boredom, or familiarity, or maybe it was just inside me, but I was itching for a fight. I felt as though I had nothing to lose.

He stood up, his six-foot frame towering over us. "You know the rule—you don't leave the boat if I'm ashore."

The force of his voice instantly conjured fear: fear of his size and fear of a beating even though he hadn't spanked us in years. At first, back then, no spankings had sounded great, like maybe life would get easier. But that was only wishful thinking. The punishments he thought up involved doing extra chores while at the same time having to apologize for whatever crime I had committed, all while being berated about how stupid and unthinking I was. The vicious sarcasm, hateful words, and demoralizing tirades were impossible to avoid.

Now I stood on deck in front of him and quickly gathered my wits, trying for a powerful voice. "We didn't go ashore. We went for a swim," I repeated. "We just ended up going a little farther than we realized," I added hastily.

Dressed in an old T-shirt and cut-offs, it was obvious he wasn't conducting any official business. I was dying to ask where he'd been and why he came back so early, but that would have only pissed him off.

"Where's dinner? Were you at least smart enough to take the spears and get us dinner?" he asked, eyes boring into me.

"We didn't take the spear guns. We just snorkeled," Karen said, her head hanging down. His eyes shifted quickly to drill into Karen's skin.

"Well, grab those spear guns and get us some fish, girls. It's your punishment for being so stupid today, and it'll be your regular job now since you're so bored every day." He returned to his seat on the aft cabin. "No excuses. Get in the water and get us some dinner," he commanded.

I looked at Monica and with my back to Dad rolled my eyes. Our nice little swim had turned into a daily chore now. *Great!* I headed for the swim locker to get our gear. While we pulled the spears out of the locker Dad said, "I have news." He paused, making sure we all stopped to listen. "Your mother arrives for a visit on July 12th."

"When is that? What date is it today?" Karen asked, jumping up and down.

"It's July 2nd today," Dad answered. "She'll be here in ten days."

It had been almost a year since we'd seen her in Oceanside. My heart filled with childish hope that things would be different. The idealized picture in my head about how our family would get back together one day and everybody would be happy, still lived on inside me. The Partridge Family, only we were sailors instead of singers.

Dad and I switched sleeping areas so that Mom could sleep in the aft cabin with him. I slept in the main cabin, but snuck up to the forward berth with Monica and Karen when they let me. The space seemed impossibly cramped for the three of us, especially now that we all had cranky "times of the month." I wondered how we were ever small enough to all sleep there.

We met Mom's Air New Zealand flight at the Papeete airport and watched her deplane onto the tarmac. Beautiful, with her coiffed locks and blue headscarf, in her matching blue flowered tropical blouse, white linen pants and white sandals, she sauntered toward us. Her trademark red lipstick and round Jackie O sunglasses made her look like a movie star. She carried a small hard makeup case and a white canvas purse, reminding me of the women from *Valley of the Dolls,* the ones who lived in New York and wore all the latest fashions. I looked at Dad and my sisters as she walked toward us. We were pathetic looking in our cut-off shorts and big, baggy T-shirts; my only somewhat-fashionable touches were my blue scarf top and puka shell necklace.

We took Mom to the boat and she marveled at the beautiful surroundings. Awkward and uneasy as she stepped in the dinghy with wobbly legs, she looked out to *Aegir.* "The boat isn't tied to a dock?"

"No, we're anchored," I said. "Isn't it pretty?"

"Yes, but it's not tied to a dock? Doesn't the boat swing around and around?"

Before I could explain, Dad jumped in. "This is the only place we have to stay unless you can afford a hotel."

The air thickened. I avoided eye contact with Mom or Dad. *Here we go again.*

Mom said curtly, "No, this will be fine."

Two days after she arrived, on July 14th, we spent the French National holiday, Bastille Day, in Papeete at a local friend's house playing games. Dad's French Polynesian friend, Pilar, attended the party and they were cozy-cozy together in a hammock, which pissed Mom off. I thought it was cruel of Dad to rub Mom's face in it, so I avoided all three of them. Mom stayed near Karen, investigating the different foods and games with her. In the evening we watched the parade of Polynesian dancers in brightly colored grass skirts and huge headdresses. I was energized—thrilled to be out among the crowds. We saw fire-eaters, and a French Navy ship with sailors lined up all around the deck in white uniforms. Coming home late to the boat, my ears filled with fireworks, my eyes with dancing girls, I drifted off to sleep happier than I had been in a while.

Over the next week Mom expressed constant surprise at how accomplished Monica, Karen, and I were at swimming, diving, spear fishing, and snorkeling, as if she didn't realize we'd been living on a boat surrounded by water for seven months.

"Girls, you've just turned into mermaids," she said in astonishment as we arrived home with our bounty of fish for dinner.

There wasn't any real emotional connection between us. Maybe I had changed so much she didn't recognize anything familiar in me. But more depressing was the fact that she made no effort to bridge the gap. She didn't spend time alone with me, or ask me privately about how life was going on the high seas with Dad. Nothing, no interest in my current life at all, which left me feeling alienated from her.

She slept late, read quite a bit, and was only mildly interested in sightseeing around the island of Tahiti. My high expectations of family life forever disappointed me—I rediscovered that all Mom thought about was herself. Exactly like her visit to Oceanside with Grandma, she arrived with an itinerary of her own. She wanted to see us three girls, but she was most interested in spending time with Dad, who did his best to avoid her, staying busy with his sailing friends, and his new local Tahitian and French friends. She wanted to get back with Dad, so she poured on the sweetness and it was awful to watch.

"Bjorn, can I pour you a glass a wine?" she crooned. Although Dad drank socially, Mom drank wine every day and night.

"Bjorn, can I fix you some cheese and crackers? You look hungry."

Dad put up with her doting on him for a few days on the pretense of trying to get along, but Mom would drink too much, slur her words, ask about Pilar and his other women, and stumble around the boat. Eventually, they'd begin fighting—screaming, and yelling at each other like the old days. A forty-five-foot boat doesn't leave much room to hide from it all.

He began counting the number of days until Mom got on the plane to return to Windsor. He'd get up in the morning, and, while eating his granola on deck, announce to Mom, "Eight days left." To which Mom would stare off at the horizon, sipping her coffee with a sour look. I retreated to the only place I could get any solitude or privacy: the bowsprit. It put me physically as far away from them as possible, hanging over the water, but still on the boat.

After two weeks, near the end of Mom's visit, the newness was gone and with it all semblance of civility, manners, or politeness. Mom constantly told Dad to "shut up." Her lip curled up and her eyes got cold as she doled out her vile words, "Shut up, Bjorn. You're a son of a bitch." In the very same breath, she'd turn to me, smiling her naturally beautiful smile and say, "Play me a song on the guitar, Leslie, I just love how you and Monica harmonize." There was a switch inside her, cold to hot, and it scared me. She'd stopped wearing lipstick and fixing her hair. It was like she was two people, or maybe three.

There was no denying that Dad treated her horribly, calling her names and disrespecting her without any thought for how Monica, Karen, and I were taking it. Dad saw me writing in my diary as the tension between them built and I got the feeling he was reading my diary again. On Thursday, July 24, 1975, at 1:00 p.m., I wrote in my diary:

> *Dear John: I don't want to explain this big problem the family aboard this boat has right now until I know what we're going to do. Dad is reading everything I write, so if you're reading this Dad, I HATE YOU!*

I hid my diary under several books, in the main salon by my bed. When I looked at it a few hours later after swimming, I saw that he had written right underneath my words, "I LOVE YOU!!!!!"

He was no longer just reading my diary and quietly returning it to its space. He was writing me notes!

I screamed, "Why are you reading my diary again? What business is it of yours?"

"Your business is my business!" he bellowed back.

"But why do you care what I write in my diary? It's mine! It's private!"

"You get no privacy until you're an adult. What's yours is mine—just remember that!"

"Bjorn, leave her alone!" Mom yelled.

"Don't tell me what to do with my daughters. You can leave now, fly back to Canada where you belong," he roared.

Mom cowered and retreated to the aft cabin for the rest of the afternoon.

I hated Dad. I hated Mom. I hated our boat and this stupid around-the-world journey. I dove into the water, swam ashore, and sat on the beach staring at our boat. Dad watched me from the deck of *Aegir*. He stared at me. I stared at him. I sat there for hours, wondering what I was going to do and how I would survive this family.

The biggest fight of all happened the day before Mom was supposed to go home. The yelling began shortly after Mom got up. Dad had taken to sleeping on deck since he couldn't stand being in the aft cabin with Mom.

That morning, I was sprawled out reading my book on the sofa that doubled as my bed. Mom came into the main cabin wearing shorts and a white sleeveless top, her hair fixed nicely but without her red lipstick. "Leslie, fix me a cup of coffee, please."

Dad sat at the navigation table looking at charts and writing in the ship's log. "Less than twenty-four hours to go, Paula. I just can't wait to get rid of you," he said without emotion or even a look in her direction.

I went to the galley and began heating the water, attempting to be invisible.

"Stop talking to me like that, Bjorn. I think we need a family meeting," she said. "Girls! Come here would you?"

Dad lowered his face into his hands and sat motionless.

Monica and Karen were in their bunk in the bow. Monica groaned as she lowered herself down from the berth and made her way to the main cabin table.

"Are we bothering you, Monica?" Dad said sarcastically through his hands.

"No," Monica said in a low voice.

I could tell by her meek expression as she slinked into the main cabin that she didn't realize how loudly she'd groaned. I also knew she didn't want to be the center of attention as she flopped down by the table, scooted to the corner, and drew up her legs, practically disappearing into the back of the couch.

Karen followed Monica quietly, wearing her white nightgown with little pink flowers and ruffles around the neckline. She took a seat next to Monica at the table. We were as ready as we could be for Mom's "family group therapy session."

Mom said, "Bjorn, if you would just stop your sarcasm, we could talk like adults."

"That's funny, Paula, you calling yourself an adult, because you don't ever act like one."

"There you go, picking on me again."

"Cut the shit, Paula. You came here two weeks ago and have been nothing but trouble, begging me for money like I'm a bank."

The whistle on the teakettle startled me. I fumbled to turn off the propane and then poured the hot water into the cup of instant coffee granules, put a splash of milk into the cup, and brought Mom the cup, a spoon, and the sugar bowl. Then I joined my sisters at the table. Nobody spoke while I did this. Afraid to be the center of attention, I avoided eye contact and sat quietly.

"Can't we all just get along for the last day I'm here?" Mom said looking at Monica, Karen, and me. I looked up and found her adjusting a curl on her head, crossing her legs and straightening out her shorts in an attempt to gain composure.

I nodded and then got up from the table and walked to the steps, itching to get out of the cabin, but Dad boomed, "Stay here, Leslie."

I sat down on the steps next to him at the navigation station, blocking the only exit from the cabin. I looked at Monica sunk into the corner. She looked far away, like she was floating on a cloud somewhere. Next to her, Karen looked upset, her face strained and pulled by fear and anger. Mom looked like a volcano ready to blow and I expected her to grab the nearest thing and fling it at Dad. I wanted to get away—to dive off the bow and swim as fast as I could to shore, run away and never come back.

In a deceptively pleasant and sugary voice, Dad said to Mom, "If you don't get off this boat then I'll have Immigration come and throw you off."

Karen burst out crying and yelled, "Stop it! Stop hurting Mommy."

She flung herself across the cabin into Mom's open arms. Mom clung to Karen as proof that somebody loved her. Mom's red, screwed up face looked alien to me as she screamed, "You can't do that! You can't deport me! I have rights!"

Dad thundered back at her, "Your stupidity is comical."

Big wet tears ran down Mom's smooth face, her mouth looking oddly large and misshapen as she emitted a sorrowful sound. Karen curled up like a kitten in her lap, her face in Mom's shirt. In a muffled voice she said, "I want to go on the plane with Mommy."

Dad yelled, "Fine, I'll go book you a ticket right now."

He almost shoved me aside to get out of the cabin. I moved just in time to avoid his foot landing on my leg. He went up the steps and I followed him onto the deck. I watched him get into the dinghy. He rowed to shore, leaving us stranded on the boat again. I sat down on the aft cabin cushion, realizing I had been chewing on my nails. They were nubs. My jaw hurt from grinding my teeth together. I stared after Dad who ran the dinghy up on shore and disappeared into the grove of palm trees in the direction of the road. I put my hands in my lap and laced my fingers together.

Monica came on deck first and sat next to me, her face twisted and drawn as she followed my eyes to our beached dinghy. Mom hesitantly poked her head up exposing her disheveled hair. Her formerly sullen eyes scanned the deck.

"He's gone," I said.

"Would you girls like me to stay and travel with you?" Mom said, her eyes big and pleading.

"Yes, Mommy, I want you to stay," Karen chirped from below. Mom came on deck, freeing the passageway up for Karen. Mom looked at me and I quickly looked down.

"Leslie, what do you say?"

With a finger near my mouth, ready for chewing, I stared at the deck and said, "I don't think you and Dad get along very well, and this boat is very small."

"Yes, I suppose you are right," Mom said in a surprisingly pleasant voice, which made me jerk my eyes up to her. She smiled at me, tears still wet on her face.

"Well, what are we going to do with the rest of our day?" she said, forcing another smile. None of us spoke. I was on guard again from her drastic change in mood. I didn't know if she would yell at me next or continue being kind. "I think I'll finish my coffee for starters," she said and went below deck.

I raised my eyebrows to Monica and Karen. They shrugged at me. And just like that, peace prevailed for a few hours. I got out my mac-ramé, Monica played the guitar, and Karen made Mom a puka shell necklace.

When Dad returned to the boat several hours later he didn't look mad anymore. He actually smiled and winked at me as he pulled himself up the swim steps from the dinghy. Still mad at him for reading my diary, I didn't smile back. It was late afternoon and we were all hungry.

"How about some pork chops for dinner? Is there a store around here?" Mom asked.

As soon as Monica and I heard "pork chops" we got up and stood by Mom. We hadn't had meat in a long time, and the thought of having pork chops just about made us go crazy.

"We already have the apple sauce in cans. Please, can we Dad? Can we get pork chops, please?" I said.

Monica's eyes begged. Karen gave Mom a big hug.

We tried to act happy but not too happy, like a family but not like a "real" family. I tried with all my might to forget the injustices done earlier in the day.

"So you girls didn't go spear fishing today?" Dad boomed.

I shook my head and looked at Monica who looked down.

"Who's going to pay for those chops?" Dad said.

"I know you have money, Bjorn," Mom said. "Why do you play games with me?"

My stomach flipped over and began churning. I walked away from Mom and took a seat facing away from everybody. I snuck a peek at Dad. He rolled his eyes and fished out ten francs.

"Leslie, come here." He handed me the money and in a voice

dripping with sarcasm said, "You and Karen go buy some delicious pork chops so we can celebrate your Mother *leaving*."

Karen and I got into the dinghy and went ashore. I was glad to be off the boat. We walked down the road about half a mile and bought five pork chops for 8.60 francs, about $15 USD, from an old Chinese guy who ran a store with his Tahitian wife. We'd been to this store many times before for butter and baguettes and other supplies. They were a friendly couple who smiled, saying "*au revoir*" as we left.

As soon as we were outside, Karen said, "Dad's going to be so mad when he finds out we spent almost 9 francs on pork chops."

"Oh well, let him be mad. It's not like he isn't already mad. How much worse could it be?"

As we crossed the two-lane road, looking both ways again and again, Karen and I ran to the dashed line in the middle of the road and stopped to let a car pass in front of us. We both saw another car coming from the opposite direction but it seemed far away. I continued on to the other side of the road. Halfway across I heard a thud and then a scream. I turned around to see Karen on the hood of a car, and then in slow motion I saw her fly through the air and land by the road.

I ran to Karen. Her eyes were closed.

Twenty-Two

"Karen!" I put my hand on her arm. She opened her hazel eyes. I felt a wave of relief that she wasn't dead. She lay near the driveway of a house, in a ditch meant to keep water off the road in heavy rain. The large grey, metal corrugated drainage pipe was dry, and a huge banyan tree gave us shade from the hot sun.

She blinked a few times, her eyes looking cloudy and confused. I looked for blood or obvious signs of broken bones and saw a long scrape on her arm covered with dirt. Her white T-shirt was smudged with brown dirt across the front. Her shorts were torn and her right leg looked strange, turned out at the knee and spread away from her body. Her cute little freckled face looked up at me, her eyes searching. She lay perfectly still, not even trying to get up.

The next moment her eyes got big and she said, "*Ou est la* pork chops?" which wasn't proper French, but I knew what she meant.

"Forget about the pork chops."

Panic washed over her face, "They're so expensive and Dad'll be mad if we lose them."

"Forget about the stupid pork chops!" But I knew she was right. I took a deep breath, looked around, and saw the bag of pork chops on the other side of the road. The bag had ripped open and two of the pork chops lay on the pavement. I hurried out to the street, past a few people who had gathered around us, picked up the bag, scooped up the two chops on the road, and brought them to her.

The woman who had hit Karen was among the crowd that had gathered. As I bent over Karen again, she stood behind me speaking

French very fast. I ignored her. When I showed Karen the bag of pork chops, she said, "What are these?"

That's when I knew something was really wrong with her.

"The pork chops you just asked me for." I sat her up. She looked at the chops and said, "Who's going to cook them?"

I wanted her to get up and brush herself off so we could walk back to the dinghy. We'd already been gone a long time. I wasn't sure what to do, but I was afraid of getting in trouble with Dad.

"Dad will cook them on the Hibachi," I said. "Try to get up, so we can get back to the boat."

But then she looked down and saw her contorted leg, and touched the scrape on her arm, flicking at the oozing blood that was escaping from under the dirt.

"How did this happen?" she asked.

"You were hit by a car, don't you remember?" She was silent for a moment and then burst into tears, which quickly turned into hysterical screaming. Dirty brown tears ran down her face and the screaming turned to a wailing cry. She shook involuntarily. I bent over and tried to hug her, but her position was so awkward it was difficult to get my arms around her. I sat down in the dirt, holding onto her uninjured arm.

Fear rose up in me. My mouth went dry.

Between whimpers she cried, "Dad's going to be so mad, isn't he Leslie?"

Scared of hurting her, I put my other hand on her back and tried to comfort her, even though I knew she was right. Dad was going to be pissed.

"No, he won't be mad—he'll be happy you're alive," I said but she kept screaming about how mad Dad was going to be about the pork chops, and how much they cost, and how long we'd been gone, and how she got hit by a car.

Behind me was the blurry far-away sound of all those people speaking French. The Chinese man from the store and his wife and various customers crowded around us. I understood a few French words, like "hôpital" and "accident," but it all seemed foggy. A couple off a boat from New Zealand recognized us from Papeete. They were talking to the woman who had hit Karen, whose name turned out to be Pauline.

I turned around and saw her black pumps and white dress with little red hibiscus print. She was petite like Karen, with short brown hair. The New Zealand couple offered us a ride back to the boat. The man helped me put Karen into the backseat of their car, which was very painful for her. They drove us half a mile up the road to *"Aulerge du Pacifique"* where the boat was anchored. Pauline followed us in her car. I left Karen with the couple and rowed out fifty yards to get Dad as I screamed, "Come quick! Karen's been hit by a car!"

Sy and Vicki heard my yelling and came on deck. I finally reached *Aegir.*

"What do you mean she was hit by a car?" Dad said his face taut, eyebrows together. I stood up in the dinghy and held on to *Aegir*. Nearly hysterical and talking as fast as I could, I explained about the store, the pork chops, the car, and Karen flying through the air and landing in the dirt driveway. Dad stepped heavily into the dinghy, pushing down hard so that I had to hold tight. He looked mad alright. Karen was right.

Directly behind him, Mom lowered herself daintily into the dinghy, speaking through her tears, her lips quivering as she spoke. "How bad is it? I want to see her."

"She's awake and talking. She's scared of being in trouble," I rowed back to the beach still talking as fast as I could. When we reached the beach, the New Zealand couple stood by the car like guards. Karen lay still in the backseat. Dad ran to her. Mom followed, standing behind him trying to peek around him as he examined her. I looked back at *Aegir* and saw Monica on deck waving.

"I wanted to come too!" she yelled. Her voice echoed off the water in the otherwise quiet afternoon. I just shrugged and she stopped waving. A few minutes later Sy and Vicki arrived on the beach with Monica in their dinghy. Monica ran up to the car to see Karen laying still in the backseat. I stood beside her.

"Are you okay?" Monica asked Karen.

Karen said, "Yes, I'm fine," even though she didn't look fine.

Pauline stood behind the car, waiting for a chance to talk to Dad. She looked exasperated and was pacing back and forth by the trunk.

"We need to get Karen to the hospital," Mom said urgently. "She needs to be seen by a doctor. She could have internal injuries."

"Can you drive us?" Dad asked the New Zealand couple.

They nodded and got into the car.

"Did somebody call the police?" Dad asked, scanning their faces.

"Yes, I believe the store owner and his wife called the police," the New Zealand man said.

"Great! Sy, will you stay with Leslie, and talk to the police, while we take Karen to the hospital?"

Sy agreed.

Pauline began speaking French at Dad very fast.

"I don't speak French. Wait for the police."

Pauline seemed to understand and stopped chattering. Dad gently picked up Karen's legs and loaded himself into the backseat. Karen cried out in pain as he placed her legs down on his lap. Mom had already gotten into the backseat and held Karen's head in her lap, stroking her face and caressing her hair.

I felt empty, spent, worthless, responsible and irresponsible all at the same time. I sat down on the sand. Monica sat next to me, throwing her arm around my shoulders. Mom and Dad drove away with Karen.

The police arrived a few minutes later. They didn't speak English, so Pauline explained in French what had happened. Monica stayed behind while Sy and I rode to the station with them and Pauline followed in her car. At the police station, they found an officer who spoke some English. I told him the story. Pauline sat next to me, watching and waiting her turn.

When it was time for Pauline to speak, she spoke French so fast that I didn't understand a word she said. I felt sure she was blaming Karen and me for the accident. I silently wished Dad were there to handle the police officers and put Pauline in her place. But he wasn't. I was alone with Sy, who didn't say a word. Kind-hearted Sy, with his friendly warm smile, wouldn't ever get mad at a police officer.

Watching Pauline give her testimony, I decided she must be rich by the way she held herself, the way she sat with her legs crossed, her gold chains and earrings dripping from her body, her long fake nails, and by the way she dug into her purse for Kleenex with such daintiness.

I didn't like her. I felt embarrassed that our family lived on a boat barefoot and in cut-offs, like we were poor or something. I hoped our cruising lifestyle didn't factor into the guilt or innocence of Karen and me.

It was dark when the police dropped Sy and me off on the beach. The warm breeze blew quietly and the full moon shone down like a spotlight on me, exposing my guilt. The longer I thought about it, the more convinced I was that the accident was my fault. I should have held her hand and stayed close to her. I should have not let her backtrack. I should have done more!

Sy and I stood on the empty beach. No dinghy meant Dad was back from the hospital. I hoped he wasn't pissed.

Sy called out in the quiet night, "Hello? Anybody there? We're back!"

Dad answered, "Be right there."

Aegir and *Resolve* sparkled in the night. The calm water didn't show a ripple, like a painting of two boats floating in ice. The moon reflected in the water like white paint. It took Dad only a few minutes to come pick us up. He was shirtless and barefoot in the warm evening, wearing only his stupid cut-offs.

As I climbed into the dinghy, Dad looked into my eyes with a blank face. I couldn't tell if he was mad or glad to see me. My heart beat fast. I chewed a fingernail.

"Thanks for taking her to the police station," Dad said to Sy. "I would have come by but I thought you'd have been done a long time ago." His deep oar strokes pulled us quickly through the water.

"No problem. Pauline took a long time to tell her side of the story. You'll get a written report tomorrow, in French," Sy said.

"Great! In French! What good is that?"

"I don't know. I guess you can have it translated. How's Karen?"

I watched the moon shine off Dad's bald head, making a small round white light on top. I perked up, wondering about my little sister.

"She'll be fine. She's spending the night in the hospital with Paula."

We arrived at *Resolve* and found Vicki standing in the cockpit. Her blonde hair was also lit up by the moon—when she smiled at me, I felt welcome. I wished I was going aboard their boat instead of having to return to *Aegir* with Dad. Sy climbed aboard his boat. He smiled at me and I smiled back. "Good night."

Vicki bent down to Dad and me in the dinghy, "How's Karen?"

"She's going to be just fine," Dad said. "Thanks again for taking Leslie to the police station, Sy. Come over for a glass of wine later if you want."

"Sure thing," Sy said.

Dad rowed in silence to *Aegir*. "I'm so hungry," I said. "I'm going to make a sandwich."

I climbed aboard and went below to make myself a peanut butter sandwich. Monica sat at the table reading her book.

"How're you doing, Lez?"

"Okay. I'm starving." I bit into the sandwich and gulped down some iced tea.

Dad's commanding voice broke the silence. "Leslie, come on deck please."

I closed my eyes and rolled my head back in exhaustion. "Okay, I'll be right there."

I took one more bite of my sandwich, another swig of my tea, and went on deck. Monica followed and we sat side-by-side on the cabin as Dad sat in the captain's chair.

"Tell me the story from beginning to end, exactly like you told the police." His tone was serious and quiet, which was never a good sign. It meant he was contemplating something. The white awning we sat under glowed in the darkness.

Drained, and sick to death of talking about it, I forced myself to tell the story again. As I spoke I stared at the outer reef, watching the white wash of the crashing waves appear and then disappear, bright and white.

"Why did you run to the other side without her?" Dad asked. His gentle tone took me by surprise. Every time I predicted his behavior, he'd do the opposite. It was maddening. He seemed genuinely concerned about wanting to know the truth.

My stomach flopped over with the stress of being responsible for my sister's injuries. "I thought she was right beside me. We were shoulder-to-shoulder and then we weren't. It all happened so fast."

Ten minutes later, as I finished, Sy and Vicki rowed up. "Permission to come aboard?" Sy called in the traditional greeting among boaters.

Relieved for the distraction and mostly finished anyway, I couldn't wait to go below and devour my sandwich.

"Permission granted," Dad answered.

As they tied up their dinghy and climbed aboard, Dad said quietly, "Okay, you can go now. Get some sleep."

Monica and I got up and headed to the companionway stairs of the main cabin. "Did they find anything wrong with Karen at the hospital?" I asked Dad, finally mustering up the courage to inquire.

Sy and Vicki took a seat on the cabin cushions.

Dad's face softened. The lines around his eyes flattened out and his velvety voice emitted love and devotion. "They found a cracked pelvic bone. Her Achilles tendon needed to be sewed back together. She also got five stitches for the deep cut in her leg, and they cleaned and wrapped the wounds on her arm and face."

I hadn't remembered so many wounds or any blood at all except the little drops of blood oozing up on her arm as she flicked away the dirt.

"Do you really think she'll be okay?" I asked.

"Yes, she's going to be fine. But she needs rest."

"Can we see her in the morning?" Monica asked.

"Yes, we'll all go see her in the morning."

"Okay, good night," I said.

"Good night," Monica said.

"Good night girls."

Monica and I went below. I finished eating and joined her in the forward bunk. As we lay quietly looking up at the starry night sky through the open hatch, I whispered, "I think it's my fault."

"Why do you think that?"

"Because I left her behind and she turned back. That's when she got hit. I didn't even know she had turned around. I was trying to time my own running to the other side as the car passed."

"It's not your fault, Leslie."

"I feel horrible."

"It's going to be fine. I'm sure Karen doesn't blame you."

As we lay in the forward bunk with all the hatches and portholes open for ventilation, we could hear Dad talking to Sy and Vicki on deck. I sat up on my knees, closer to the open hatch. I strained to make out the words. Monica joined me.

"A policeman came to the hospital and made me sign a note saying I'll pay for everything—the dent in Pauline's car, Karen's hospital bill, and the gendarme's time if it's determined that the accident is Karen and Leslie's fault," Dad said.

"It isn't like the United States here. It's opposite," said Vicki. "French law says you're guilty until proven innocent."

"Karen's hospital room alone, is 3,000 francs a night, and the doctor thought she needed to stay a few nights at least for observation," Dad said. "At that rate, I can only afford two nights."

I fell back down on the bed and buried my head in the pillow. Monica lay beside me. "Leslie! It's not your fault!"

I rolled over and looked at the square block of night visible through the hatch opening. The sky was midnight blue, and the stars were few. I got out my diary and recorded the day's events for the final time.

The next morning Monica and I slept later than normal. Dad was gone with the dinghy when we woke up, but by the time we'd finished our cereal he had returned with Karen and Mom. We scrambled up on deck when we heard him yelling to us from the dinghy.

Karen and Mom sat in the back of the dinghy, facing us. Mom waved and smiled when she saw Monica and me watching them. Karen looked even smaller than usual. Mom's hair was messy and unkempt, but her smile was warm. Karen's arm was in a sling, and a Band-Aid covered her right cheek. Her hair was pulled back into a

DRAWING OF THE ACCIDENT THAT HAPPENED ON JULY 26 1975 At 4:00 - 4:15 pm in Punaua at the store "Man yine"

X - Karen
● - Leslie

PAEA

300 meters ↑ I came

CAR

SPEED LIMIT 80 KL

MAGASIN "MAN yine"
Parking Lot here

CAR

stream (bridge)

RIVITE EPA
TARE EPA

CAR

CAR

CAR

PAPEETE

"MAGIR"

① We were standing there then we both crossed. Karen Right beside me or a little behind me.

② A car was comming. Karen got scared so she ran back on the way back she got hit. This is where Karen landed. Karen landed on the gravel almost in the gutter.

③ This is where Karen landed.

ponytail. She wore a blue and white pareo—we found out later Mom had bought her that because her other clothes were gone, cut off her by the hospital staff before examination. As they got closer, I saw Karen's leg wrapped from her foot to her shin with white gauze bandages. Dad lifted Karen aboard the boat and she hobbled on her left leg to the cushion on the main cabin and sat down, wincing. She couldn't put any weight on her right leg. Dad handed up the crutches and helped Mom aboard. We swooned over Karen, hugging, kissing, and making her a big breakfast. Dad explained that she had no signs of internal injuries so they'd released her.

After all the commotion, Mom went below to sleep. Both Mom and Karen looked exhausted. Karen and I sat on deck staring off at the waves breaking on the reef that protected our little lagoon. The waves broke higher than ever before that day—maybe fifteen to eighteen feet. When everybody had gone below, I leaned over to her and whispered, "I'm sorry if the accident was my fault."

She looked into my eyes. Her hazel-green eyes looked strong and wise. "It wasn't your fault. I should've never run back across the road. I should have stayed with you."

I felt better knowing she didn't blame me for the accident, but a lingering feeling of guilt persisted. I had not been a good sister that day. I silently vowed to do better in the future.

Twenty-Three

On July 29, 1975, Karen and Mom flew back to Windsor on Air France. After all that had happened, Karen got her wish to go with Mom, but seeing her little body loaded on the plane from a wheelchair was difficult. We stood on the tarmac waiting for the plane to taxi down the runway.

"How long will Karen be gone?" I asked.

"I don't know. We have to wait until the Canadian doctor examines her. Your mother will send a telegraph soon with news."

We saw Karen's face through the first passenger window on the big silver jet. She waved like crazy and blew us kisses. Monica and I blew kisses back, jumping up and down and waving. The plane climbed into the clouds from the seaside airport in Papeete. It would be many months before I'd see Mom or Karen again.

A week later Dad got the telegram that Karen needed six weeks to recover.

A week after that, while still anchored at Puna'auia, Monica, Dad, and I sat on the deck of *Aegir* under the white awning eating bowls of Grape-Nuts with mangoes. He broke the sound of crunching with another life-changing announcement. "Girls, I've agreed to deliver a boat back to San Diego while Karen heals."

"What boat?" I said.

"Do you remember the Finns Ollie and Chuck from our time in Papeete?"

"Yeah, sort of," Monica said. I nodded, but only vaguely remembered them.

"I'll be delivering Ollie's boat, *Patricia*."

I thought I was past the point of being surprised by Dad, but I never saw this coming. Without missing a beat or even acknowledging our astonishment, he explained that he needed to pay for Karen's hospital stay and Pauline's car, since Karen had been deemed the guilty one. Dad explained that Ollie had health problems and could no longer continue his voyage, and that he would pay in cash. Dad said he couldn't pass up the money.

"Leslie, I could use your help sailing back to San Diego. Will you join me?"

Before I could answer he looked at Monica.

"I assume you want to go to Windsor, Monica, and not do another ocean crossing if you don't have to."

Monica nodded emphatically. Dad's gaze landed back on me. His eyebrows went up, waiting for an answer.

I squirmed a little under the ever-present pressure to please him. I felt responsible for the accident and guilty about the money he owed. But I didn't want to be alone with him at sea. All the feelings ricocheted around inside me.

"I don't know. How many days will it take to get back to San Diego?"

"My guess is about forty."

I swallowed hard and looked off to the horizon. "That's a lot of days at sea."

I felt on the spot to decide right that minute. Dad said the over-all plan included delivering *Patricia*, then collecting Karen and Monica from Windsor and flying back to Tahiti to continue our around-the-world-voyage.

We sat in silence for a minute and then he slapped my leg gently and said with a big smile, "Let's go see the boat. She's a bugeye ketch!"

Dad went below to gather his things. I wrinkled my nose at Monica and she shrugged her shoulders. I knew a ketch had two masts, but wasn't sure what the "bugeye" part was about.

Monica and I loaded into the dinghy. As we sat waiting for Dad, Monica smiled and punched me in the arm. "I'm so glad I don't have to go!"

"Ouch! Don't punch me so hard. I don't know if I'm going either."

We rode *le truck* along the coast in silence. Dad read his sailing magazine while Monica and I stared out the open-air windows. Papeete was still an assault on the senses. Cars rushed past, buses honked, and crowds flooded to the fish market across from the quay.

We found *Patricia* tied up on the quay. She was sixty-feet long, old and dilapidated, all wood, with two masts leaning backward. We went aboard and looked around. She had two cabins, the main cabin where the navigation station and bunks were, and the aft cabin where the galley and eating area were. The peeling white paint on her hull revealed blue as her original color. Rust stains tarnished the hull where water drained off the deck. She looked pathetic and ancient. The squared-off, raised up stern reminded me of an old pirate ship—it was surrounded by a rust-colored wooden railing like I'd seen in the movies. She had a peeling varnished wood spoke wheel and a helmsman chair for steering. The only thing I loved was her long bowsprit and netting, which stuck out five feet over the water. I could see myself lying on that netting, watching the water go by beneath me. Below the netting was an intricately carved wooden mermaid painted gold and seaweed green, its paint flaking like the rest of the boat.

"Can she even sail? I mean look at her, she's so ugly." I said, my nose in the air.

Dad laughed a big, all-knowing laugh. "Don't judge a book by its cover. She's a seaworthy Chesapeake Bay bugeye ketch, modified from the original bugeye ketches built to dredge for oysters over one hundred years ago."

"She looks a hundred years old," I said.

"Yeah, she looks like she'll sink at any moment," Monica added.

"Girls, all she needs is a little love to spruce her up."

Monica punched me in the arm again, lightly this time, and smiled at me. I knew she was especially grateful she didn't have to sail on that wretched thing.

"Why do her masts lean back?"

"Ollie explained it to me. It's a long story, having to do with pulling up heavy nets of oysters and balancing the boat under reefed sails. I'll explain it to you at sea. We should have plenty of time for long

talks." He smiled a great big toothy smile and flung his arm around
my shoulders like I was his best friend.

"Where's her spreaders?"

"We'll talk about her design later, okay?"

I nodded.

Dad squeezed my shoulders and kissed me on the cheek. "What
do you think? I could really use your help."

God I hated it when he wanted something from me. He was just
so sweet and awful and I felt scared to say no, but scared to say yes. If
I didn't give him the answer he wanted who knew what he might do.
We stood on the sidewalk again facing *Patricia*. I squinted and sized
her up. Going back to Windsor with Monica didn't sound like any
fun either. I was confused and unsure about what to decide.

Dad continued. "I'll look for two men to help me with the sailing.
Can you cook for us, sweetie?"

"Is that why you want me—to cook?" I didn't like being his
"sweetie," especially when he needed me so badly. "I want to do more
than just cook, okay?"

"Sure, I'll put you to work on the navigation and regular crew
watches."

"You have to find a girl, too, somebody to cook with me. I don't
want to go if it's just two boys and you. It'll be awful for me."

"I'll do my best," Dad said, patting me on the back.

I really hoped he could find another girl to sail with us, otherwise
I might have to back out on him. I wondered if he would force me
to go with him. I rolled my eyes at Monica, not sure what I had just
signed up for.

During August, Dad looked for crew, took inventory of *Patricia*,
and provisioned her for the crossing. He seemed happy to have an
adventure before him and something to focus on. Monica and I had
more freedom than we'd ever had. We explored Tahiti by *le truck*,
discovering every part of the island. We went to new beaches on
Tahiti-Iti—some with beautiful coarse black sand, others with white

sawdust sand. We snorkeled and dove in pristine bays, far from the city. We hung out at the swanky hotels in Papeete, drinking Cokes and swimming in their pools like we owned the place. We visited the Gaugin Museum and were successful in getting money from Dad for ice cream and food. It was a fun, carefree time, not anything like the boring time before Mom came.

Unsuccessful in finding crew in Papeete, Dad decided we needed to take *Patricia* and visit some of the outer islands like Moorea, Huahine, and Bora Bora. If we were successful in finding crew there, we could leave for San Diego directly.

On September 1, we moved our boat *Aegir* to Papeete and tied her up on the quay, putting her in "storage." Dad enlisted several cruising families and local Tahitian friends to watch *Aegir* while we were gone. It was hard to batten her all up, feeling she would be neglected and ignored for several months. I loved *Aegir*, and was loyal to her—I tried to reconcile that with the feeling I was betraying her by sailing on *Patricia*.

Monica, Dad, and I moved aboard *Patricia* and settled in. She smelled musty and felt damp, so we opened all the hatches and aired her out. The wooden decks looked rotten in spots, but Dad said she was sturdy.

Dad slept in the main cabin as usual, near the navigation station. Monica and I slept in the forward bunks, of which there were six. *Patricia* was fifteen feet longer than *Aegir*, and we immediately felt the increase in space. I kept telling myself that although she was longer and we had more room to spread out, she definitely wasn't as good a boat as *Aegir*. The galley took up the entire aft cabin with a big crew table surrounded by a horseshoe-shaped cushion. I imagined everyone would eat there together once we were under way. After a few days of getting settled on *Patricia* and stocking her with more canned food, we took her on a shakedown cruise to Moorea, a half-day sail away.

We anchored in iconic Robinson Cove with its world-famous jutting peak. Down the island from the Cove we visited Club Med for dinner. Dad spoke to every surfer and traveler living in tents along the beach to scrounge up crew members for our trip home. Nobody was interested, maybe because he wasn't paying, but only offering work experience in exchange for passage to the United States.

After a few days anchored in Moorea, without any luck finding crew, we sailed ninety miles away to Huahine. While every French Polynesian island certainly looked idyllic, there was something special about Huahine. Maybe it was the overgrown lush vegetation, or the beach shacks and houses built right at the edge of the water. All this set against the bluest sky, and the calmest, clearest water overflowing with populations of sea turtles, dolphins, manta rays, and an abundance of fish swimming over the silvery white sand. The beach was fringed by palm trees that hung over the sand, peeking into the lagoon like they wanted to swim. I fell completely in love with Huahine.

We anchored in the bay most populated with sailors and travelers, just inside the reef near Maitai Lapita Village. Dad set out to find two men and one woman who were looking for work on a boat.

First, he found an eighteen-year-old surfer from France with a name I couldn't pronounce. "I found him sleeping under a tray of copra with his backpack and surfboard. He'll be here tonight to move aboard."

"He's a bum probably, without any money," Monica said to me under her breath.

We sat on deck as the surfer approached the boat that evening with just a small backpack. He looked foxy from afar. When Dad introduced us to him, I couldn't pronounce his name so I just called him "Jim."

After many corrections on how to pronounce his name, Gibus De Soultrait, I'm sure I confirmed his belief that Americans were stupid. He explained to me that Americans talk like they have clothespins on their noses. Gibus's smile was nice and he was kind of cute, but he made me nervous. He made me that feel either he, or the entire French population, didn't like Americans.

But one thing he did like about America was our pancakes. One morning he said, "We no have thick ones in France." On top of the pancakes, instead of using syrup, he put "peanuts butter." I tried to tell him that in English we don't say the "s" in peanut butter, but he said, "It takes more than one peanut to make the butter so I will call it 'peanuts butter.'"

Dad also met a young woman who'd taken to sleeping in a tent on the beach just down from our anchorage. A twenty-year-old American named Annie Musselman, she was ecstatic that we were going to San Diego because she needed a ride home to see her ill father. She had sailed to Tahiti on a small, twenty-six-foot boat from Maui and had been sick the entire time. When she arrived in Tahiti, she left the boat and took up camping on various islands, trying to find a new boat and a new adventure.

She moved aboard immediately and I was overjoyed. Monica, Annie, and I hung out together for a week or so, snorkeling, playing the guitar, cooking, and laughing. She grew up in Pacific Beach and went to Mission Bay High. She was blonde, smart, adventurous, artistic, and had a great smile and fantastic sense of humor. She and I instantly bonded as big sister and little sister.

Our final crew member was an older Swiss guy, twenty-four-year-old Roland Hofer. He spoke French and German and some broken English. Roland was fit, thin but muscular—a quiet type, with dark curly hair and a reddish moustache. We found out later he used to be a ballet dancer in Switzerland. A perfectionist, neat and clean, it seemed he always had to do everything the "right" way. Though he had kind eyes behind the metal-framed glasses he wore, he hardly smiled or laughed, at first. He put lotion on his body every day to keep it soft and he loved to bathe, which he did at least three times a week, which may not sound like a lot, but even at sea, when taking a shower on the foredeck was difficult and cold, Roland never missed his bath.

Our crew was assembled. Dad had two deck hands in Gibus and Roland, and I had a girl to keep me company, to protect me from my father if needed, and to help me cook. Everybody moved aboard and we gelled instantly. We laughed about the language difficulties and made do with pantomime when needed. Everybody seemed happy and easy going. It was time to begin our long journey, but first we had to say good-bye to Monica. We had a special dinner aboard—fish that Monica and I caught that afternoon—and raised our tea glasses to her for a safe journey to Canada. We said a tearful good-bye, and I hugged her tight, knowing I would miss her terribly. She flew out on Friday, September 12, 1975, and joined Mom and Karen in Windsor.

Roland Hofer

Twenty-Four

*W*e set sail for San Diego two days later under long cotton ball skies, with fat rolling seas and a warm steady wind. The night before we left Huahine, I helped Annie prepare her "15 Hungry Oarsman Stew," which we hoped would feed everyone the first two days at sea as we adjusted. Excited about making the passage now that we had interesting crew aboard, I readied the galley and the boat as instructed by Dad.

Aboard *Patricia,* Annie and I joked that we were galley slaves. In addition to our cooking responsibilities, we also had to stand two watches a day, which meant we had to be on deck paying attention to the weather, checking our heading, and reporting any changes to Dad. My watches were from 0600-0700 and from 1900-2100 Annie's immediately followed mine, from 0700-0800 and 2100-2300 Gibus and Roland were aboard for the heavy lifting, to change the sails and do anything on deck Dad required, but mostly to hold the most difficult watch: 2400 to 0600

That first evening at sea, we were all gathered around the wheel chitchatting, laughing, and telling stories—excited about our first night. Annie couldn't manage going below into the galley without getting sick so I served the special stew by myself with bread and butter. Lips smacked and nobody spoke, which I took as a compliment. Roland wore a thin white T-shirt with the Swiss flag on it. Gibus was shirtless, suntanned, and hungry as he scooped spoonful after spoonful of stew into his mouth. Annie wore a sour expression, her blonde hair blowing around her face. As the sun sank into the ocean behind us, launching us into our first full night at sea, we sailed northeast, toward the United States.

Dad finished chewing a carrot from the stew and broke the silence. He wore no shirt, and his belly hung over his blue corduroy shorts just a little. "Let's go over a few chores while we're all together." Everyone looked up from their bowls.

"The two main chores I want done daily are sweeping the main cabin carpet and cleaning the heads. Each person will take a week, starting tomorrow. Leslie, you start with a week of cleaning the head, and Gibus you start with the floor."

There were two bathrooms aboard the boat, one in the forward cabin (where we all slept), and the other near the main cabin entryway, so I had my job cut out for me. I looked at Dad with pleading eyes but he looked away. There was no arguing with the captain's edict. I knew Dad picked me first for this job to make his point about being in command, and although I felt I was carrying more than my weight with cooking three meals a day and doing two watches a day, I didn't complain. I wanted everyone to like me, so I remained silent.

The crew meeting continued as Dad explained the finer points of reading the compass, and how to signal for help if we needed it at night by ringing the bell. The tropical wind blew, pushing *Patricia* into the open ocean over large rolling waves. As I looked around to Roland, Gibus, and Annie, I felt good about being fourteen and having more sailing experience than all of them, except maybe Annie. I considered myself first mate, but was hesitant to ask Dad if he agreed with me.

"We'll be hand-steering *Patricia* tonight, because the wind vane doesn't work sailing downwind, so listen up on how to steer a course." He explained how to avoid over-steering and said the boat responded slowly so we should be patient. "Later, when the wind shifts, we will use the wind vane, which will steer for us automatically." He pointed to the metal contraption with a metal sail sticking up, mounted on the stern of the boat

Roland, Gibus, and Annie paid close attention to Dad. When he was done with his opening speech for the trip we scattered, with Annie heading to her bunk to sleep off her seasickness. I headed to the galley to make tea when Dad grabbed my arm. "We can split Annie's shift tonight while she gets over being seasick."

"Okay," I said, disappointed. I hoped Annie got over being seasick soon. I had visions of Monica dancing through my head and got a pretty sick feeling myself at the amount of work I'd have to pick up.

That night, as the wind gusted and we plowed through the darkness, a crashing noise woke me. I lay quiet for a second and then heard Dad. "Shit!"

After a minute he called, "Everyone on deck."

I climbed down from my bunk wearing my white long johns with blue clouds, dolphins, and breaking waves airbrushed all over them. Roland followed behind, shirtless in a pair of shorts. Annie groaned. We headed for the steps out of the cabin, Annie trailing behind, wearing a long Tahitian flowered shirt. On deck we found Gibus looking sheepish, a mixture of guilt and fear on his face. He sat at attention, straight and stiff at the helm, fingers wrapped tightly around the wheel, aware of the audience. It was 1:30 a.m., the wind blew a steady twelve knots, and the ocean sparkled with moonlight. I shivered and wrapped my arms around myself as we all waited for instructions from Dad.

"I don't do dat," Gibus blurted out in his broken English.

"The boat jibed," Dad said loudly, his voice, lips, and face tight.

I knew he was furious just by that look. He hid his anger from the rest of the crew by checking equipment and quietly surveying the damage.

Roland leaned over to my ear and whispered, "What's a jibe?"

Dad was half a boat length away, examining the connection between the mast and boom so I whispered to Roland, "It only happens when the boat is off course, sailing downwind. The wind catches the main sail from behind and violently slams the boom from one side of the boat to the other."

I wasn't sure if Roland understood. Annie had leaned in to hear the explanation, too. I stopped talking as Dad got to the stern. "Look at this," he said.

I walked toward the stern with Roland and Annie behind me, but with only the light of a three-quarter moon we couldn't see much.

"The wind vane is gone!" he boomed, as if we all should have known. "Ripped from the stern, and now at the bottom of the ocean, no doubt."

The contraption we had seen a few hours earlier, which would have automatically steered for us in conditions other than downwind sailing, was missing.

Gibus lowered his head to his chest. "I am sorry."

I sat down next to Gibus, who looked terrified. Roland and Annie sat, too. Knowing how my father operated, it was clear to me that we were brought on deck to learn a lesson, not because we were needed in any way.

"What happened exactly?" Dad stood in front of us all, legs straddled for balance, looking like the King of Siam with his eyes bearing down on Gibus.

"I don't know. That piece over there," he said pointing to the boom, "flew across the deck and I don't know why."

"It did that because you were off course." Dad glared at Gibus. "Remember what I told you guys earlier?"

Gibus looked down at the compass. "I steer sixty degrees. I believe I keep that amount."

Dad walked away shaking his head, stopping in front of the main cabin hatch. We all watched him stand quietly, waiting for him to speak.

The loss of the wind vane was immensely bad news for everybody aboard. Roland and Gibus probably didn't understand the magnitude of the loss, because they had no sea experience, but it meant that we'd have to hand steer the boat every hour of every day, trying not to jibe it again. Aboard *Aegir* we had an autopilot that steered twenty-four hours a day. Not having the wind vane was going to require focus and concentration to keep a constant course.

"That's all. I have nothing more to say," Dad announced unexpectedly, and then went below to the main cabin.

"It'll be okay," I said to Gibus. Roland patted Gibus on the back.

"Yeah, we'll all work together," Annie chimed in.

I went below to get a cup of tea for Gibus and found the Oarsman Stew fell over on the galley sole. Annie poked her head into the galley.

Brown gravy, chunks of meat, potatoes, and little orange carrots slid into the corners. I nearly gagged at the sight and smell. Annie actually did gag, racing up on deck to put her head over the side of the boat. I cleaned up the mess alone, while Annie went back to bed, saying she could smell the stew from her forward bunk.

I brought Gibus tea and an oatmeal cookie as he continued to steer and sat next to him for a few minutes. Roland sat on the other side of him. None of us spoke as we stared ahead to the horizon in quiet solidarity. It felt like we were a family now, having survived our first trauma and needing to support each other against our hostile parent.

The next morning on my watch, Dad sat with me and explained how we had lost the wind vane. "The mizzen lines must have wrapped around the wind vane and ripped it right off the stern."

"Wow," I managed, visualizing the jibe again. Why he was giving me all this information baffled me. I wished he would tell somebody else, but guessed he didn't have anyone to talk to, so I listened. I also wondered if this exclusive information was just a warning, since Dad was always hard to figure out.

"Gibus was lucky," Dad continued, staring out into the ocean. "Lucky he didn't do more damage to the boat. He could have cracked the boom and the mast, and ripped the sails, too, on an old boat like this."

I tried to focus on steering while he talked. Sometimes it was hard to do two things at once. The wind was steady and the wheel felt easy in my hands. It scared me to think of jibing the boat and of what Dad would do to me, since I knew he'd held his temper with Gibus.

As the sun beat down on the deck, Dad called us to join him at the helm for another lesson in steering. Clearly concerned about our abilities to perform the task, he took a deep breath and explained. "We probably have to sail more than forty days to reach San Diego, and without the wind vane each of you will get very good at steering," Dad began.

He talked to us about "feeling the boat," as he put it. At night he instructed us to pick out a star to steer by, and during the day, when the horizon looked the same in every direction, to try "feeling the boat's movement." We would all have to hone an extra sense.

On my watch that night, the bright moon lit up the ocean and sky. I focused on feeling the boat. It didn't take long before *Patricia* and I got into synch and I could steer her with my eyes closed, like riding a bike without hands. The ocean had a rhythm and I thanked her kindly for tuning me into it. I could feel her motion low in my body as I sat in the helmsman chair, grounding me to the boat and to her. She was a gracious and giving hostess. I thanked her for cradling us on her surface and I said a prayer of hope that we reach San Diego safely. The moonlight showered me with peace and understanding. I felt in synch with my world making me feel special that I was alive.

As the days ticked away and everybody got better at steering, we would become inventive in order to get a cup of tea or a cookie, or go to the bathroom while on watch. I don't remember who started it, but without Dad's knowledge, we rigged a system that allowed us to tie the wheel down for a few minutes. It worked very well and we began to rely on it more and more. Halfway into the journey Dad found the wheel tied down and me below eating bread and honey with Annie, laughing and giggling when I should have been on watch. He used me as an example and made a huge scene, yelling and screaming about my laziness and complacency. He forbade us from tying down the wheel any longer, saying we had to shout for help, or ask for relief if we needed to use the bathroom.

A few days after leaving Huahine, Dad had quietly told me I was the best helmsman aboard. "The others aren't doing so well with steering a straight course. I'm worried we won't ever get to San Diego if we keep zigzagging our way across the Pacific, wasting precious time and adding miles to our journey."

Compliments by Bjorn Johansen to me, his middle and only

daughter on this voyage, didn't come very often. I took his words to heart and swelled up considerably.

So that day, as I sat among the crew on deck listening to the rules of using our safety harnesses and doing a man overboard drill, I felt proud, self-important, and puffed up. The man overboard drill was old news for me and I felt a little cranky anyway because "Flo" had come to visit me. As Dad explained the process of the man overboard drills, I felt confident that even though I was only fourteen, I had wisdom and experience to bestow on my fellow crew members. After all, I was the captain's daughter and the second best helmsman aboard (only they didn't know it).

I interrupted my Dad. "I've done many drills with my sisters before, and during our sail to Tahiti. With this being my second ocean crossing, I can tell you that it's very important everybody work quickly."

Roland and Gibus stared down into their bowls of food. I tried to get Annie's attention to see how proud she was of me, but she fixed her gaze on the horizon.

"That'll be enough out of you, Leslie," Dad said. "I think it's time the heads get cleaned."

"What? I already cleaned them yesterday."

"You heard me. *Now!*" he boomed.

The rest of the crew looked out to sea, avoiding the entire interchange. I jumped up, partly at his booming voice and partly at my own embarrassment. I stomped across the deck and went below as Dad's eyes followed me. I glanced sideways at him and saw the scowl on his face. I felt six years old and I fumed, grunting the time away scrubbing the toilets, the sinks, and the floors—the most disgusting job aboard the boat, especially with three men aboard. I didn't think I could ever show my face on deck again.

Annie and I took our first salt water shower after four days at sea, together on the foredeck topless, with just our bathing suit bottoms on. Nobody was on deck when we started and I felt comfortable following Annie's lead being topless, but of course by the time we were done Dad was on deck taking pictures of us. Annie giggled and laughed while Dad took the pictures, just like Monica, Karen, and I had done on *Aegir*, but she looked extremely uncomfortable. I explained later what we had endured when Dad took our pictures every time we showered. Annie rolled her eyes at me, "Well, I might just tell him to stop it next time."

I couldn't wait until next time. I wanted Annie to tell him off. I made light of the whole thing, not wanting to get into the weirdness, the abuse, and my fear of Dad. I didn't want this trip with Annie to be infected with those stories so I just laughed it off.

About a week into the trip navigation classes began for Roland, Gibus, and Annie—on deck each day at 1000.—just like they had for Monica, Karen, and me. Roland was especially anxious to learn how to use a sextant to take a noon shot of the sun. I sat through classes too, even though I knew everything Dad was teaching and felt a little feisty about it. Just like with the man overboard drills, I wanted Annie, Roland, and Gibus to know how much I knew.

"You should have seen me when I started navigating," I began, my head held high and my chest out just a little. "My shots were so bad, we ended up in Texas one time. But I'm an expert now."

"Leslie, humility is the mother of all virtues," Dad said.

"Whatever that means." I rolled my eyes, "Tell them how close my shots are to yours when we plot them. Go ahead, Dad, tell them!"

"I think the heads need another cleaning."

"No way!" I ran into the galley, angry at him for not supporting me.

I knew I was a good navigator. Dad just wouldn't admit it to the rest of the crew. Sitting in the galley, I dreamed of the day Dad would point to me and publicly announce to anybody who would listen, "Yes, Leslie's an expert. Her shots are so good I would use them for my own." But he never did that, and my heart was crushed that he wasn't proud of me.

There were days when Annie and I worked together on our shots and plotting, which made it fun for me. There were also days when Dad got mad at me when I made a little mistake, or because I forgot to add and subtract in sixties instead of one hundreds. As punishment he made me figure out every noon shot he had taken since we left Huahine, just to get me back in the habit of adding and subtracting in sixties. I began to hate him again.

Early in the lessons of navigation on deck each day, Roland misread my arrogance as ignorance, or something was lost in translation, because he told me in his superior voice, "Greenwich Mean Time is where everybody in the world measures time from. It's located in Greenwich, England."

I rolled my eyes, knowing this already from the lectures I endured from my father a long time ago. I politely replied that I already knew where G.M.T. was located, but then he started explaining where Africa was located on the map—maybe because I was fourteen and a girl. Why did everybody want to lecture me? Didn't they know I already knew everything about sailing?

The days were long and hot, bright, and sunny. The calm ocean reflected the sun like a mirror, making it hard to see the water without squinting. After a few days at sea, we hit a gale, with rain and winds gusting up to fifty knots. It was our first storm. Dad, Roland, and Gibus deep-reefed the main, took down the mizzen completely, and put up the storm jib. And still we moved through the water at a nice clip of four—six knots. The watch schedule changed during the first storm so that none of us had to be on deck steering for more than one hour in the rain. The storm came from the north, which made us bundle up like we were Alaskan. As soon as the front passed though, the heat returned and we were in our bikinis during the day again. But at night, the winds stayed cold and we continued to dress warmly as we sailed into the Northern Hemisphere.

During the one-day storm, Dad lost his brown leather hat, which he called his "Five-cent Mexican hat." He'd had that floppy hat since we lived on the ranch and he was heartbroken over losing it. It fell into the "drink" he said, referring to the ocean. "I watched it float away," he said. "I was frozen and unable to think of what to do next. And then it sunk."

"Why didn't you call a man overboard drill to test our ability to retrieve something quickly?" I asked.

"I didn't think of it," he said.

I wasn't sure if somebody had stolen my father and replaced him with a kindly twin, that comment was completely out of character for him. From then on he wore a red or blue bandana knotted at the four corners. It took on the shape of his head, hanging down toward his ears. It made him look funny, like a clown, but it did the job of keeping his bald head protected.

Annie and I worked together cooking three meals a day, taking turns being the lead cook. The backup cook did side dishes and served the meals and drinks. We did the dishes together. We made pancakes and bacon for breakfast, tuna sandwiches for lunch, and some kind of fish or meat with potatoes for dinner. We began making bread every day, putting it in a pot on deck with a damp towel over it so the sun would coax it to rise.

We fell into a routine. After breakfast was cleaned up we would either play the guitar, write, read, or paint. Annie was reading *One Flew Over the Cuckoo's Nest,* about a man who is admitted to an insane asylum. I was reading *The Girls At Huntington House* by Blossom Elfman, about unwed eighteen-year-old mothers living in a house together. My book was a real eye-opener, educating me about the "real" world. I continued reading my racy choices, and Dad continued to be totally unaware of what I was being exposed to. I couldn't wait to grow up and leave home. Adulthood sounded like great fun—having the freedom to go anywhere I chose, eat in any restaurant I wanted, stay out late with a handsome man who adored me. I felt confident the books were giving me the "inside scoop," so I would be wise and not make the same mistakes as the women I was reading about.

Annie and I spent hours and hours writing in our diaries. Annie wrote exciting, thought-provoking stories she shared with me.

"We are fellow galley-slaves and scurvy knaves," Annie said one morning. Her thin, freckled face always had a smile for me. I didn't know what she meant, but I was glad to be anything with Annie! She was so creative and talented. I looked up to her and was grateful to have a mentor and older sister.

One day as we sat alone in the galley Annie said, "Why don't you wear a bra? You really should. You're beginning to sag."

Embarrassed, I decided to trust her and told her the whole bra story. I had never said anything about my struggles out loud, and it felt strange to summarize my traumas. When I was finished telling her about Raine and me stealing the bra, hiding it, and then having to leave it behind, she watched me intently, hanging on every word.

"He's always been sort of weird about raising my sisters and me as Europeans instead of Americans," I twisted my fingers together under the table. "Being Norwegian is better than being American, according to him. That's why I don't wear a bra or shave my legs, or under my underarms either. I hope it doesn't gross you out."

"Are you kidding? I might just join you, as proof that I'm on your side. That way your father can have two hairy European women aboard!" If she was disturbed by anything I said, she didn't show it.

We both laughed. Sweet and supportive during the entire story, she hugged me when I finished and said in a serious tone, "You'll be out on your own soon, and then nobody will be able to tell you what to wear or not wear."

It felt good to share some of my secrets with Annie. I silently promised myself I'd get a bra after I got back to California, even if I had to steal another one.

Ten days into the trip, on the autumnal equinox, September 23, 1975, we passed over the equator into the Northern Hemisphere at the same time the sun passed over the equator into the Southern Hemisphere. We were going north and the sun was going south, exactly at the equator. There are probably only a handful of people who have ever been on the equator at sea on an autumnal equinox. Nothing overtly happens, of course, and it was probably only cool because Dad pointed out to us the concept of watching the sun pass directly overhead, headed in the opposite direction.

We had very little wind at the equator, and the sun pounded down on us, so we stopped for a few hours, swam, and did some laundry. I sat near the helm when Dad announced swim time and I watched Roland prepare himself. He had a particular procedure for bathing and hygiene and it fascinated me. He took his nicely folded towel, body lotion, and toothbrush on deck and then brushed his teeth using red and white striped Swiss toothpaste that, if I stood close enough, smelled minty and fresh. He brushed his teeth for many more minutes than I ever brushed my teeth, moving up and down rhythmically and consistently, forward to back, before he spat into the sea—downwind of the boat of course, so the spit floated away.

Gibus was earthier than Roland and just stripped down and jumped in, as did Dad. I couldn't calmly watch the boys getting naked so I went below into the galley where I felt safest and peeked out the porthole at Gibus and Roland. I wondered about Gibus, since at eighteen he was closest to me in age. I didn't want to see Roland naked because he was too old and not my type at all. I liked scruffier boys than Roland, and although Gibus was scruffier, he wasn't the "right kind" of scruffy. He thought highly of himself and had an attitude about it.

I finally got to see that Dad was right about the Europeans not caring if they're naked or not. Dad, Gibus, and Roland lathered up and dunked in one more time and then got out naked, scrubbed their underwear and hung it on the lifeline to dry.

Annie came down into the galley and caught me peeking out. "I don't want to swim naked," I said.

"Me neither, so let's get our suits on. It's hot down here."

I loved Annie and felt safe with her. She understood me without my having to explain myself.

When we came up on deck, the sun was scorching. The ocean was navy-colored, almost black, with bolts of sunlight disappearing into the depths. Dad, Roland, and Gibus sat around various places on the boat, scrubbing their laundry. Annie and I held hands and jumped from the main cabin top into the water, doing a cannon ball together. The water was refreshing and clear but a little cold at first.

The strong current forced us to hang on to a rope Dad threw overboard. I climbed out and lathered up, then dove from the bowsprit. I had seen Gibus do it and wanted to try. The netting under the long wooden pole forced us to climb out to the very end to jump. It made my heart pound to dive off the end of the bowsprit.

Annie and I did our laundry and hung our underwear in the galley to dry so "the boys" wouldn't see them. That afternoon, with our underwear hanging all around us, Annie and I made watercolor certificates for everybody, as a token for crossing the equator. I water-colored all the pages and Annie used a special calligraphy pen and ink and wrote in fancy letters on the certificates a language she made up on the spot.

This artistic certificate is issued to galley slave and scurvy ney,

Nesles Ann Johansen

On this seemingly endless voyage from Huahine to San Diego she successfully ate herself across the equator on the Mighty Bug-eyed Ketch, Yacht Patricia. Longitude W. 146° 33'

September 23, 1975 1200 hours

Captain: Bjørn
1st Mate: Leslie
2nd Mate: Annie
3rd Mate: Roland
4th Mate: Gibus

Signed,

Annie
(co-galley slave)

The day had been perfect, although we weren't making any headway toward San Diego. Dad let us languish in the heat and stillness of the doldrums until evening when he turned on the "iron wind," and after finishing his navigation, went to bed.

It was my watch and I steered as Annie strummed the guitar. The light wind and motor made it easy to steer as the stars lit our way. Gibus and Roland appeared on deck together around nine o'clock, as if in cahoots. They made their way back to the helm. Gibus smirked at us, holding up a joint, and uttered the words "It *could* be good."

Gibus used that phrase about everything he had encountered in the past week, from tea to stew to soap to a reefed main sail. It was his go-to English phrase, and his using it twenty times a day drove me crazy.

When he brought out the joint, I saw a new side of Gibus, which made me wonder if he was cool and not such a French brat after all. Every time I thought I had decided about him, I began to wonder again. Was it the French in him, or the surfer in him that intrigued me? As Gibus lit the joint and handed it to Annie, Roland eyed me like an older brother wanting to protect his younger sister.

I took the joint from Annie. Roland raised his eyebrows at me when I lit it with expert dexterity.

"Here, take it Roland, it's your turn," I said, after taking a big hit. I handed him the joint and burst out laughing. With his mouth hanging slightly open, Roland took the joint. I punched his arm. "Mellow out, would you?" I said. He shook his head with a grin on his face, looked away, and took a hit.

"This is my first time sailing this many days across an ocean. I miss the good food." Gibus said.

"Hey! What do you mean?" Annie said, laughing. "You don't like our food?"

Gibus took the joint from Annie, trying to avoid her eyes. "No. I like the food of my country more than I like the food of the boat."

"Well, I'm going down to get those chocolate chip cookies we baked today, and there'll be none for you, Gibus," I said.

"Ah, come on, I just mean ... " He stopped talking and then after a while said, "It *could* be good," and we all laughed. Roland and I went below and made hot tea. We sat under the stars eating chocolate chip cookies and drinking tea, mesmerized into silent meditation. I was higher than I'd ever been, fascinated with the sparkling water, the night sky, and the sound of water rushing past the boat.

"I think I'm too high to steer," Annie announced.

Nobody responded.

She continued, "Hey you guys, we're shell backs now and able to have our left ear pierced to prove it to the land lubbers of the world."

Gibus looked intrigued, but Roland shook his head no. "I already have both of my ears pierced, so that's out for me."

The jeweled sky beckoned and held my attention more and more as Roland, Gibus, and I sat for hours together through Annie's and then Gibus's watch. So high I knew I couldn't coordinate my movements enough to put a sail up, or steer the boat, I just let myself sit. I held the guitar, feeling it was part of my body, as I sat cross-legged, unable to move.

That Tahitian pot was strong.

Twenty-Five

The orange and red glow of another sunset filled the sky as I steered on my evening watch. The waves built into rollers and were spaced far apart. White caps reflected the auburn sun, making the ocean look like it had whipped cream tips.

The horizon ahead darkened, blurring the horizon. I stared off, alone on deck, the crew all below eating, resting, or writing letters. Sunset was my favorite time of day, unless the sun was rising, then sunrise was my favorite time of day. I was assigned both the sunrise and sunset watches, but I never thought to thank my Dad for that. The swells gathered strength in the fading light while the warm wind, with a hint of chill, blew fifteen knots. *Patricia* moved along, pushing the water aside on an imaginary line in my head as I attempted to steer a perfect course to my beloved California. My mind wandered to John—I idolized him in my diary and in private, but I never spoke about him, not even to Annie.

I imagined John pining away for me in Oceanside as I pined away for him at sea. I let myself fantasize that he'd been loyal to me even though he would have graduated from eighth grade by now, and started Oceanside High without me, and even though we had not exchanged one letter in the nine months I'd been gone.

My trance was broken as Dad's bald head appeared out of the galley hatch. He ascended onto the deck and sat next to me. He handed me a peanut butter cookie and a cup of tea. "Thank you," I murmured, trying to guess the reason for his visit.

I spent most days avoiding my father, choosing to be with Annie. Alone with him on deck or in the galley, he might praise my advancing sailing, navigating, and steering skills. But in front of Roland, Gibus, and Annie, he put me down, treated me like a child, and embarrassed me. I yearned to be worthy of his praise in front of the crew. Roland and Gibus knew nothing of sailing before this journey, but they seemed to have my Dad's approval and admiration in all things. When they did something wrong, he seemed to let it slide. The idea of being held back because I was a daughter instead of a son tapped into a well of resentment from long ago. We sat quietly for a few minutes in the final glow of the setting sun. I took a bite of my cookie, waiting for him to speak.

"I've taken two more deliveries after this one, a boat named *Solar Wind* from Hawaii and *Impossible Dream* from Tahiti. After that I think I'll have enough money saved to continue on with our voyage."

Dad was making a dollar a mile to sail *Patricia* back the four thousand miles to San Diego. I wasn't ready to think of leaving California and going on another delivery before I had even returned. I wanted to go to an Oceanside High School football game and kiss John De La Cruz again. And yet, I also knew it wasn't likely that Monica, Karen, and I would be going back to Oceanside. And I certainly didn't want to live with Mom while Dad traveled the world delivering boats. I had to admit that Dad had been pretty nice to me for months, not stalking me or making me uncomfortable. I didn't get that creepy feeling when he looked at me anymore. He had taken a big step back and I was grateful. I could relax and be myself—whoever that was at age fourteen. All I knew was that I wasn't afraid all the time. So sailing with him, as long as we had other crew aboard, sounded better than going to school in wintry Windsor.

Confused, I steered the boat a little too hard to port. I quickly spun the wheel to starboard to compensate, admonishing myself for steering like a novice with Dad right next to me.

"Do you need crew for the Hawaii trip?" I asked, hoping he wouldn't notice the spinning wheel.

"Sure do, and I'd love to have you, too," Dad said. "Stop letting the boat swerve so far off course. Feel the motion of the boat. I know you can do better."

It was just like him to scold me after saying something nice. I shrunk, also knowing I could do better. I'd learned to admonish myself alongside him. I made a small adjustment to the wheel and the boat responded nicely.

"Better," he said.

"Can I bring Raine or Katie on the Hawaii trip?"

"Yes, I think that can be arranged," he said with a smile. "We can even see the islands while we're there, and pick up some more crew."

He knew how to suck me in with his charms and make me feel important and needed when he wanted something. And I knew, though he never said as much, that he relied on me at sea. The bond between us had strengthened in a positive way for the first time in my life.

"You're a good helmsman, Leslie. Keep up the good work." He brushed his hand across my cheek like he'd done since I was a little girl, smiled at me kindly, and went below.

When he closed the galley hatch the yellow light from below disappeared. Darkness surrounded the boat again. The sound of whales breaching the surface of the water made me jump. Sitting straight up, I saw a pod of dolphins jumping off in the distance. We sailed on, and they stayed in the same spot.

A few minutes later, by the green glow of the compass light, I saw Annie, guitar in hand, climbing out of the main cabin to join me on deck.

"Have you been practicing our song?" she chirped, "Do you know the words yet?"

Annie had a way of "checking" on me after Dad and I spent time alone. She'd told me she felt the tension between us, and I adored her for feeling protective of me.

"I've practiced a little, but I'm probably not good enough yet."

A few days earlier she had played the Bobby Goldsboro song, "Leaving a Straight Life Behind," and then wrote the words and chords in my diary so I could learn them. I focused on steering, staring out at the horizon as she played and sang. I joined in singing the melody while she harmonized. When the song was over, I laughed a little at how good we sounded.

"That was fun! But I'm freezing. I'll be up for my watch in an hour, okay?" Annie said. She turned and looked at me with a serious face, "Is everything okay after your talk with your dad?"

"Yes. I'm fine." I smiled at her.

The hatch closed, leaving me alone again. The world of stars and ocean took over my heart and soul. The comforting sound of the ocean sloshing against the hull filled my ears as the boat pushed forward. I was back with an old and cherished friend and I enjoyed my time alone on deck. I felt love and devotion for the ocean, seeing her as a confidante and protector. I had shared my heart and soul with her last time I was at sea, throwing letters of distress in bottles to her in my desperation. I didn't feel that way this time, but instead felt gratitude for her vastness and beauty.

The black night was moonless, making the stars pop out and appear unusually close. Melancholy gradually descended on me. I missed singing with Monica. I wondered how Karen was recovering from her injuries. My sisters were worlds away from me, living in the city with buildings and cars, getting ready to celebrate Canadian Thanksgiving. I pushed the sadness away—I was headed toward them.

The melancholy stayed with me through the night. On my morning watch the next day, the rising sun looked like a yellow tulip bulb ready to bloom. I was cuddled up with my blanket and socks on, sipping my tea, leaning back in the chair steering the boat with my feet. The wind died down, it got very calm, peaceful, and quiet, the water still and flat.

We had picked up a hitchhiker ten days previous when a huge white albatross landed on the boat, claiming *Patricia* as his new home. I had wrangled with words, brainstormed with Annie and meditated on the alliteration I was aiming for. Finally coming up with an appropriate phrase for our feathery friend, I wrote in my diary: "A fat, fartin' frigate flew freely by to freedom's festivities."

The albatross came and went each day to someplace we couldn't see. We expected him to leave us for good every day, but each morning I found him sleeping, perched on the wooden railing that surrounded the stern. After a few days we named him Albert, which Gibus and Roland pronounced with a French accent, "Alberrrr," making it sound exotic. Alberrrr's wingspan was breathtakingly long and sleek—like a seagull but ten times the size. His bright orange beak stuck out of his white face. Annie and I remembered the story of *Jonathon Livingston Seagull*, and imagined Alberrrr in the storyline. He appeared wise and confident as he sat quietly on the stern.

That particular morning I turned around to find him sitting with one eye open and one closed. I said, "Good-morning, Alberrrr." He closed both eyes and I returned to steering *Patricia*. I looked over the bow and saw a black cloud in the distance—a squall, very defined in shape, just off our port side. I could tell it was raining because it was dark from the bottom of the clouds to the ocean with no light behind it.

About ten minutes later, the rain started on our bow and I watched, fascinated, as the boat moved forward into the squall and the rain fell on deck until it got to the steering wheel, and then it stopped. The squall had moved to the side of us just in time for me to miss getting soaked. I considered it my daily miracle. Annie came back up on deck just then and together we saw the most vibrant rainbow I'd ever witnessed. It started in the ocean, went high in the sky in front of us, and ended back in the ocean, a complete arc. Annie and I laughed that the ocean itself was the pot of gold, a worthy thought to begin the day with.

The days ran together so similarly it was hard to distinguish one from another. One afternoon at the galley table, Annie said, "Let's make the popcorn now, and then bake something!" Her freckled face was animated, her brown eyes wide.

We had gotten in the habit of making popcorn in the afternoon for the night watches. Everyone loved it—that morning at breakfast Roland, who always had the last watch of the night, requested his own bag because we were all eating too much and he was only getting a few corns and some old maids.

As we began to collect the ingredients, Annie dropped the big bottle of oil on the galley floor and most of it glugged out before we could grab it. We watched the oil seep into all the crevices and down into the bilge. The remainder of the oil laid slick on the floor.

With bright eyes and a grin Annie said, "This floor has needed a good scrubbing for some time now."

"Ah, come on! I don't want to clean the floor now! You do it and I'll watch."

"Not a chance, Nearly Normal. Get your butt down here on the sole and let's get to scrubbing."

"Nearly Normal?"

"That's your new name. I decided a few days ago."

The only nickname I'd ever had was Lezzie, which I hated, of course. But I liked Nearly Normal, because it suited me. It felt good to be unique.

We boiled up some water and got down on our hands and knees and scrubbed the galley sole, moisturizing our legs in the oil as we slid from side to side singing "Surfin' USA."

When we were finished we sat at the table and ate the shortening cookies we'd baked. We came up with nicknames for everybody else while munching cookies. She would be Almost Alright Annie; Dad would be the Voice of America (of course); Gibus had already been nicknamed Quick Draw McGraw (QDM for short) because he was so slow at doing everything. We never came up with a fitting name for Roland, although we tried Ravenous Roland, Random Roland, and Reliable Roland. But none of them felt like the perfect fit, and so none of them stuck.

A constant source of entertainment was our shortwave radio. Sitting below in the main cabin, near the navigation station, we listened to the Japanese fishing boats talk to each other while figuring out our navigation shots. Of course we couldn't understand anything they said, but it reminded us there were other people in the world. I heard two Germans one day and called Roland to translate, excited and thinking he would be excited as well. But he was irritated with me for waking him up and stomped back to bed.

Dad heard news items every so often, and one day heard that Patty Hearst had been released from her captors, which fascinated him and Annie. I didn't know who she was, and wasn't very interested even after they explained. Another day we picked up a Mexican radio station playing music and I danced to the mariachi music while everybody laughed at me.

Dad had been communicating with Sy from *Resolve* on the shortwave every afternoon for the first two weeks we were at sea. He sent our coordinates and would check in to see if Sy had heard of any bad weather coming our way. The Carkhuffs were back in Huahine, but we could still talk to them after seventeen days of sailing. Sy's voice became more and more muffled as the weeks ticked on, however, until one day we couldn't raise him on the radio anymore. Dad continued to send our coordinates every day anyway, believing that Sy could hear us and we just couldn't hear him.

After twenty days at sea, halfway to San Diego, while Dad and I sat alone in the main cabin listening to the weather report, the radio began smoking and then caught fire. Only a small flame or two appeared and Dad quickly extinguished it with his blue bandana. After the radio had cooled off, he turned it on. I kneeled on the couch, looking over the edge of the navigation table, watching intently as he fiddled with our only source of long-range communication.

"It's a miracle if it even powers up," Dad whispered under his breath. He wore his beige cotton Mexican tunic and ratty old blue corduroy shorts, and one leg bounced up and down nervously. His burnt blue bandana lay on the navigation table.

Static and white noise spewed out as Dad retuned the dials to the weather report on the National Weather Channel. Dad's eyes got big and he smiled.

"Hallelujah, I'm a believer!" Dad sang out as he raised his arms in the air. "We must be living right. I can't believe we're picking up the weather!"

After a few more tests, his good mood vanished when he discovered we could not send messages, only receive them. He frowned, "Let's hope we don't need to send a distress signal."

"Why would we need to do that?" I asked.

He pursed his lips and stared off. I could almost hear the wheels turning as he ran through the scenarios. Then he said quietly, "No need to alarm everybody. Let's keep this quiet for now."

"At least we still get the weather reports," I said, hoping he'd be happy again.

"Yes, I suppose we should be happy about that."

But Dad didn't look happy. We were more alone than ever in the middle of the Pacific Ocean. He spent the next few hours fiddling with the radio, trying fruitlessly to fix it.

After twenty-five days at sea, someone flipped the month to October (four days late) on a calendar that hung in the main cabin and began X-ing off days like we were prisoners. I had just finished reading *Bonjour Tristesse,* written by a French girl not much older than me named Francoise Sagan. It was a hauntingly sad story about a young girl and her father's various mistresses. The mother is dead and unable to guide the young girl. It made me sad, which is how the main character felt and why the book title translates to "Hello Sadness." I tried to imagine writing a book at seventeen but couldn't. Francoise had to be an amazing girl. At dinner that night we discussed the books we were reading. Roland told me he had read *Bonjour Tristesse* in German and Gibus said he had read it in French which made me feel closer to them somehow and excited that we all read it in different languages. Sometimes I was a real dork.

Annie was hot to read *Jaws,* though I warned her against the dreams she would have, like Karen did, of giant sharks jumping on deck and eating her. She laughed and said I had a vivid imagination. I took *A Separate Reality* by Carlos Castaneda since Annie had just finished it. She wished me good luck with it, saying it was "difficult and very existential." I had no idea what that meant and couldn't wait to start the book. I found it almost too difficult to read. It made my brain hurt to follow Don Juan's way of thinking. I could only read the book in small doses and then I'd have to think about what I read for a while. In between doses I buried myself in *One Flew Over the Cuckoo's Nest.* I read every moment I wasn't cooking or steering *Patricia.* The fun and frivolity of the early weeks had worn off and everybody kept to themselves, reading and sleeping, talking only when necessary: "Pass the salt," or "Wake up, it's your watch."

In between navigation, cooking, and watches, I spent long

stretches alone on the netting under the bowsprit. I would lie on my stomach over the sea and stare at the water, especially before my sunset watch with a blanket, curled up cozy. Just four or five feet above the water, I was mesmerized by how the boat carved through the water, pushing aside the sea as she made headway. The water calmed, soothed, and cleared my mind. Sometimes I laid on my back in the netting, staring into the limitless starry sky and daydreaming about Friday night high school football games, beach parties, surfing with my friends, or traffic jams on the 5 freeway. I couldn't imagine being able to see a person to my right and then another to my left. Being in such close proximity to so many human beings seemed a galaxy away and I yearned for it.

There were fewer and fewer niceties as the days ticked away. People's real feelings about things began to surface. Food became an issue as Annie and I sunk into a self-imposed eating frenzy where we ate everything without reason or restraint, partly for fun and partly from boredom.

More than once we ate so many thick slices of just-baked bread with butter and honey that there was none to give the crew at dinner. One time we made a lemon cake and then sat in the galley and ate the entire warm tangy sweet thing ourselves. It tasted superb going down, "but after a while it catches up to ya," Annie roared, and we grabbed our aching stomachs.

Though neither one of us were hungry, we'd make fudge and then eat it all. It seemed we would kill ourselves. When I was sure I couldn't eat anything else, I'd stuff another piece of fudge or cookie down and then roll on my side, aching, near vomiting. It was a downward spiral, brought on by boredom and an insanely matched love for baked goods, and it seemed impossible to get a handle on it. We each gained at least ten pounds though neither of us cared.

The boys claimed we ate too much between meals and they didn't get their share of the bakery items, which was true. Tensions began rising. One night Roland and Gibus refused to eat our spaghetti dinner—throwing it overboard in protest and demanding another dinner. Roland went on and on about how bad the food was. We defended our basic culinary skills and took offense to being challenged in the galley by a couple of European boys. As far as the spaghetti went, we knew it tasted bland, but it wasn't rancid or anything. This was the second night in a row we'd served it but that was due mainly to the fact that Annie and I had been busy eating ourselves sick with baked goods all afternoon. Roland was a skinny guy and seemed to be getting skinnier as the days ticked on. His complaints about the food became more vocal. "I am allergic to your tuna salad sandwiches," he said, "and your cornbread is like thick paper (he meant cardboard, I'm sure), and your oatmeal makes me sick at my stomach."

What could we say? Nothing! So we ignored them.

Like any family forced to spend too much time together, we needed our parent to help us work it out. Dad stepped in and brokered a deal between our two camps in order for the yelling at dinnertime to stop.

"Get along and figure it out," Dad yelled at all four of us.

Consumed with fixing the radio, performing some engine maintenance, or doing his daily navigation, Dad was distracted and tuned out until the yelling got too loud. He had never been picky about food, always content with meat and potatoes, like his mother used to make in Norway. Also, not having super delicious and appetizing food didn't bother him much as he wanted to lose a few pounds before reaching California and seeing his lovely Shirley.

The real fireworks happened one night when Annie and I weren't hungry at all. We'd cooked a few cans of meat called "Corned Meat Loaf," which we found on the boat from the previous crew. We didn't know what it was or how to serve it, so we just heated it up and served it with potatoes. It smelled awful, and tasted awful too. Roland and QDM threw it overboard.

"That meat requires a sauce on it," said QDM. "In France we eat everything with sauce."

Roland agreed. "We need some butter and garlic, cream and cheese to make a sauce. In Switzerland I eat three courses, and the main course comes with a beautiful sauce, but with American cooking the only sauce is ketchup to smother the taste."

QDM demanded to cook and we reluctantly agreed. Giving up control of the galley meant we wouldn't be able to bake and eat what we wanted. Maybe that was a good thing, though, since Annie and I didn't seem able to control ourselves. On one hand I loved the idea of the free time, but on the other I felt insulted that the crew hated our cooking so much. It was embarrassing.

On the first night QDM cooked, I purposely waited until he had made dinner to tell him that the cook has to clean up, too. I actually think he expected Annie and me to clean up after him. When we told him to forget it, Roland offered to help him. The two of them cleaned the galley as it had never been cleaned before.

The next morning as Annie and I sat in the galley alone, looking around at the sparkling counters and cabinets and table and cushions, Annie said, "I hate those boys."

"I know! I hate them too."

QDM continued to cook dinner sometimes, and Roland jumped in as well and they were actually good. Sometimes QDM made a sauce with the canned Cheese Whiz and some spices we had aboard. We never threw any of QDM's meals overboard. I had to admit he used the spices better than Annie and I did. He and Roland tried to show us how to use the spices and sauces, but we weren't interested in learning. Annie and I had a bit of an attitude—we just wanted to make dinner, not "create" it. We would have rather baked than cook with spices for those ungrateful French/German scallywags.

Annie and I tried to make more of an effort to serve food that was appetizing. One dish consisted of what Annie called "flied lice," which was rice smothered in butter and salt, corned beef hash, onions, mushrooms, and green beans.

"I'm getting tired of their persnickety European taste buds," Annie said one evening as we did the dishes after Roland and Gibus threw another dinner overboard. I began to hate those European boys for causing so much trouble in the galley. "We're not French chefs, you know," I yelled one night when they threw our dinner over the side again. "I'm fourteen and Annie is twenty. So leave us alone."

Twenty-Six

The wind blew ever so lightly from the stern. We had been motoring on the "iron wind" for five days and nights. I wanted to scream from all the vibrating and shaking. The rattling of the cabinet doors, the squeaking hatch cover, the clinking dishes, and the clattering of the very wood holding the boat's old hull together went on ceaselessly. The engine lay between the main and aft cabins, infecting both spaces with the noise and smell of oil and machines. The insulation was completely gone, if the *Patricia* ever had any to start with. Everyone scowled and complained and was generally in a foul and impatient mood.

Annie felt seasick again and I seemed on the verge of being seasick, too, with a tinny taste in my mouth all the time. The only time I'd been seasick was the day we lost *Aegir's* mast off the coast of Newport Beach, when I was thirteen. It was a point of pride for me that I'd only been seasick once.

The engine noise was deafening. Shouting gave us all headaches and sore throats.

Eventually, after the first or second day of motoring, we just pointed. If we needed to speak we made the effort to get close to each other's ears to talk. It was much more humane.

On the fifth day of motoring, Dad rang the bell and called a general crew meeting. Roland was already sitting next to Dad when Annie and I came up from the galley. Gibus, as always, was nowhere to be found.

"Leslie, get him," Dad said.

I went below and found Gibus sleeping. I shook him.

"Crew meeting now, on deck," I shouted.

Gibus stumbled up the stairs a few minutes later, half asleep, and found a seat near Dad on the deck, leaning his nonchalant head against the cabin.

"Our progress is very slow. We only made thirty miles yesterday, which is partly due to the lack of wind, but mostly due to the horrible job everyone is doing steering. If I could fire you all, I would."

I looked around, sure Dad didn't mean to include me in his rebuke.

A blank expression from Roland seemed like he didn't think the problem was with him.

Annie squirmed a little next to me, and Gibus's eyes were slits in the sunlight.

"I will work with each of you again on steering. We only have another ten days or so until we reach California. We all need to focus on steering a straight course."

Annie spoke hesitantly. "That's good. I don't think I'm doing such a good job." Dad smiled at her, clearly glad she recognized the need for a refresher.

He continued. "On top of that, fuel is getting low and we won't be able to motor forever. If we don't get some wind soon, I'll have to shut down the engine. We need to save fuel for emergencies, so pray for wind, people! Pray every moment of every day." His serious eyes travelled from one person to the next.

"It's a good idea," Roland said. "I will begin my prayers immediately."

Gibus nodded his agreement, and Annie put her index finger in the air and chimed in, "Yes, prayers for the wind are coming up."

My mouth hung open slightly, as I listened to Dad.

"That's all for now. I'll see you all on your watches today to work on steering."

Roland got up and left. Gibus followed. Annie went back down into the galley and I went to the bow.

I was shocked—I couldn't believe Dad had asked for prayers. It was so out of character for him. He didn't believe in prayers, or in God for that matter. He prided himself on being an atheist. I shuddered a little inside, feeling the seriousness of our situation.

My religious training was nonexistent. Mom gladly left the Catholic Church when she married Dad. I was baptized Catholic, and I remembered being little and wearing fancy dresses with ruffled bobby socks and shiny black-heeled shoes to church on Easter and Christmas with Grandma. Except for dressing up, I didn't like going to church, always feeling stifled and uncomfortable in the hard seats during long sermons. As I grew, my church became the sixty-three acre ranch in Paradise and the Pacific Ocean.

But being stuck at sea with no wind for nearly a week was torture, so I began to pray to the heavens for wind, entreating the ocean to do her part, too.

Reading on the bowsprit later that day, I looked up and saw a black bulge on the horizon. I crawled out of the netting and yelled to Annie, who was lying on the main cabin reading.

"A ship! Look! A big ship!"

We waved like crazy. I yelled at the top of my lungs, "Bring us cheesecake!"

Annie yelled, "Do you have any ice cream or salad?"

The tanker, as if he could hear us, blew a deep belching horn three times, which made us squeal, jump, and wave harder. At the wheel, Gibus smiled and just shook his head at us. Roland and Dad came up on deck.

"What's all the screaming about?" Dad said irritated.

"Look! A ship!" I pointed to the horizon.

"Leslie, get a hold of yourself. It's a ship. So what?"

"Come on, Dad, you're not excited to see another boat after thirty-two days at sea?"

"Ugh, not really. I'd be happy to see the coast of California," he said, and went back below deck.

Like hearing voices and music on the radio, seeing that freighter on the desolate waterway lifted my spirits and I watched until it disappeared over the horizon.

An hour later, oodles of trash floated by—plastic milk jugs, a two-by-four piece of wood, Styrofoam cups, and pages of writing like from a diary.

"Dad! Come up on deck. Look at all this trash!" I hollered.

He came up huffing and puffing, but then seemed genuinely interested in the trash. "This *is* unusual. I hope a boat hasn't met an ill fate ahead of us."

On our sixth day with no apparent wind, and our first full day praying, the torture continued. Body odor in the bunk area got increasingly worse. My pillow, sleeping bag, and sheet were moist and musty. At first I tried to ignore it. But the smell became so overpowering nobody wanted to be below deck.

"We must bathe today," the Voice of America announced. We shut off the engine, lathered up, and braved the frigid water. Each of us screamed a little, including Dad, who yelled, "Uff-da!" when he landed in the water. The dark, unwelcoming water must have been sixty degrees. Nobody lingered to swim like we had at the equator. Each of us rushed to the swim steps and hauled our freezing selves out. But those few minutes of precious quiet without the engine droning on were welcomed, even as we hopped around the deck, trying to dry off and get warm. After thirty minutes, Dad started up the stinkpot again and we pushed forward to California.

Bathing improved the smell below decks slightly, but the dirty, wet clothes and mildewed bedding overpowered any positive change brought on by our better hygiene. Nobody but Roland attempted laundry during the overcast day because we were unsure if anything would dry by bedtime.

I'd have to sleep with the smell of diesel and dirty clothes again. Before my watch ended, I looked out over the ocean, calm and serene, and earnestly entreated the breeze to return, trying to channel and visualize the boat sailing and all the natural elements working together in peace and harmony.

Hallelujah! As the sun went down on our seventh day of motoring—and our second day of praying—the wind started picking up, slowly at first. We put up all the sails and turned off the awful engine.

We hadn't seen the sun in a few days, but nobody complained because *we were sailing!* The wind blew from the north and the cold began to sink in. Hot tea helped, but only for a short time. It felt like mid-December with the nights becoming unbearably frigid. None of us had enough warm clothes, so everyone but Roland borrowed and shared dirty clothes during watches at night. Annie borrowed my ski jacket every night, in addition to bringing her blankets and sleeping bag on deck. She would then pass the jacket to Gibus.

The diesel odor disappeared from the cabin, which only made the dampness and mildew smell in the main cabin more obvious. If it hadn't been so cold and wet on deck overnight, I'd have slept up there to avoid the stench from below, but as it was, I could only put off going below until I absolutely couldn't keep my eyes open any longer.

October 16, 1975. From my diary:

"Wonderful, beautiful, starless night
Thank you, whoever, for such a misty night.
The wind was strong, chilly and cold
And the course 80 degrees I could not hold!

"The mountains lift us up with the breeze,
And set us back down with such great ease.
We all have a friend while out on the sea,
She's big, white and free as can be.

"We sat in the doldrums for 164 hours
It seemed like a year, but just 164 hours.
But Patricia's been hauling since yesterday
And supposedly we only have ten more days.

"Winds, waves, and currents are with us,
We'll make it to San Diego
With just a little luck."

I woke that night, out of a dead sleep, to the sound of a large thump followed by the ear- splitting sound of cracking wood. I held my breath for a minute or so, and then heard rustling covers and pillows by Dad's bunk. The boat was heeled over. I smiled in the dark to myself, happy the wind was back. The ocean rushed against the hull as I drifted off, but I was awakened again to find myself sliding across my bunk to the opposite side. The sounds of ripping metal, another large thump, and another huge crack made me scrunch up my face in the dark. These were very bad sounds.

Dad got up, grumbling under his breath something I couldn't make out, then yelled, "What happened?" as he climbed the stairs out of the cabin.

I lay very still, hoping he wouldn't call my name. I didn't want to get out of my warm bed. But before I knew it, I was being awakened by Roland for my watch. It was 5:50 a.m. and I slowly got dressed.

On deck, the morning wind blew hard and the seas were thick with developing white-tipped waves. Roland scowled at the compass. Bundled up, he wore a black wool ski hat pulled down low to his eyes.

"Good-morning," I said as we switched places so I could take the helm.

"It's not a good morning."

"Why?" I adjusted my blue ski jacket and put my socked feet up on the wheel to steady it. My hair was tucked up in a white fluffy ski hat with a pom-pom on top, the ties hanging down on either side of my face.

"Because I almost killed the boat last night."

The noises I had heard the night before rushed back to me. He started speaking as if confessing. "I was at the wheel around four this morning. It was a beautiful night, and I was somehow happy alone at the wheel. The moon and stars were peaceful and so beautiful. The wind became stronger and stronger, the boat started to surf on the waves. What a wonderful feeling surfing on this big boat."

Roland continued in broken English, "Suddenly the sails were beaten to the other side of the boat, and there was a loud *incroiable* crash—the rope went around the air vent and ripped it off and threw it to the sea."

I looked at the main cabin and saw where the air vent should have been was now patched up with a stiff fabric of some sort. The surprise must have registered on my face.

"Wait, there's more," he said. "After the vent was gone I had a wrong reaction—I turned the boat in the opposite direction, so the sails crashed back again to the other side, making the boom crack."

"Wow!" I said. I sat silently, taking in his explanation, remembering the sounds. Roland had jibed the boat twice! "I'm sorry," I said. "Did Dad get very mad at you?"

"Your dad came and saw the mess I caused." He pointed to the boom on the main sail and I saw a large crack down the middle of the boom.

"Your dad yelled at me and he should! I am a bad sailor. He yelled for a long time. He said how could I wait so long and not to call him to take the sails down in this strong wind. I do not really remember all the words he said. But I remember his anger. He was completely right!"

"He can get pretty mad about stuff. I'm sorry if he yelled at you too long," I said.

"No, he yell for ten minutes, and then stop and say, 'Let's fix the problems,' so we tied the wheel down and reefed the sails. Then we covered up the hole on the cabin and we tried to fix the crack in the boom, but in the dark we could not. Today we will fix it for good."

We sat silently. I was grateful it wasn't me who had jibed the boat. I knew Dad would not have been so kind to me. I kept expecting Roland to go below to get some sleep, but he continued to sit beside me in silence. The waves built and the sea looked on the verge of being angry. *Patricia* surfed down the waves as I steered her with little more than a double-reefed main and a storm jib. It was obvious Roland felt incredibly guilty about the damage he'd caused. We sat together as the glow of the sun became brighter behind the clouds and the lumpy waves rolled under us.

"Looks like my prayers for wind worked," I teased.

"No, my prayers worked," Roland said, and finally smiled.

Dad, Roland, and Gibus fixed the boom with big screws and tie straps later that morning. The collective mood of the boat lifted slightly with the onset of the wind.

That afternoon, as Annie swept the main cabin carpet, she yelled, "Hey Bjorn! Come quick! I'm sweeping water here!"

Gibus de Soultrait and Roland Hofer

Twenty-Seven

*D*ad went to investigate. I joined in, too, curious to see how much water Annie was talking about. As Dad went below into the cabin, water squished around his feet. He bent down and felt the carpet, sinking his fingernail deep into the carpet.

Gibus peeked through the hatch. "Is it bad?"

Dad moved the dripping wet carpet aside, took the floorboard up to reveal the bilge full of water.

"How did that happen?" I said, looking at three or four feet of water in the bilge sloshing at floorboard level.

Dad's eyes were small and serious, his lips tight and drawn. He turned on the electric bilge pump and within an hour the main bilge was dry. Water remained in the rib-like sections going up the hull on either side of the bilge, though, and as the boat moved and heeled, the water spilled back over into the main bilge.

Later that afternoon Dad sat down at the navigation station, as I sat at the main cabin table figuring out my navigation shot for the day. "The bilge is full of water again and it's only been about four hours," he said. "I can't figure out where it's coming from."

He clicked his tongue and sucked on his bottom lip in a rhythmic nervous habit as he stared at the water sloshing around the bilge and engine room.

The afternoon and evening passed without a solution to the problem, but we continued making headway toward California.

When I got up for my morning watch, I stepped onto the sole of the cabin. My feet sunk ankle-deep down into freezing cold water. "Dad! Dad!"

He stirred in his bunk, Annie groaned, and Gibus rolled over. Sleepy faces looked over the edge of their bunks down at the pond of water swishing back and forth over the carpet with the movement of the boat. I sat on the edge of my bunk with my legs pulled up out of the water.

"Go do your watch, I'll handle the bilge," Dad said, as he stood up.

I waded over to the stairs and put on my shoes and socks while sitting on the steps.

On deck, the bitterly cold wind howled at fifteen knots. The ocean and the sky looked pissed off—the dark clumpy waves crested with white caps all around, and dark clouds filled the northern sky. The boat heeled, going nine knots with her railing in the water.

"Wheeeee!" I yelled at Roland, trying to be funny, but my words flew away before he could hear them.

Completely bundled up and only showing his stubbled cheeks, nose, and tired eyes, Roland smiled. He looked like somebody who needed a break.

Halfway to the helm, I yelled, "Man it's blowing! I need to get my harness, I'll be right back."

He raised a sock-covered hand and I saw his thumb strain the fabric. Roland didn't own any gloves and his socks did double duty.

Back below decks I found Dad watching the bilge water, looking perplexed as the bilge pump churned.

"I think we need to reef the sails. It's blowing steady and gusting hard up there with threatening clouds on the horizon." I spoke hesitantly, not wanting to pile on any more work or bad news.

I took off my shoes and socks, left them on the steps, and waded through the water. Grabbing my safety harness, I put it on. I stood on the steps before leaving the cabin, waiting for an answer about reefing. Dad was a million miles away with wheels turning as he studied the bilge. After a short silence, which I read as anger, he said in an exasperated tone, "Okay, I'll be right up."

I took over the helm from Roland, and Dad appeared on deck

with his harness and bright yellow foul weather jacket. Somehow he owned foul weather gear, but the rest of us didn't. He stood still for a moment, taking in the weather, looking from horizon to horizon, assessing the oncoming storm.

"Go get your harness, Roland, and let's reef the main."

Roland disappeared below.

Alone on deck with Dad, he looked at me with a smile and said, "She's blowing nice this morning, isn't she?"

"Yes, she is." Dad loved a good blow—no matter how bad his mood, a good squall always pleased him. "Did you hear of any weather coming our way on the radio?"

"I haven't listened since yesterday," he said, "but I will as soon as we get this main reefed."

Roland came back on deck and Dad met him at the mast. He looked back at me and yelled, "Bring her into the wind!"

I steered the boat so that the sails flapped back and forth and they could lower the sail down half way, called reefing. The boat was level but rocking and rolling over the seven- to nine-foot waves. Dad yanked on the sail fabric, pulling it downward as hard as he could, but it stayed put.

"Ah, Goddamn it!" I thought I heard him yell, or maybe I read his lips and knew that expression all too well.

Dad stared up the mast. He pointed to something and Roland strained to see it. I looked up the mast but couldn't see anything—I was thirty feet away. The wind whipped, gusting up to twenty-five knots, the seas confused, waves coming from every direction and getting bigger.

Dad and Roland came back to the helm.

"The mainsail won't come down. The lines are tangled near the middle of the mast. There are at least three lines wrapped around a wire halyard in a mess."

"What are we going to do?" I asked nervously, looking around at the building storm.

"Let's get some of these other sails down until we can fix the problem. We need Gibus."

Roland woke up Gibus and they took down the mizzen, making it easier to steer, and replaced the big genoa with a small jib. Still we did seven knots. I knew Dad wanted to use the storm as much as possible to pick up miles.

I envied Annie, tucked in her bunk, warm and cozy.

"We'll have to send somebody up the mast to untangle the lines." Dad looked around waiting for Gibus or Roland to volunteer. After a short silence Dad said, "Roland, what about you?"

Roland grimaced at the horizon, leaned his head back and looked up the mast, and then reluctantly said, "Yes, I'll do it."

Gibus and Dad slowly hoisted Roland, one pull at a time, half way up the mast. Roland clung with all four limbs around the mast between hoists. The mast rocked back and forth on the waves the way branches on a tree move back and forth in a strong wind.

As I watched, guilt seeped from my pores. The tangled lines were my fault. A few days earlier Annie and I had hoisted Roland's red European bikini underwear up the mast in a camp-style joke, thinking it would be funny. We laughed, and Roland even had a good sense of humor, saluting them, saying, "There is my underwear of love flying as our Swiss flag." But when Dad saw it, he got mad and made us take them down. When we did, I yanked and jerked and pulled at the line and got the underwear down but the lines were tangled with the halyards. Afraid to admit what I had done, I left the mess and kept my mouth shut, for fear of Dad's punishment.

Roland worked to untangle the lines and halyards for a solid forty minutes as we rocked and rolled over the building waves and wind. My stomach soured and churned with guilt. When he arrived back on deck, his lips were thin, eyes bulging, and his entire face was as pale as the white caps around us. I felt so relieved it was over, I nearly confessed my sins right there to Dad, but stopped myself. Dad didn't hover. He was anxious to get down below and deal with our leaky bilge problem and so disappeared quickly. Gibus went back to bed and Roland came to sit with me. "I never do that again."

"Thank you Roland, from the bottom of my heart. I think those lines were tangled because of our underwear joke a few days ago."

"No, I don't think so."

"Don't tell Dad, please?"

"I don't think that was the problem but I won't tell your dad anything."

The storm continued building. The waves grew and the wind gusted to forty knots. The day turned dark. I sat on the steps of the main cabin watching Dad work on a solution to our leaking problem. The sound of the electric pump stopped and he screamed out in frustration, "I hate you, Murphy!" I scrunched up my nose and tilted my head to the side, not knowing what he was talking about. I went on deck to see Annie at the helm. The wind howled. She explained to me about Dad's comment. "You know, Murphy's Law—anything that can go wrong will go wrong."

Dad fixed the electric bilge pump instead of trying to find the leak. But after several hours, the water appeared again over the floorboards and we had to start manual pumping shifts.

I stayed with Annie that morning. We did our watches together that day as moral support for the increasingly tough job of steering. The weather on the horizon in front of us looked ominous, but to the stern it was clear and bright. The wind howled and blew the still-reefed *Patricia* toward California at eight knots. Somehow another albatross hitchhiker joined us. He sat on the stern, just like Alberrr, huddled up, a smaller white-winged glob than Alberrr. But just like Alberrr he kept one eye on us as he bobbed up and down with the stern. How he didn't get blown off in the gusting wind was a mystery to everyone. We named him Eterno and he became our company during watches that awful day. He lightened all of our moods just a bit in the building storm. Annie and I took turns going below to the galley for slices of bread for Eterno and learned later that Gibus and Roland fed him crackers while on their watches.

The storm gathered and organized itself more every hour. The waves got bigger and stronger, the ocean blacker and rougher. The cold cut deep, my feet turned blue, and I couldn't get warm. All my shoes and socks were wet from wading through the water so I went back to wearing flip-flops. My shoulders began to hurt from the manual pumping shifts, which had now been increased to two hundred strokes before and after our hour-long watches. Life was miserable. And still the storm built.

Late in the afternoon on the first day of the storm, we changed course and tacked, and miraculously the water stopped filling up the bilge so fast. Something was wrong with the hull on the port side. Roland, Gibus, and Dad combined their efforts and set out to investigate, but after hours of looking they couldn't find anything. Dad suspected a leak in the hull somewhere but it was hidden.

The wind gusted to sixty knots, Dad said. The gusts were turning into steady blowing wind as the breaks between gusts got shorter and began to disappear altogether. The twelve- or fifteen-foot waves did not match the blasting wind, but they were quickly catching up. We continued hour-long watches through the first night, although Dad took a two- or three-hour watch himself.

I prayed it would be all over by morning and that the sun would shine and the seas would calm down, but when I woke up for my watch at 2300 it was worse. The waves had built to the size of small mountains. I pumped two hundred strokes five minutes before Roland pumped his strokes, but the water went down only slightly. Instead of being ankle deep, the water just wet the bottoms of our feet, but it never seemed to go below the floorboards. Dad pumped between watch changes.

I dozed off and got up for my next watch at 0500 to see the sun struggling to light the day from behind thick black clouds. The rain poured down. The wind still blew steady at forty knots with long, angry bursts to sixty knots. I hung onto the railings, using my harness to clip on to deck hardware in case I was washed overboard, and slowly made my way to the helm. The hill-size waves from the day before had turned into monsters who seemed to be wrestling some giant underneath the sea. Eterno wasn't on deck—we never saw him again. I sat next to soaking-wet Gibus whose eyes were big and fingers tightly wrapped around the wooden wheel. He sat sideways looking behind us every few seconds. I looked too. Fear crept up inside at the size of the wave coming after us.

I watched Gibus expertly surf the boat down the face of one enormous wave at a forty-five degree angle. I looked behind us and saw the top of the wave get blown off, unleashing torrents of heavy, cold water on Gibus and me.

"Jesus! How long has that been happening?" I yelled.

"It happened once before a few minutes ago."

Dad pushed the hatch back and stuck his head up. "What the hell was that?" he yelled.

"A wave broke on deck," I yelled back.

"Water's pouring into the cabin!" He pointed to the gaping hole in the main cabin where the air vent that he and Roland had patched days earlier used to be.

"Jesus, look at that wave!" Dad yelled.

I turned around to see another monster just feet off the stern. Gibus surfed down the face while Dad watched and then handed over the helm to me.

"Dad!" I yelled before he went below. "I'm scared. I need your help steering."

Some of the waves were now reaching halfway up the sixty-foot mast. The ocean was completely white with only small patches of black where the water lay undisturbed for a few seconds.

"I'll be right up."

I steered for a few minutes, trying to emulate Gibus's surfing tactic down the wave but it was harder than it looked. The bow of the boat wanted to head back around, and go up the face of the wave. I had to hold tight to the wheel and only let the boat turn slightly. As the wave picked up the boat from behind, raising the stern and lowering the bow, we headed down the face into the trough. I looked behind us and a wall of water threatened to break on me. It didn't, and somehow disappeared underneath us. I let out an involuntary scream but then looked back again and saw another wall of water coming at us.

"Dad! Come quick. Help!" I yelled to nobody since everybody was below deck and the hatches were closed.

"Dad!" I began to cry. I steered the boat as best I could down the

face of the next wave, spearing the black water in the trough at the
bottom when the boat seemed to fall off a cliff and we free fell what
felt like several feet. The cracking sound as we hit the concrete floor
of water reverberated through the boat. I could feel the vibration in
the wheel, through the deck on my rear end, and on my feet, which
were planted between the spokes of the wheel.

Dad pushed the hatch back. He was bundled up in his foul weather
gear with his safety harness on. He yelled, "What the hell was that?"

"I don't know!" I shouted. "The wave just disappeared and we fell!"
I could almost see my words being carried away on the wind before
they reached his ears.

Dad came back to the helm and as I steered down the next wave,
the boat fell again into the trough of the wave and again we heard the
cracking sound.

"It seems like the boat's going to do a somersault." I said.

"Right, well we don't want to pitch pole," he said. "So steer more
to a forty-five-degree angle." I knew that to pitch pole was to flip end
over end.

"I'm trying but I can't keep the wheel in place. It pulls to the starboard too hard!"

We were yelling at each other even though we sat right next to one
another. The wind buzzed in my ears.

"Let me try." He bumped my arm and I gladly scooted over.

Dad steered the boat down the wave at more of an angle so that
the bowsprit didn't spear the water at the bottom. Another wave
broke over us and drenched us. I licked the salt off my lips, my hair
drenched and clinging to my cheeks. Frantic and shivering, I looked
up into Dad's eyes. He was calm.

"It's going to be fine," he said.

"I don't like this. I don't want to steer anymore." I could feel the
tears building.

"Well, you have to. Use your feet to hold the wheel steady as she
goes down the face. Your legs are stronger than your arms."

"I don't want to. I'm really scared we're going to go over."

"Stop crying, Leslie. You can do it. Just take the wheel."

I took the wheel and began to steer down the next huge wall of water rising up behind us. Dad stayed next to me. I wedged my soak-ing-wet running shoes in the lower spokes of the wheel and held on with both hands as the boat tried to turn to the starboard. I held tight, my arms quivering a little at the strain. I didn't let the wheel turn. We made it to the bottom of the wave and *Patricia* began to climb the next mountain. Dad stayed with me for the next thirty minutes, coaching me and eyeing the storm in every direction.

"At least we're making good time to San Diego," Dad said.

"Yeah, we're flying here."

Roland appeared on deck, wrapped with his safety harness done tightly around his chest.

"Looks like you're off." Dad told me. "Do your pumping and then go see Annie in the galley. She's keeping it warm and has food." Dad stayed on deck with Roland and coached him through the skills needed to keep the boat from falling off the wave.

When I climbed down the wet slippery varnished stairs of the main cabin I was shocked to see so much water below. The cushions around the main cabin table were wet, the table itself had water on it, and the navigation station was soaked with puddles of water all around the charts. I sat on the stairs, dripping wet, shaking from cold. The letdown was immense and I cried with relief, sniffling and wiping my nose with the back of my jacket. It was somebody else's turn to fight the monsters. I had survived.

I pumped two hundred strokes on the bilge pump and felt the warmth come up in my muscles even though I still shook. I headed to the galley. My face felt the warmth first as a blast of heat. I longed to feel the warmth all over my trembling body.

"Look at you, little girl! Take off your clothes and I'll hang them to dry on the lines," Annie said.

I found out later that Dad had given Annie the day off from steer-ing that day, which I resented a little. She apparently didn't want to go on deck at all and offered to keep the galley warm and the hot food available.

The lines we had used for our paintings and stationary the previ-ous week were being used now for everybody's wet clothes.

I peeled off my ski jacket, my hoodie, my button-up sweater, and

T-shirt, which were all dripping wet. The last wet layer was my air-brushed long johns top, which I kept on. The oven dial read four hundred degrees and the heat poured out. I rubbed my numb hands together. I'd forgotten my gloves before I went on deck that morning and my hands were bright red. I shook uncontrollably. Annie put a dry towel around my shoulders, rubbing my arms up and down to create some heat. I peeled off my jeans and my long johns bottoms, which had to be wrung out before we hung them. We let the water fall to the floor since it was already wet.

Our largest pot was wedged next to the teakettle and another empty pot and filled with a small amount of soup so it wouldn't slosh out. The gimbaled oven and stove rocked back and forth violently as we rode up and down the waves, threatening to toss the pots onto the sole. I sat in the warm space, legs drawn up near my body in only my wet underwear and wet T-shirt with a bath towel wrapped around me, shivering, but glad to be there with Annie who sang a pirate song and was in a great mood.

"Aren't you seasick?"

"Not today, Nearly Normal. Today I'm the galley slave that's going to take care of all of you brave souls who steer the Mighty Bugeye Ketch *Patricia* through this storm."

Her mood lifted mine, the fear of the storm and of *Patricia* sinking leaving me briefly. I savored more deeply than I thought possible a hot cup of tea and a cup of soup with crackers.

A few hours later as Annie and I sat in the galley, all warm and mostly dry, the hatch slid back and Roland yelled down, "The jib just ripped!"

"Do you need any help?" I forced myself to ask. I didn't want to go on deck again. My toes and fingers had just thawed.

Dad yelled down the hatch, "Stay down there, Leslie. We can handle this."

I had never been more grateful to have Roland and Gibus aboard. I thanked my lucky stars Dad didn't have a lesson to teach me at that moment, which he usually did, and when the galley hatch cover closed, Annie and I did a high-five.

We stayed in the galley reading and keeping warm, losing track of time, living in a sort of denial about what was happening on deck. About forty-five minutes later, Roland and Gibus fell, dripping wet, into the galley from above, disheveled and spent. Annie lit the fire on the stove and put on the teapot and warmed up the soup. As each one silently peeled off their wet clothes, I noted the look of fear and anxiety on their faces.

"What happened?" I asked. "Did you get the torn jib down and the storm jib up?"

Annie handed each a cup of hot tea. Gibus nodded.

I looked first at Gibus, whose face stared into his cup of tea and then at Annie, whose sand dollar-sized eyes stared out from underneath her puffy white knitted hat.

Roland started, "I kneeled down, holding on, waiting for your dad to say to me what to do as the boat climbed a huge mountain of water. Finally Bjorn climbed out to the end of the bowsprit, which was under water every few minutes. But he crawled on his hands and knees out the wooden pole. A wave came and he hugged that wooden pole and went under."

"Wow! Really?" Annie said.

I was speechless, staring at Roland, waiting for the next part.

"He came up and kept working. This happened three times. The line was stuck on the sail up there." Roland continued, "Then Bjorn pointed down and I lowered the sail. He pulled the sail to him, all in a ball, and scooted back to the deck. Next we put up a tiny small sail."

"Geez! Where's Dad now?"

"He took the wheel from me." Gibus said.

I felt sorry for Dad out there being pounded by the ocean. Night was falling and we faced our second night of watches in this dreadful weather. Roland and Gibus went to their bunks to lie down.

"I don't want to go up there for my watch," I confessed to Annie. "It's so scary!"

Sitting safely in the warmth of the galley just a few feet below the freezing wind and pounding water, I worried about the coming night.

After an hour, Annie left to lay down as Roland and Gibus came back to the galley for some warmth. We sat quietly, sipping hot tea and listening to the transistor radio, which picked up the Los Angeles station KLOS. "Stairway to Heaven" played as Gibus laid his head on his folded arms on the table and rested. Roland also closed his eyes, knowing he was next up on watch. I wrote and read alternately. After more than an hour, Annie returned to the galley claiming that the bunks were wetter than the floor. She was heating up some chili when Dad slid the hatch back and descended into the galley, dripping wet. We all stared at him gape-mouthed. Annie turned the radio off.

"What are you doing? Who's steering?" I said, astonished.

"The spaceship Annie said she saw—the one with the little green men—well, they came and took over the wheel," Dad said in a completely serious tone.

Over the course of the trip, Annie had mentioned seeing lights on the horizon hovering and then disappearing. Even though Dad assured her every time that it was a freighter, Annie said she thought it could be an alien spaceship. The joke aboard the boat was that Annie might be abducted by aliens.

"Dad! Be serious. Who's at the wheel?"

He ignored me. "You're probably wondering who the little green man is. Am I right?" His gaze travelled between Roland, Gibus, and Annie.

"Dad! What's wrong with you? Who's at the wheel?" I nearly screamed.

He held up his hand to me in a stop motion and launched into the story about who the little green man was. From the looks on Roland and Gibus's face, the silly joke didn't translate very well. They were as confused as me.

I squinted at my father, thinking that he hadn't gotten enough sleep, or the cold water had frozen his brain, or his mind had checked out. But what I screamed out again was, "Who's at the wheel?"

With a sly smirk, Dad looked directly at me. "A wise seaman once told me if it gets too bad, let the boat go by itself."

"What does that mean?" I prodded. "Nobody's at the wheel?"

"I've tied the wheel down and back-winded the storm jib, heaving us to in the storm," he said.

At that moment I finally noticed it—the motion of the boat was nicer, not nearly as abrupt and treacherous. It almost seemed as if the storm had gone away, like we were parked or anchored somehow, but when I looked out the galley porthole and tried to find the top of the oncoming wave, I still couldn't see it.

"I'm giving up on trying to stay on course and ride the storm to San Diego. It's just too big of a storm. We're headed south now, riding the waves to Baja," he said, and then did a little jig and said, "Olé!"

Something like happiness began to grow inside me at the thought of not having to go on deck for my watch that night.

Dad continued, "We'll be blown south and have to deal with sailing up the coast of Mexico later. Let's make it through this awful storm. Now can I get a cup of tea or what?"

Dad had done this my entire life: taken a left turn, changing the plan and springing it on me without warning. Up until that moment, doing our watches and steering the boat on course was his main concern. I breathed a sigh of relief that we were hove-to in the storm. I think Roland was the second happiest at that moment to hear he didn't have to go on deck for his watch. I got up and lit the fire under the kettle.

The second night of the storm, exhausted, we doubled up, sleeping together in the only two bunks that were relatively dry. Everything below deck was either sopping wet, spongy wet, or just plain wet. Annie's and my bunks, the two top bunks in the bow, were the driest, and even though we didn't have steering watches, we still had pumping shifts. The motion of the boat was definitely better, but the situation was not improving below deck. The waves kept crashing on deck, sending water through the ripped vent hole, and through the

openings in the hatch slats and hatch cover. Dad fashioned a tempo-
rary fix for the air vent hole, but it constantly needed shoring up as
the waves beat on it. In addition to taking on water from the ocean
above decks, the water continued seeping in from below. Water was
everywhere and it looked like we were sinking.

Needing sleep, I crawled into my wet bunk, trying to think posi-
tively. I wore damp clothes that were half-dried from hanging in the
galley: my long johns, jeans, button-up blue knit sweater, hoodie
pulled over my head, and my ski jacket. I also had a half-wet blanket
that I pulled over myself. It was unbearably frigid as I lay in a wet ball,
feeling salt crystals on my arms as I wrapped them around myself. I
swished my bare feet back and forth trying to find warmth. I wasn't
present for any conversation about who would sleep with whom but
when Annie said, "Scoot over," I was relieved. I lay facing the hull
when she climbed in behind me and I could feel her warmth.

Across the aisle from my bunk was Annie's bunk where Roland
and Gibus had climbed in. Dad was in the galley on the first pump
shift of the night. We'd agreed earlier that we would each maintain a
below-deck watch for two-hour shifts throughout the night, looking
around and pumping fifty strokes every fifteen minutes.

As I lay frozen, thinking about *Patricia* slowly sinking, the
huge monster waves outside, and the whipping wind. I must have
drifted off to sleep. The next thing I remember was that my bunk was
empty—Annie was gone. I was pressing up against the hull, trying
to find more warmth, when Dad climbed in the bunk with me. My
hackles went up. I was facing away from him and my eyes flew open
in the darkness as he pulled the covers over himself and snuggled
in. I remained very still for a long time, not itching my nose or rubbing my eyes or swishing my feet back and forth for warmth. I lay
still, wondering how I could sleep. After a few minutes I heard Dad
whisper, "Please let us make it through this storm." Then he began to
snore lightly. I relaxed a little.

This was the second time my father entreated something bigger
than himself to help us. Visions of past encounters with him in the
dark in a bed flashed through my head. I listened to his rhythmic
breathing and snoring for a while and willed myself to relax just a

little more. *He's not going to try anything tonight. It would be crazy. Roland and Gibus are sleeping right over there.*

My muscles began to relax, the tension left my body, and exhaustion set in. My mind wandered as images raced through my mind of waves and wind and Dad holding onto the bowsprit and going under the wave, and me at the helm trying to fight my way down the face of a gigantic wave so *Patricia* didn't pitch pole. All of it played in my head like a movie as Dad lay sleeping next to me. My mind wouldn't shut off.

I felt betrayed by the ocean, my friend and confidante, whom I had given my secrets to for months now. *Patricia* was slowly sinking under the punishment being inflicted. It was only a matter of time before the water overtook us all. I wondered how long it would be until the boat broke apart in the waves, me clinging to a piece of wood, trying to survive. If Dad was praying we must be close to dying. Wedged between the hull on one side and Dad on the other side, fear filled me and my heart pounded as my wide eyes stared into the black night. I tried to escape the reality around me by joining Dad in sleep.

I decided I didn't want to be scared out of my mind when I died—I wanted harmony and acceptance. Fear left and I accepted my fate of dying at sea. Quiet filled my heart and body, unlike anything I'd experienced before. *If it's my time to die it's been a good fourteen years and I am ready. Thank you for a wonderful life.*

I hung on to that warm feeling of gratitude and must have fallen asleep because the next thing I knew sun rays came through one of the port holes, waking me up with a spear of light. I was in the middle of a dream where Monica, Karen, and I played in a thick forest of redwoods at Henrik Ibsen Park in Redwood City like we did when we were little. The forest was cold, wet, and dark just like my bunk had been, but it was a place of safety and love for me. In the dream my sisters and I played with the forest debris, making a little village out of bark and pieces of wood, playing make-believe.

From my bunk, I looked down at the floor to see the water still above the floorboards. Gibus was pumping and looking very tired and cold. I got up and found everybody awake and working to save

Patricia. How had I slept through such commotion? I went on deck to find Dad at the helm. The day was spectacular! He smiled his great big proud smile at me. I smiled back, grateful for so many things.

I walked toward him. The clouds were gone and the sky was blue. The water was green.

"Strange color," I said.

"Yeah, it's all the oxygen in the water from the storm, but it's also because we're getting close to land."

Those words made me look up at Dad and smile again.

"Look! There's a chunk of seaweed," I said. "I love seaweed. I love land."

Dad smiled again.

The storm had died down considerably. The waves were still fifteen to eighteen feet with white caps, but the wind only blew at fifteen knots. The sails were all up and we were on course, sailing seventy degrees east-northeast. I sat down next to him and looked ahead at the clear blue horizon, remembering the range of emotions from the night before and feeling happy we didn't die.

"A few minutes ago I saw two redwood logs as big as telephone poles float by us, only two feet away from the boat."

"They were redwood? Are you sure? Neat!" Nothing could squelch my happiness at that moment—it was a sign from the ocean, I was certain of it.

"No! Not neat. Imagine if those poles would have come at us during the storm?"

"Oh, right," I said envisioning two redwood trees slamming into the hull, doing the final bit of damage from the outside to poor broken-down *Patricia*.

Secretly I remained happy about the redwood trees floating by, knowing it was a sign from my dream that things would be okay.

A few hours later, Dad took a sun shot to find our location. He plotted it and found we were at 120 degrees longitude, only 180 miles out, just one or two days away from San Diego. We had not been blown down into Baja, in fact, we were almost exactly where we'd been three days ago, directly in line with the great city of San Diego. A miracle! How we didn't get blown to Baja, to smithereens, or sink, was another miracle. I loved the ocean and her majesty and power. She had the power to kill in an instant and also the power to save.

We were saved.

The rest of the day went by uneventfully as everyone tried to find a dry piece of clothing and a hot meal. Each hour the ocean calmed down a little more, returning to normal. That night on my watch I saw a big red light off the port bow. It was huge and I imagined a cruise ship or military ship bearing down on us. I rang the bell as hard as I could. It was 2000 and everybody was dead tired and sleeping. Annie and Dad came up on deck, startled, and I pointed to the red light that had gotten bigger by the minute and Dad began to laugh.

"It's the moon, Leslie. We're getting close to smoggy California."

The moon rising at sea had always been a spectacle with the white light glowing at the horizon, and then peeking above. I had never been tricked by the moon before and felt silly to have woken Dad and Annie. But my Johansen specialness, which I had associated with the moon since I was a kid, filled my heart. I studied the orange ball rising in the sky. Annie came and sat down with me. There were white dots of light all around us on the horizon. Civilization was near.

Twenty-Eight

*T*hursday, October 24, 0730 I finished my morning watch and handed the wheel over to Annie, staying by her side in hopes of catching some of the building morning heat. My clothes were still wet and I shivered most of the time. *I will never get warm again.*

"Your lips are still purple, Nearly Normal."

"I think my whole body is purple under these wet clothes. I'm going to do some jumping jacks."

As I jumped up and down, flagging my arms over my head, I felt the blood begin to move and my limbs start to warm. Annie laughed her giggly laugh, smiling at me. We had pushed through the windless night with the stinkpot running, making only about three or four miles an hour headway. I ached to see Point Loma, the entrance to San Diego Harbor. As we sat sipping our tea, hands wrapped around our warm mugs, Annie's feet steering the wheel, we squinted in the ever-brightening sun and then we saw it: a brown bump on the horizon in front of us.

There are times when sailors feel like desert survivors and don't trust their eyes—mirages abound when spirits are low.

"Could it be?" I said straining my eyes to see through the rising sun in front of us.

"I think it is, but go up on the bow and look closer," Annie said. She was jumping up and down, stretching to bounce higher each time and look over the bowsprit.

I ran to the bow and squinted, shielding my eyes from the brightness. The island climbed above the horizon in front of me. Sure enough, there it was.

"San Clemente Island off the bow!" I yelled and ran back to Annie. I yelled it a second time. Then Annie stood up and yelled it, too, even louder.

A minute later, the main cabin hatch opened. Slowly, as if from hibernation, Roland, Gibus, and Dad crawled out, peeking around in the bright sun, shading their eyes with their hands to see land, right where Dad had predicted it would be. A huge grin lit up Gibus's face and he raised his arms to the heavens. Roland threw his head back and laughed. Dad looked downright pleased with himself, taking his King of Siam stance, puffing out his chest.

"You did it again, Dad," I said. "You navigated us all the way from Tahiti to one precise location off the coast of California!"

Dad smiled and put his arm around my shoulders, and kissed my cheek. We stared ahead. Just seventy-five miles off the coast of California, and directly in line with Solana Beach, we had landed perfectly after the storm.

There were times I was proud of my father, proud to be his daughter, and this was one of them. He had his rough and funky edges, was hard to deal with at times, but I had to admit there were things he did that were amazing. And, though I wasn't nearly ready to forgive or forget his abuse, he seemed to have changed toward me, so—as long as I kept my armor up and was on guard around him—I could afford to be generous toward him for now.

The island was a glorious sight to see after so many watery days. My eyes drank in the treeless brown landmass that rose from the sea directly in front of us. From a distance, it looked bald, like Dad—but upon closer inspection with the binoculars, we saw scrub brush covering the military island, giving it a desert look. The island was dry, unlike *Patricia* and her crew.

We were entering day five of living with misery and wetness all around. Roland and Gibus sat on the main cabin staring at the island. Dad went below and turned on the radio.

I headed to the galley to make a pot of warm oatmeal for everybody when I heard Annie screaming and hooting on deck, "Look! Look!"

I ran up the stairs and peeked out.

"It's a monarch butterfly! It almost landed on my face!" Annie said, sitting at the wheel, still on her watch.

I looked around, not seeing it anywhere. "Where is it?"

"I don't know. It was right here. The bright orange and black wings were so big and beautiful. It almost landed on my nose!"

I kept looking around, walking all the way around the aft cabin and the wheel, but I didn't see anything.

Dad yelled from the steps of the main cabin and I could just hear the smirk on his face, "Sure, Annie, we believe you. We're ten miles from San Clemente Island, but there are butterflies all around."

"Not butter*flies,* a single butterfly."

"Just like the aliens?" Roland said, smiling.

"Go on, you guys. Stop teasing me. I saw the darn butterfly. I swear it!"

I smiled at her. "I believe you, Annie!"

I counted it as another miracle, like seeing the redwood logs after my dream. The energies surrounding us kept revealing signs that we were on the right path, just like in the Carlos Castaneda book. I had become a "seer," a believer in that book, and although it had taken me weeks to make it through, I was hooked. I could see the energies surrounding us and called them the "ocean goddess energies" rather than Neptune because Neptune was male and I didn't connect with that image. My ocean goddess was a beautiful woman with wild hair, almighty, powerful. She wanted us to feel happy and secure because we had made it through that awful storm and had been saved.

I finished cooking the oatmeal and brought the pot on deck with a stack of bowls, spoons, and the last of the brown sugar. I ladled up the steaming hot cereal for the whole crew except Annie, who was still at the wheel. We all sat staring at the island ahead of us in silence. The air was chilly and I could see my warm breath. My clothes were still wet in places, and damp in all the other places. I shivered a bit in the morning air. The sun hadn't climbed high enough yet to produce any serious heat, but we knew it was coming and were hopeful. For the first time in days we were hopeful!

The morning was windless, the engine churning on, when the sound of rushing water like a large waterfall made us all turn around.

Coming from our hind quarter, a mega pod of dolphins flew past us in such a rush it reminded me we would soon be back in civilization again where everything moves fast. Seeing the humps of the dolphins break the surface to breathe, side-by-side, the pod a hundred feet wide, barely any water between them, made me feel like I could walk right out onto their backs. A few jumped high in the sky, flying over those in front of them, wiggling their tails mid-flight, to get further ahead I guessed. Teenagers probably, anxious to get ahead of Mom and Dad and make the destination first.

Together, as a crew, we witnessed this amazing sight of nature, marveling at it in complete silence. Nobody yelled "wow," or "ooh," or anything. The sound of rushing water diminished as the pod left us behind. Shocked from the sight, we sat in complete awe and wonder.

I looked after the dolphins. I wished they would come back and circle our boat for a minute, acknowledge our accomplishments in making this forty-two-day journey. But that's not what happened. Five minutes behind the dolphins, a mega-sized herd of seals flew past, sleek and shiny with whiskers and bulging eyes. They flew through the water, just barely clearing the top in an up-and-down motion. They followed the dolphins at almost the same incredible speed, maybe to the warmer waters of Mexico, or to a plume of fish so large it could feed all the wildlife off the coast of Southern California.

Lifted up for the second time that morning, I knew we had seen another sign from my ocean goddess. Land was straight ahead, and wildlife was all around us. Two days after the storm, gratitude still filled my heart. I felt we had been spared by the ocean—that mighty wicked wonderful queen, in all her glory and ferociousness. The humbled feeling of being so small, nothing more than a pin in the vastness of the ocean, stayed with me. I felt small and yet large at the same time for having survived this journey.

Through it all, I had changed. I left California nine months earlier a scared little girl, wounded and on edge. Somehow I'd found power and strength inside and ultimately took care of myself by speaking up at the critical moments. How prophetic that would be in the years to come as I had to learn again and again to speak up for myself. My Dad never touched me again. I wished I would have known this at the time, but living with the fear lasted years more. He was completely predictable in his unpredictability. I loved him desperately as any little girl loves her hero father, but I also hated him fiercely and would have done just about anything to get away from him. He was the best and the worst father in the world to me, and that would be a hard fact I'd have to reconcile in the years to come. On this day though, I loved him and was bonded to everyone on the trip.

The beautiful goddess ocean looked so calm on the surface, blue and inviting. But below in her depths were secrets and darkness, as well as wonderful things to behold, just like in me. Her power was reflected in me and I would hold her strength inside forever, remembering the fine string of life we all hung by and the grace by which we were saved.

Author's Note

I wrote this book with the help of my diary, our red leather-bound Logbook entitled "AEGIR" where many people wrote stories of their time with our family sailing, our Daily Sea Logbook where I wrote stories of the days' events on the back of the logbook pages. I also referred to Annie Musselman's diary for detail and help in remembering. Most everyone in the book is real and I obtained their permission to include stories about them. Some names and places have been changed, but not the events. There are some composite events to save time and interest but combining them did not affect or effect the stories or the outcome.

The journey is not over in the story of the Johansen family. Leslie is currently writing the end of this family saga.

Pictures by chapter can be found at www.lesliejohansennack.com

Acknowledgments

I'd like to thank my husband, David, whom I love dearly and who always believes in me, no matter what. To my two children, Dylan and Marina, thank you for your support while I wrote this and always. Thank you to my mother for supporting the idea of this book. To my sisters, I love you both dearly. I'm extremely grateful to my Read and Critique Group in San Diego, where I wrote this book, led by the fabulous Judy Reeves, who always believed in me, even when I didn't believe in myself. Thank you to my other R&C group members: Greg Johnson, Elizabeth Marro, Elle Brooks, Scott Barbour, Jonathon Heller, and Dawne Ellison, you guys are the absolute best! And a special thank you to Anita J. Knowles and Helen Chang for being so enthusiastic in your support and meeting me for breakfast to let me vent about the process.

Thank you the amazing Brooke Warner for helping me finish and for being so positive and supportive every step of the way. Jennifer Silva Redmond, who edited and shaped my manuscript into the book you see today, thank you for somehow stealing the vision in my head and making it come to life. Thank you Adriaan Veldhuisen for your research skills and enthusiasm. Thank you Ivory Small from NOAA who researched the storms for me and sent me the data. And for the multiple e-mails and facts about Bugeye Ketches, thank you Pete Lesher, chief curator, Chesapeake Bay Maritime Museum.

And to my school friends Raine Oliver and John De La Cruz, you guys are the best. Thanks for being there and for all the fun we had. My dearest friend, Annie Musselman who's been my big sister all these years, thank you for being there when I really needed you. To Roland Hofer and Gibus de Soultrait, thank you for your encouragement and enthusiasm as I wrote this book and for helping me remember. Barbara Nack, Rita Harding Burke, Eva Friedlander, and Carol Doupe Canterbury thank you for helping in editing and reading. And finally, thank you Terri Brewer and Kelly Casey for reading my ARCs and for helping me find all the little left over errors before publication.

Taken from First Logbook of "AEGIR"
By Bjorn Johansen
March, 1973

*T*he desire to go sailing (at least on Bjorn's part) must have started the first time he encountered that big – beautiful – lonesome and powerful ocean. Since an introduction starting that long ago would fill a book by itself, starting there would be impractical. The starting point is difficult to determine because the dream of travel has always been with the Johansen's. For simplicity let us start when firm plans to purchase a boat capable of long ocean voyaging were made, and explain how the events leading up to it took place.

As you already know by now, the Johansen family consists of Bjorn, Monica, Leslie, and Karen, who will accompany 'AEGIR' on this long voyage, which we hope will enrich – educate and broaden their experiences.

Bjorn of course has a father living in Norway, who promptly denounced the trip as silly and stupid. Then we have Monica's, Leslie's, and Karen's mother, Paula, who at one point was coming along, but since became sick and went back to Canada (where she was born) to a hospital, and has since decided to stay there for good. Bjorn also has a son**, Rune, from a former marriage in Norway, who he has not too much contact with, (not enough), but when he heard of the trip labeled his father to be struck with '*vandrelyst*' (wanderlust).

Bjorn has since his early years realized that one's education and experiences broaden considerably with travel, and has always said that his girls were to go to Europe for one year to learn another language fluently before entering college. That of course he has said since before the girls entered grammar school. Time passed, but not before the last few years did he realize that he better do something about it before it was too late. And that is when it all started.

A warm balmy spring afternoon at 'Midgaard' (B. J.'s ranch) in 1971, Paula (the girls' mother) was present at dinner that day, when the subject was brought up regarding the girls' final schooling before entering college. In the conversation the family was caught with the adventure of it all, 'Midgaard' was mentally sold and the money used to go to Europe. The countries to go to range from close to Bjorn's homeland Norway, to the rest of the continent like Spain, Switzerland and France, etc.

After many months of considering the problem BJ estimated for one year in Europe the cost would be about $20,000 to $30,000, a lot of money for a young man who came to Canada in 1958 with $10.00 in his pocket. If they went to Europe for one year and spent that money, that would leave Bjorn all but broke and back to the factory again, a thought not very encouraging, at least not to Bjorn.

Another idea cropped up – maybe they could 'kill two birds with one stone?' Could Bjorn's lifelong dream of the sea be combined with the girls' education?? Why not sail to Europe? Use the money to buy a boat, work and educate the girls on the way, stop in Europe for one year and then return to California. In theory it sounded fine, but would it work?

Bjorn started to work on the problem in the fall of 1971, laying out tentative time tables, estimating what money was available for a boat, and all the other details which would encompass such a venture.

After fall and early winter studying and estimating if the project as feasible, Bjorn announced his decision – it was feasible, practical and most of all desirable.

In late winter of 1971-72 a vote was taken by all that were to partake in the venture and the vote was an enthusiastic 'yeah' let's go!

Bjorn started immediately looking for a boat. Starting on the west coast and after a while encompassing all of the U.S.A. without very much luck. When the price was right, the boat did not meet with Bjorn's specifications or approval, and when the boat was right, the price was out of sight. The problem that seemed so simple on 'Midgaard,' to find a boat that could take them to Europe and back for approx. $25,000 was impossible to find. <u>Cruising boats</u> were far and long between, and when one was found, it was too expensive. It seems like the whole thing was coming to a halt due to lack of capable boats in the right price range. Bjorn's father in Norway was contacted, but nothing was available in Scandinavia either.

Then in November, 1972, B. J. heard about a boat in Newport Beach. The boat was supposedly built to be cruising to Alaska – heavy, big and solid, but rather run-down. The asking price was $39,950.00. The boat was owned by a doctor in Newport Beach, Linda Isle, to be correct. Linda Isle is a private island so there was no way to see the boat without an appointment. A month of long distance phone calls and letters was rewarded by getting to see the boat one night by flashlight. To Bjorn the boat looked like it might be usable, and he obtained permission to see it the next day in daylight. The boat was ideal, but the price was too high, but asking price and paying price are sometimes far apart. A sea trial was set on December 31, 1972. She behaved like a gentle lady in 50+ knots wind. Bjorn was sold. An offer was made, survey taken and B. J. ended up paying $10,000 more than anticipated, digging deep in to the cruising fund. But the boat was what he wanted and after over 9 months of looking, this was the best deal he had seen. Compromises would have to be made.

On March 15, 1973, he took possession of 'Serenity' a 45' LOA, 16 ton net, fiberglass over plywood sloop, and promptly renamed her 'AEGIR.'

On the following pages you will find her story."

**I didn't read this "Introduction" until I was an adult. I did not know he had written a narrative of our lives and didn't find out for three years after this (1978) that I had a brother.

About the Author

© Kelci Gilley

*L*eslie Johansen Nack graduated UCLA with a BA in English literature. She is a member of the National Association of Memoir Writers and San Diego Writers Ink. She lives in San Diego and has two children with her husband of twenty-five years.

SELECTED TITLES FROM SHE WRITES PRESS

She Writes Press is an independent publishing company
founded to serve women writers everywhere.
Visit us at www.shewritespress.com.

The S Word by Paolina Milana
$16.95, 978-1-63152-927-6
An insider's account of growing up with a schizophrenic mother, and
the disastrous toll the illness—and her Sicilian Catholic family's code of
secrecy—takes upon her young life.

The Coconut Latitudes: Secrets, Storms, and Survival in the Caribbean by
Rita Gardner $16.95, 978-1-63152-901-6
A haunting, lyrical memoir about a dysfunctional family's experiences
in a reality far from the envisioned Eden—and the terrible cost of keeping secrets.

All the Ghosts Dance Free: A Memoir by Terry Cameron Baldwin
$16.95, 978-1-63152-822-4
A poetic memoir that explores the legacy of alcoholism and teen suicide
in one woman's life—and her efforts to create an authentic existence in
the face of that legacy.

A Different Kind of Same: A Memoir by Kelley Clink
$16.95, 978-1-63152-999-3
Several years before Kelley Clink's brother hanged himself, she
attempted suicide by overdose. In the aftermath of his death, she traces
the evolution of both their illnesses, and wonders: If he couldn't make it,
what hope is there for her?

*Don't Call Me Mother: A Daughter's Journey from Abandonment to
Forgiveness* by Linda Joy Myers $16.95, 978-1-938314-02-5
Linda Joy Myers's story of how she transcended the prisons of her child-
hood by seeking—and offering—forgiveness for her family's sins.

Say It Out Loud: Revealing and Healing the Scars of Sexual Abuse by
Roberta Dolan $16.95, 978-1-938314-99-5
An in-depth guide to healing the wounds caused by sexual abuse, writ-
ten by a survivor who's lived the process firsthand.